Alone Near Alice

✦

Australia's Outback

Harold Harbaugh

iUniverse, Inc.
New York   Bloomington

Alone Near Alice

Australia's Outback

Copyright © 2008 by Harold Harbaugh

All rights reserved. No part of this book may be used or reproduced by any means, graphic, electronic, or mechanical, including photocopying, recording, taping or by any information storage retrieval system without the written permission of the publisher except in the case of brief quotations embodied in critical articles and reviews.

The views expressed in this work are solely those of the author and do not necessarily reflect the views of the publisher, and the publisher hereby disclaims any responsibility for them.

iUniverse books may be ordered through booksellers or by contacting:

iUniverse
1663 Liberty Drive
Bloomington, IN 47403
www.iuniverse.com
1-800-Authors (1-800-288-4677)

Because of the dynamic nature of the Internet, any Web addresses or links contained in this book may have changed since publication and may no longer be valid. The views expressed in this work are solely those of the author and do not necessarily reflect the views of the publisher, and the publisher hereby disclaims any responsibility for them.

ISBN: 978-0-595-53386-2 (pbk)
ISBN: 978-0-595-63444-6 (ebk)

Printed in the United States of America

iUniverse rev. date: 11/07/2008

for Lynette and Robert

"Don't worry about the world coming to an end today. It is already tomorrow in Australia."

Charles M. Schulz

Table of Contents

Chapter One

Groggy Anticipation

I detest, really detest, getting up early. Nothing civilized, in my opinion, happens between 5 and 8 a.m. in any time zone. This part of the day, at least for me, is about shaking off sleep and facing, with lots of coffee, the day ahead. Like a teenager, I begin to really function about 10 a.m. and peak after midnight.

But this morning I was in Eastern Standard Time on the other side of the world and not on my own schedule or in my usual comfort zone. My brain urged, "You're in Canberra. Wake up."

"Can...?" I asked.

"berra. Australia," my brain concluded.

Despite the fact that it's the size of the United States minus Alaska, Australia has only three time zones plus one oddity. On its four day journey across this Continent/Country, somewhere in the middle of the Nullarbor Plain, the Indian Pacific train creates its own time zone for scheduling purposes. Out there in truly no where, who's to notice, or care?

Ruth, a lifelong morning person, and I were in New South Wales for the sixth time, Canberra for the fourth, and it was already our sixth day in Australia. On the first four days we explored Sydney, among our five favorite cities in the world, and had only one small crisis. I put the card into my new digital camera backwards and it jammed beyond retrieval, so don't ask to see my pictures of The Rocks.

And now Ruth was moving about the dark room, getting dressed and bumping into the furniture. So I rolled over and the bedside clock showed 6 a.m. At home in Camas it was noon. Yesterday.

I always struggle with the International Dateline concept and feel disoriented or dumb when I take the time to try to reason it out in preparation to make flight arrangements or a phone call to anyone Down Under.

I'm not alone. Rob, our dear friend in the bedroom downstairs, sometimes rings us at 3 a.m.

"Give me just 10 more minutes," I bargained while trying to roll back over.

But Ruth, fully dressed and now arresting my shoulder, wouldn't let me. "We have to meet the bus at 7:30," she reminded, applying more, not-so-gentle pressure.

Then Rob knocked purposefully on our door.

"HANK! Let's go," Ruth said in her insistent teacher voice, so I stumbled out of bed instead of tunneling under warm blankets and began putting on my traveling clothes. It was freezing in the room since it was August and, therefore, still winter. Another disorienting concept when I'm Down Under. It never stops feeling odd to call January summer and July winter.

Downstairs, Lynette had prepared a light breakfast of fruit and toast. It was already on the dining room table. I reached first for the coffee.

The three early risers engaged in animated conversation about the bells in Goulburn and the trip we were about to take together while I ate mechanically, hoping they would ignore me.

Yesterday morning, Lynette and Rob's son John had come to Sydney to drive us to Canberra, and on the way an unusual event occurred. It started to rain, dismally, coldly. So instead of strolling the streets of this once merino sheep capital, we opted to see Goulburn's massive cathedral where, just by coincidence, the chief bell ringer was there. Unused to visitors interested in and asking questions abut his passion, he invited us up into the tower for a demonstration and regaled us with some fascinating information. To summarize, bell ringing is not a job, it's an art.

Ruth and Lynette disappeared into the kitchen, and the sounds of closing up and final checking began to stir my blood. Or perhaps it was the second cup of coffee.

"Rob, John's here," Lynette sang out.

We were soon standing in the alleyway behind their condo with our extra-light luggage. As was typical of a Canberra August morning, the city was a bit under the weather, foggy with rain imminent but never assured.

Since it was god-awful-early on a Saturday morning, the wide streets of Australia's planned capital city were empty, except for the five of us.

John, always cheerful no matter what time of day, dropped us at the parking lot of an IGA, waved a cherry goodbye, and drove off.

Funny, I didn't remember that there were IGAs in Australia. Even funnier, we could have been standing in any small, store-front shopping center in the United States. But we were not. We were in the ACT, or the Australian Capital Territory, and the four of us were about to take off on a nineteen day trip to The Outback, not the restaurant but the hot, even in winter, so-called desolate place with the famous rock in its middle.

Up very late last night while attempting to catch up on the lives of our geographically distant friends, I was still fighting my eyelids and experiencing thought deprivation despite the caffeine. Maybe it was just my mood, but this parking lot hardly seemed like a place to leave on such an unusual and long-anticipated trip. No scenic harbor, no rising gang plank. No champagne corks. The IGA was anonymous, not even opened.

The trip yesterday from Sydney had been far more celebratory, and the rising, super highway had me imagining the roads to and in the Red Center, or Centre as it's spelled in Australia. The wattle was in bloom all long the freeway to high-country Canberra as winter fitfully inched toward spring. We had lunch in Berrima, a historic stage coach town established in 1863 when Abe Lincoln was President on the other side of the Pacific. The restaurant's name, The Bushrangers' Bistro, sounded a bit like an oxymoron to me. I envisioned men with whips ordering a field greens salad with raspberry vinaigrette. The Bistro was in the Surveyor General Inn, the oldest continuously licensed inn in Australia.

The IGA was clearly newer than the Surveyor General since Canberra didn't officially become the capital until 1927 and real growth didn't occur until after World War II.

I looked for Ruth, who had wandered away. Always more of a people person than I, she was already deep in friendly exchange. "Bell ringing is far more complex than one might imagine," I heard her say to Gwen, who had arrived before us. Gwen and her husband Angus were Rob and Lynette's best friends, and they had signed on for Out and Back to the Red Centre too.

I walked over and greeted them. After a brief re-introduction, I drifted away as did Angus, who is rather retiring and has a hearing problem. We stood together in silence like two men at a funeral parlor visitation.

Soon enough others arrived and became engaged in animated conversation. The other participants, all strangers to me, clearly knew each other. As circles formed and tightened, I could see Ruth standing there stoically. Alone. Feeling a bit left out, she eased away and came toward me.

"Old friends, it seems," I said, recognizing the easy, social pull of long term acquaintances.

"Of course. I certainly understand that," Ruth agreed. "I just learned that we're the only couple who isn't Australian," she added.

"Think that'll be a problem?"

Before she could answer, Lynette was at her side, taking Ruth's arm in delight. They hadn't, after all, been together for two years. We immediately felt less left out.

Others arrived. Car doors slammed. Hands waved goodbye. Luggage accumulated in a perfect row.

The other travelers were, like us, all married couples. The single female who had been listed all along had dropped out at the last minute fearing 17th wheel status, I suppose.

Ruth and I attempted to introduce ourselves, and the now assembled Aussies were courteous, if reserved. I shook hands all around without remembering a single name, and both men and women immediately, a bit dismissively, turned back to interrupted conversations.

We listened on the periphery as the others, all from Canberra we quickly learned, spoke about the futility of trying to keep up with technological change. Telstra was repeatedly mentioned. I knew that this was a telecommunications company, but I didn't know enough about it to participate in the talk. Instead, I flashed on Rob taking us to the top of the Telstra Tower on our first visit to Canberra. But I had forgotten whatever I had learned so could add nothing to the conversation. Being the outsider, I wondered if this would be true throughout the long trip ahead of us. I felt a bit like a Red Sox fan at a Yankee game.

When the talk turned to the glories of Tasmania and the quirks of Tasmanians, Ruth and I, despite having been there, totally faded into the background and huddled in our coats.

It was certainly an unexpectedly blustery, cold Saturday morning, and all of the shopping center's parking spaces were still empty except for, I now noticed, a bus that looked like a veteran of many tough excursions. Attached behind it was a separate, two-wheeled, enclosed luggage cart. The bus dwarfed the boxy carrier, making it look like an afterthought. I suddenly understood the severe luggage restriction.

A somewhat stocky, mid-thirtyish man came from around behind it and began stowing the luggage in the carrier, whose wheels bounced with each heave ho. The suitcases were small but, apparently, densely packed.

Having stuffed my own, I understood. We had been repeatedly warned to bring only one small piece for the 19 days plus a single carry-on—only if we needed it—that could easily fit under the seat in front of us. Nothing more. Nothing. That meant I had to squeeze 19 days worth of toiletries, travel paraphernalia, extra layers of clothing for unpredictable weather, photo equipment, notebooks, etc. inside my smaller Travelpro, which reminded me of a Volkswagen full of circus clowns. Packing had been especially difficult for me since, being a writer, I was planning to record this experience and to collect as much information as I could find. Where would I put it? Ruth, blithe travel vet, had less of a problem. And Rob and Lynette's miniscule suitcases when we had traveled together over the years always seemed to be packed with Styrofoam.

The group was called to attention and we were introduced to the man who had been loading the carrier, Dave, our tour director. He seemed a jolly guy, or mate. Or matey. Since we were in Australia, it was time to start thinking and communicating in Strine. When in Rome, or Canberra….

A curious silence instead of hearty greetings followed.

Intro over, there was suddenly an anxious buzz among the assembled. Faces registered disappointment, dismay, maybe even anger. Something was clearly not as it should be.

I took Lynette aside and asked what was going on.

"He's not the usual…what we expected."

"Dave?" I asked.

"Yes. Rob and I thought that Garth would lead us."

"Garth?"

"The National Trust's Tours Coordinator. That man over there who just introduced us to…Dave." She pointed to a middle-aged man who looked like a museum curator counting the days until retirement.

"What do you know about Dave?"

"Nothing," Lynette replied, looking a bit uncertain, maybe even a bit upset. An acute observer and my source of information about just about everything, Lynette's demeanor forecast trouble ahead. "Garth organized the tour, but he seems to have hired another guide for us."

"Is that OK?" I inquired.

Lynette's raised eyebrow spoke volumes.

"It's time, mates!" Dave said cheerily, and we lined up to get on the bus.

Since Ruth and I straggled, we were the final couple to board. The somewhat cramped interior had just enough seats for the group. Outside, the towed carrier had made the bus seem larger than it actually was.

To our left were double seats. To the right were singles. The only empty double seats remaining were the two in the very back.

Ruth and I separated. Noticing quickly that Angus had taken a single seat, Ruth sat down gratefully next to Gwen, whom we had met at a cricket match in Melbourne on our previous trip to Australia. I took the seat in the back, leaving one empty space next to me and one single seat two rows up.

Garth's grey head popped through the door and, taking a final count, he looked a bit sheepish. He seemed to be a man holding back an apology that didn't get made.

I learned later that Dave was part owner of an EcoTour company that the National Trust had used on previous occasions. Dave had somehow, without prior warning, become part of the deal and responsible for our experience.

Since 1956 the National Trust has been working towards conserving and protecting Australia's heritage. It's the major operator of house museums and historic properties that are mostly opened to the public in all Australian States and the Northern Territory. The local Trust, the one that had offered this tour, had 23 properties under its umbrella, or brolly. Since Sydney's The Rocks is this Continent's first European settlement, and Cadman's Cottage, built in 1816, is Sydney's oldest house, this meant that the Trust oversaw no building over 200 years old. This still young nation had the advantage of recognizing its heritage before a lot of it was destroyed in the name of development. Not part of the government, the National Trust is independent, non-profit, and supported by communities. Ruth and I were soon to find out that all of the others on the tour were members.

But for now, a blank page breathless with anticipation, I settled back and watched the IGA's parking lot recede. It may not have been the starting point I had been anticipating for months, but we *were* on our way to The Outback.

Chapter Two

Getting Underway

We headed, not toward the open road as I expected, but into downtown Canberra. Driver Dave interrupted his greeting to announce that he had to stop at a motel to pick up the final couple.

They were waiting on the sidewalk, suitcases at their feet. While Dave stowed their bags in the back, the man climbed into the bus and took the single seat, so the woman had no choice but to sit next to me. Without hesitation, she turned, extended her hand and said, "Hello, I'm Karin."

Effortlessly gracious and very attractive, Karin was obviously the kind of person who leapt into conversation with a stranger as if she had known him forever. We got on immediately and within minutes she was telling me that she and her husband Brian had been involved in wine making for the last nine years.

A big fan of Australian wines, I was delighted by this sudden opportunity to learn about this important Aussie industry from a source, my very first Aussie vintner.

"Nine years?" I asked, probing for details.

"Yes, ever since Brian retired from government service. Wine-making was his second career," she explained. "And we both loved it, absolutely loved it."

"Why do you talk about it in the past tense?"

"We just sold our vineyard," she said, not sounding too happy about it and quickly changing the subject.

She asked where I was from and if I had children. "Washington. The State," I replied. "Two."

She spoke of her three sons and three grandchildren, but then she returned to the subject of their retirement venture. It was clearly occupying her thoughts. She said wistfully, "I truly loved viticulture."

"Then why did you sell?"

"A young couple came to our door recently and asked if our property was for sale by any chance. It wasn't. But Brian and I looked at one another… and…."

"You sold your beloved vineyard," I concluded for her.

"It seemed the right time. The right thing to do. So we just moved back to Canberra a week ago, and our new house is still so disorganized that we've been living in a motel."

"You moved one week ago and are leaving on a long trip?"

"It does sound a bit daft," she admitted. "But we had this trip planned long before the sudden move. We've never been to The Outback. So we just walked away from stacked furniture and unpacked boxes."

"Are you glad?"

"About moving back to Canberra? Not really. The vineyard was our project together. But one does get tired of recycling laundry water."

I flashed on this land's chronic problem with perpetual water shortages. Lynette always reminds us to get wet when showering and then turn off the water to lather up. She is appalled by anyone, Aussie or American, who leaves water running for any reason. She barely rinses the soap off of dishes.

"I always washed the sheets first," Karin continued. "Next the more soiled items, and then I used the dirty water to flush the toilets."

As she went on about collecting sparse rain in cement tanks, I was increasingly aware of her sophistication. It was like listening to a New York socialite at the Russian Tea Room, or perhaps more accurately a London Dame at the Ritz having high tea and talking, incongruously, about mopping floors.

Like most affluent Australians, Karin was well traveled. She had lived in Manhattan for a year and Washington, DC for two. "I was 17," she said matter-of-factly. During that time she had taken a trip across Canada "tracing the route of my great-grandfather," she explained.

The conversation kept returning to wine, and I began taking notes. I wrote Penfold's Grange Hermitage in my log book, and Koonunga Hill Shiraz/Cabernet.

The eager student in me was interrupted by Dave who drew our attention to the approaching town of Cowra. Until now, his comments had been the standard how-are-yas and criticism of the bleak weather. "A Japanese interment camp existed here in World War II," he informed. "Built in 1941. It was the scene of the largest mass prisoner of war escape in British military history three years later."

I was impressed with Dave's knowledge and decided that maybe he wouldn't be, as rumored, so bad after all. Was he a history buff? A World War II expert?

"At the time," continued Dave, turning the word *time* into a roughly three syllable word, *toim*, "the camp had 4,000 prisoners in 4 separate campgrounds. In their bid for freedom the inmates used knives, forks, saws, ax handles, baseball bats...." His voice trailed off. After a dignified, professorial silence, he continued. "Many buildings were burned to the ground. After 9 days, 334 prisoners had escaped. But they were all recaptured."

There was no reaction on the bus, no questions from the Australian passengers. Were they embarrassed by this recounting? Was this perceived as a black mark in history, like Manzanar in the US? I wanted to ask Karin but was afraid the question from an American might not be appropriate. This escape attempt was news to me, but perhaps numbingly common knowledge here. Were they bored?

Ruth turned in shock and looked at me. I shrugged. She and I were, apparently, the only ones surprised by this information.

"230 Japanese killed, 4 Australians," Dave added. Then he spoke of the comprehensive media coverage that accompanied the 50th anniversary commemoration of the big breakout, so I had at least a partial answer to my queries about his detailed knowledge and the passengers' reactions. I gazed out across the rain-soaked, rural landscape and looked forward to seeing this first historical landmark of the trip.

But we bypassed Cowra. "Have to stay on schedule," Dave explained.

Only I seemed disappointed.

Was this setting a precedent, I mused, for drive-by attractions? This was the reason why I had always avoided group tours. You see only what the guide allows and for only as long as you are permitted. I had hoped that the Trust's thrust would be different. Maybe they let drivers set their own agendas. It was too soon to tell, but, in the meantime, Cowra was in the rear view mirror.

We were gliding along the Barton Highway at a purposeful rate of speed and it was still raining, the weather front casting a dismal grey pall over some low, green hills dotted with sheep, like Ireland or New Zealand. But no roos. So far and in four previous trips, I had seen kangaroos only in zoos and on nature preserves, where they seemed lethargic and tame. I wondered how long it would be before I actually saw one of the estimated 20,000,000 wild kangaroos sharing this large landscape with about as many Australians.

There were almost twice as many people in California at the time as there were on this entire continent.

We stopped at exactly ten a.m. for tea, a ritual that would repeat every day. Ruth jumped in and helped with the setting up. I watched her chatting casually, ice already broken with the other women.

Among the men, conversation was reserved and mostly about the weather. I stood on the fringes of two or three small clusters saying nothing, acting as though I couldn't possibly drink tea and talk at the same time. I was uncomfortable and not sure why, concluding that we just hadn't yet had a real opportunity in the form of a bonding experience, a shared adventure, to get to know one another. I made a vow to approach each person during the next 24 hours, one at a time, starting with the men.

I walked over to the nearest male, whose name I had forgotten. He too was standing apart from a group, nibbling a cookie. I grinned like a car salesman and asked, "Is this typical weather for this time of year?"

"No," he said as if done with the subject. He turned toward the nearest circle of men and blended in. They began discussing the lack of snow in the Snowy Mountains this year.

After hot drinks and what everyone was calling biscuits but were actually store-bought cookies, Ruth and I stood together, she smiling and me frowning. "Will you sit with me for a while?" I asked.

"No. Gwen has to finish a story."

Back on the road, Dave, who seemed an outsider as uncomfortable as I was, put on a tape. "This is Barry Cohen and James Killen," he said, and there were appreciative nods and noises from the other passengers. It sounded a lot like thawing. I knew nothing about either man and made a note to ask Rob about them later. Rob and Lynette, our only real connections in the group, were seated behind the driver at the opposite end of the bus.

All of the Aussies, especially the men, listened in rapt attention and laughed regularly at Cohen and Killen, who sounded like practiced after-dinner speakers. I didn't get the humor at all, but I didn't know the players. Or the politics.

Curious, I leaned over to Brian, Karin's husband, and asked whom we were listening to.

"Barry Cohen was a member of Parliament. Labor. And James Killen was in the House of Representatives. Liberal," he said, and I knew about as much as I did before.

Brian saw my blank expression and added, "Cohen is a very popular public speaker. Very funny. He also writes books. He's a master of the witty anecdote."

I tried again but just couldn't get involved, so my attention drifted to the landscape, which had changed to wheat fields. I once asked Rob, a courtly gentleman who has the mien of a high court judge, if he could think of something that couldn't be grown in Australia. He thought this over for a long time and finally said, "Actually nothing." In the back seat of a car and traveling together through orchard country around Shepparton at the time, I began to list cash crops from apples to zucchinis. Rob would say "South Australia" or "up around Darwin" to each. By the time the game ended, Rob could think of nothing that didn't grow somewhere in Australia. This is admirable, a testament to Australian grit, since this is among the toughest and driest places in the world. No natural Eden of kiwis and pineapples, which grow in abundance in Queensland, Australia had a full, varied cornucopia.

We drifted through Canowindra, a town of historic old buildings surrounded by wheat fields, but there were no golden waves of grain at this time of year, August.

We were experiencing steady rain, but Dave turned off the MPs and went on and on about drought and its affect on farmers. He told a crude joke about two dogs fighting, which I didn't get. Aussie humor, I had decided long ago on our first trip Down Under, was often inscrutable, at least to me.

The road was not as good now, the edges deteriorating. The broad multi-lane highways of populated eastern New South Wales were already behind us. I supposed that government officials wisely used money to build and maintain roads near population, which made sense, but I wondered what was ahead. The Northern Territory, roughly 521,000 square miles and slightly smaller than Alaska, had fewer than 200,000 people, most of whom lived in Darwin and Alice Springs. In the NT, doctors flew to emergencies and patients to appointments. What would its roads be like?

Dave droned on about hard times. He spoke about the boom and bust experiences of an uncle who in bad years borrowed from the bank and never got ahead. He caught my drifting attention when he said, "18 years of below average rainfall."

Can that be? I wondered. 18? Maybe he meant 18 months.

Ironically, I was staring out the window at a consistent downpour.

Dave segued into emus, flightless birds whose feathers reminded me of once-popular shag carpeting. "There are only ten emu farms left in New South Wales," he said, sounding really regretful and adding, "Emu oil from the US is far inferior to Australian."

I wanted to retort, "Ha! Is not! Our emu oil is *better* than yours." But my only experience with this lubricant that is said to penetrate glass was a few radio commercials about its miraculous soothing properties, the tout clearly Australian.

I gave up on trying to recall emu oil's uses and tuned back in to Dave's patter. He was telling everyone about a couple he knew who had 1,600 of these gigantic birds, second only to the African ostrich in size among avian species. I envisioned an Australian Western with Emuboys rounding up the herd and heading them, flouncing and screeching, toward the corral.

We were entering Eugowra, yet another seemingly deserted small town. A sign whizzed by informing that for the next ten kilometers the road would pass through the "long paddock". I was about to ask Brian what this meant but immediately lost the thought because the next sign said, "Kangaroos next 10 km" and I became totally focused on spotting them.

We were on the outskirts of Parkes, described by Dave as a government town. "We'll stop here to use the facilities," he said, slowing down. Aussies call them loos and laugh at Americans who request directions to a bathroom where they can't bathe or a restroom where they can't rest.

Parkes had its fifteen minutes of fame in 1969 when, through a series of unforeseen glitches, the Radio Telescope just north of town beamed the historic image of Neil Armstrong walking on the moon to an audience of 600 million people—not from NASA as expected but from right here in rural Australia. The incident is lightly and lovingly portrayed in the Aussie film *The Dish*.

Ruth and I had actually seen this film. Not in Sydney as one might expect but in Kansas City. Despite the success of *Mad Max* and others, few Aussie films make it to the US market, so we never passed on an opportunity to see one. We had probably seen more Australian movies than most Australians.

Back on the bus after sharing a typical communal urinal with a bunch of men all pretending to be alone, I sat next to Angus, the only other man besides Rob with whom I had some acquaintance. It was time to break the proverbial ice. I told him that I was looking forward to seeing a wild kangaroo.

Harder of hearing than I remembered and, ironically, very soft-spoken, Angus mentioned that we would more likely see some camels along this highway.

I wondered if he was a bit dotty, but he went on to explain that camels had been brought to Australia in the 19th century, used as draft animals, and then set free when they were deemed no longer useful to breed and prosper on their own. They adapted extremely well. "They're rounded up in the wild and exported to the Middle East," Angus said with such assurance that I no longer doubted the information. At the same time I appreciated the irony of that particular mental picture and now envisioned camel rustlers with hump-grabbing lassos.

Now traveling due north on the Newell Highway, we passed through Peak Hill, population 1,400, and Dave put on another tape. "Spanish Eyes" filled the air, and I wondered both how many music tapes Dave had brought along and where I might purchase some industrial strength earplugs in The Outback.

We passed a sign for an emu farm, a welcomed temporary distraction and entered Dubbo, one of only two big inland towns in New South Wales. The other one also had a great name that sounded to me like the street name for a social disease, Wagga Wagga, which I can't say like an Australian to save my life. Knowing about Aussie love of casual nicknames, I wondered if Dubbo began it existence as Dublin.

We were heading northwest on the Mitchell Highway when we stopped for lunch, a sandwich and a home-grown banana, at Narromine. The landscape was very flat in this cotton growing area and the midday still very cold and now windy too. As I fought hypothermia, Brian came over to formally introduce himself. He had distinguished grey hair, a classic Englishman's face, and a hesitant manner, as if he had to weigh every word before speaking. Neither of us knew enough about the other to start a real conversation, but I did appreciate the gesture.

Barbara had an empty seat next to her. I knew her name because, at morning tea, I overheard an exchange she had with Ruth, something about playing the organ. I knew that by evening Ruth would be able to give me enough information about the other women for me to write sizeable biographies. Barbara took charge and was putting food on the picnic table, demonstrating obvious host skills. I watched her arrange the meats and condiments attractively and wondered if she was or had ever been in show business. She had a lilting voice and seemed naturally self-possessed, a member of royalty with a lady-like but lusty sense of humor. I watched and listened as she and Gwen ate together. Talking to Barbara seemed very easy. Bubbly and extraordinarily nice, she laughed heartily and enunciated very clearly as if she had had voice training. Each word demonstrated a quick wit and joie de vive. I was enamored and soon confirmed my suspicion; she was a semi-professional singer.

After lunch I sat on the bus with Ruth for the first time that day. Like most long-marrieds, we didn't have to talk to communicate. While I off-and-on studied the detailed New South Wales map that John had gifted me with that morning along with several others, Ruth scanned the landscape looking for wild kangaroos.

Just after 4 p.m. our bus, tough and not exactly five-star, reached Nyngan, where we would spend our first night on the road. Because I had done the calculation, I knew that we had traveled 650 kilometers, or in American, 400 miles. It seemed like much more, and we were still in New South Wales, far, in fact, from the Queensland border. I began to wonder where The Outback officially began. The map didn't clarify and I began to consider the possibility that it might be a state-of-mind rather than a geographic demarcation.

I waited in line to gather our two suitcases from the carry-all and stashed them in our modest, generic room. Ruth wanted to rest and was curious to see what was on TV way out here away from any city. After being confined in a not-too-comfortable bus seat all day, I was full of pent up energy and craved a long walk.

The rain had stopped hours before. The sky was cloudless. It was not yet 4:30 on a Saturday afternoon, but nothing in Nyngan, pronounced *ning' un,* was opened. Nothing. The single grocery store had closed at 4. This town, described as the Gateway to the Outback in our lengthy itinerary, was nondescript and uniformly hardscrabble. I covered every street in less than an hour.

Some Gateway. Nyngan didn't seem like the beginning of anything. It was more a middle-of-nowhere kind of place. Many of the residents were sitting on their front porches, staring into space like extras in a zombie flick. There was no one approachable and nothing to see, so I had plenty of time to think about the other travelers. Some were friendly, most, so far, were not. I sensed a strain of anti-US sentiment among some, especially the men, and I wondered if I would ever move beyond outsider status.

In our first and only exchange, Allan, Barbara's husband, asked me point blank, "How did two Americans qualify for an Australian Trust excursion?"

He may have been simply curious, but I interpreted it as judgmental and felt defensive. "Lynette and Rob sponsored us," I replied, not knowing if this was truly correct. The subject of our eligibility had never come up while making arrangements. For all I knew, Ruth and I were no different from illegal aliens in a smuggler's van barreling down a Texas highway.

Driver Dave was friendly enough. But his subjects were mostly beer drinking, fishing, and lame, politically incorrect jokes. Based on the Trust's description of the trip, I had anticipated some erudite scholar who would wow me with cultural insights while the riveting history of every passing landmark unfolded. When Dave did comment on what we were passing, as opposed to stopping, his words were dry facts and his tone dutiful. Instead of thrilling information, I was listening to crude dog gags and the plans for his upcoming fishing trip.

I returned glumly to the Sundowner Motel, which was barely passable, kind of like the first day of this so-called dream trip had been so far.

Ruth had the TV on and was totally focused on a sports event. The sound was down low and I could see men running up and down a field aggressively kicking a ball. Ah, Australian footy. Ruth must be desperate for distraction, I surmised.

Rob and Lynette were huge fans and followed every sport, every tennis tournament, each cricket match, with extreme Aussie pride. Perhaps Ruth figured this was her entrée with the others. Had she overheard someone passionately discussing a football game? Was she trying to fit into the group by learning something about Aussie sports? I decided not to interrupt and break her concentration to find out. Her eyes were glazed. Does everyone here in Nyngan, even visitors, become a zombie? I decided not to sit with my back to her.

Instead of footy, I settled into the only chair in the room, planning to read until dinner. I had brought along a book by Alan Marshall, a fine Australian writer. On my first visit to Oz, I went into a bookstore and asked the woman behind the counter to tell me the name of her favorite purely Australian author, and I walked out with *I Can Jump Puddles*. I was now reading a collection of Marshall's essays about rural folks called *Australia*. The stories were charmingly authentic and totally without pretension. Highly entertaining. A good thing since the chair was uncomfortable in any position.

Next I read my notes of the trip so far. A little more than 2 ½ pages. That was it. Ten hours, less than 50 lines. I put pen to paper and wrote, "18 more days. 432 hours. How do I avoid going crazy?"

Dinner was a surprise, as in succulent perch and surprisingly good pumpkin soup, an Aussie passion that's on almost every menu. The conversation was lively. I sat across from Lynette, who was drawing everyone out with lots of questions.

Next to me was a lady named Jane. She reminded me of Margaret Thatcher's weathered and indomitable persona. Jane and her craggy husband Michael, who exuded self-possession, had been literally everywhere in the world, and they regaled us with tales of India, Sri Lanka, and Cyprus.

"Where is your favorite destination, Michael?" I asked at one point.

Without hesitation, he replied in a voice that reminded me of fine, single malt scotch, "Easy, Hank. Bhutan." I was pleased that he used my nickname, and I felt more included.

I considered myself fairly world-wise, but at the time I drew a blank on Bhutan. "Tell me about it, Michael."

"It's the world's first non-smoking country. Do you know its most important export?"

"I haven't a clue," I replied.

"Postage stamps!"

Michael spoke with first-hand knowledge about Bhutan's quirky laws. Visitors when he was there, for example, were allowed in only as part of a group and had to stay together like a class on a field trip. He entertained me with stories about his illustrious Irish ancestors long after the dessert and coffee cups had disappeared.

Jane spoke lovingly about her grandfather, a World War II general whose name I never caught. She said of his official biographer, "He was a nice man who unfortunately died of cancer one year after publication." I realized then that Jane and Michael were the kind of people whose lives are routinely recorded in lengthy entries in who's who type books, not in brief 20 words or less newspaper obituaries.

Michael had an unquenchable love of history, especially the events that his ancestors had shaped. While discussing birth dates, he asked mine and I said, "June 18."

"Ah, the Battle of Waterloo," he said from the depths of his historical compendium of a mind without missing a beat.

So, Day One certainly ended on a high note, and I decided that I might not have to worry about slipping into insanity in The Outback after all.

Chapter Three

Tenderfoot Meets Gidgee

The sunrise was spectacular. How did I know? Ruth and I were rambling, or as they say in Australia *having a walkabout,* and taking photos of an old Nyngan movie theater when the sun broke free from the horizon with an explosion of color, mostly nuclear orange. With nothing to do after last night's dinner, we had gone to bed early and, of course, risen early. It felt strange to be so active and alert at sunrise.

I had awakened in a dark motel room, kick-started my brain, discovered where I was, remembered yesterday, and wondered if I could doze off again. But then an inner voice prodded, "When do you expect to be back in Nyngan?" And I answered quite quickly and astutely, "Never." Hence the early morning walk with a new attitude.

Nyngan was a rather nice, small town after all. Of course, nothing was open at this hour. It was Sunday, too, so I wondered if anything would open all day.

I had read a bit after dinner the previous night and learned that Nyngan was an Aboriginal name meaning "long pond of water" and that the town, so very dry today, was completely under water in 1990. That flood was labeled the worst of the century and verified in my mind one inescapable fact about Australia—it's either flooded or on fire.

On our previous trip here, we went to the Blue Mountains west of Sydney in the aftermath of some bush fires started by arsonists. The devastation was shocking. Eucalypts, the common indigenous trees, burn interestingly. Fire might affect only their lower portions, or it can creep all the way to the top, creating what's called a crown fire. From on high, wind-driven balls of flame can and do catapult for great distances in any direction.

When I read about Nyngan's epic flood, I recalled our very first trip to Oz, as Australia's sometimes called, in 1993. Daily back then and strictly out of curiosity, I combed newspapers seeking information about the United States. I wanted to see what there was in the print media, namely the Australian press, about us and how they expressed it. Only two items comprising three paragraphs appeared in two weeks—John Wayne Bobbitt's angrily amputated penis and a brief mention of flooding in the Midwest. Ruth and I lived in St. Louis at the time, and this news was not especially unusual. When you live at the confluence of two mighty rivers, you get used to periodic inundation.

As our plane approached home a few days later, the announcement came on about tray tables and seatbacks, and I pulled my nose out of my book and glanced out the window. Instead of rolling hills and farms, I saw below a huge, inland body of water. For a split second I panicked, thinking that the disoriented pilot was taking us down in Chicago. But the expanse below wasn't the color of Lake Michigan. It turned out to be an unprecedented 500 year flood, worth, say, 25 words in the *Sydney Morning Herald*.

Day Two's travel towards The Outback, wherever it began, was shorter then Saturday's—Nyngan to Nardoo Station via the Mitchell Highway. The day was brilliant, cool, and sunny.

As soon as we reached the outskirts of Nyngan, which took about 20 seconds, Dave grabbed his microphone and said that the music tape he had played yesterday was the only one on board. He apologized for the oversight and said he would not be playing it again. I looked over at Lynette who had a satisfied smile on her face.

I leaned toward her and said, "You had a hand in this, didn't you, Lynette?"

Negotiating for all of us in her caring way, she admitted, "I merely asked Dave if he had any other musical choices." On previous trips with her and Rob, Lynette had always done all of the driving with Ruth navigating. Ruth and Lynette also did the daily food organizing. Rob and I selected the wines and the evening restaurants. Not a bad deal.

"I do have some books on tape," announced Dave, "but first you might be interested in Lynn Bedall, the last true Australian XP before 1923."

XP? Did I hear him correctly? Did he say, or mean, MP? Still not quite used to Dave's richly Australian diction, I wasn't sure that I heard even the name correctly. I had no idea what an XP was, but the Aussies aboard nodded approvingly and laughed regularly at Bedall's laconic humor. Again, I didn't get it, but I knew neither the player nor the historical references.

In a permanent caddy to my left were some well-thumbed travel books, a tiny on-board library. I checked the pile instead of listening to the tape and selected a few. In the first I learned about what the writer called the Gunbarrel Highway from Alice Springs to Perth. Ah, yet another road to explore. Built in the 1950s, it displaced some Aboriginals. I wondered why a travel book would mention this since building projects always displaced someone. Was it guilt? I also wondered why I couldn't find the Gunbarrel Highway on any of the maps John had given me.

I read next about some astronomical observatories, which were somewhat common here in a land of little artificial light once you're away from the coast. I later discovered that there were 17 professional observatories in Australia and many more public, 14 in New South Wales alone.

I examined pictures of the Simpson Desert's sand dunes in a *Time/Life* tome and began looking for a map, any map, that would define this Desert's perimeter. I didn't find one, nor did I determine the size of the Gibson, Great Sandy, or Great Victoria Deserts. They all morphed together in the vast interior. I turned a page and found some pictures of Ayers Rock, now mostly called Uluru by everyone here except for the very elderly and the culturally insensitive.

I was being secretly observed, probably a lot more than I realized. Gwen saw my awed reaction to several photographs of The Outback landscape around Uluru near Australia's true Red Center. She leaned toward me and said, "Angus and I were in a museum in London one time for an exhibition of paintings from around Alice Springs, and the next day a critic in the newspaper said that the colors had been overdone. We had a bit of a laugh about that."

We pulled into Byrock Village, more of a one building way-station than a community. The few dwellings looked abandoned. Total observable population this morning—one man, one dog.

A major railway stop in the 1880s, Byrock was now a sleepy outpost surrounded by miles of nothing much. Its name derived from a pioneer family, *Bye's Rockhole*, or from the Aboriginal word for rockhole, *bai*, or from a misspelling on a Station Master's rubber stamp. No one knows for sure.

In the 18th century the National Government was pushing out the frontier, very much like in Nebraska and Montana at about the same time, and those in power were determined to make Byrock a major hub. The Government offered land for sale cheaply. A railroad arrived. Five-hundred people took a chance and moved here. What The Feds hadn't thought about beforehand was water. Since there proved to be no reliable local source, it had to be brought in during droughts, which was most of the time, for a penny a gallon. So much for governmental planning.

Near Byrock was an important Aboriginal site, the first of several we would visit. As Dave led us to it, he said, "This rocky outcrop trapped rain and provided a water supply for the Abos, so they made this a sacred camping site." As I was making a mental note to check and see if the term *Abo* was politically correct, I noticed that the woman standing next to me at the time, Jan, was wincing. I had my answer.

I walked completely around the water hole, which was the size of an average municipal swimming pool, and looked into its eerie depths. It seemed only inches deep, but it was hard to tell. Strange growths of peculiar color seemed to wave in a beckoning way from just below the surface near the shoreline. Towards the center it became opaque. I looked across at the group from our bus on the other side where most had wandered. No one was wading. No one was even leaning down to touch its surface. If a waterhole is ever discovered on another planet in a distant solar system, it will probably look like this. I read much later that the Aboriginal creator god Biamee drank here during Dreamtime.

Dreamtime is yet another concept, like infinity, that will probably always baffle me.

Nearby was a forlorn cemetery that brought to mind the certain struggle of any pioneer who tried to make a life in this largely unforgiving place. The headstones recorded falls from horses, sudden epidemics, and cruelly short lives.

We moved on to the town of Bourke for a picnic lunch alongside the Darling River, Australia's second most important inland waterway. Everyone photographed the historic lock and weir from several vantage points as if the world media were hungry for images of it and paid accordingly. But truly, the actual results were the kind of images that, when found much later in a drawer or file, induced the question, "Where the hell is this?"

Bourke has been around since 1862 when it was established as a center for sheep herding and wool export. Camel and bull teams provided transport until a bridge was built across the Darling in 1883.

A train arrived two years later. Cobb and Company, a coachworks builder, had hired Americans to plan and implement the operation. At its height, Cobb's network of tracks was the most extensive coach system in the world, all horse drawn. It had branches as far distant as South Africa. Reportedly, 6,000 horses from a herd of 30,000 pulled cars along 28,000 miles of company track each week. Bourke was one of Cobb and Company's five major Australian facilities, but the coachworks here shut down in 1899 due to little demand for its services—delivering mail, people moving, and getting the gold to market from a rush that never amounted to much.

Bourke's history is blotted with the usual shearer strikes and floods. Riverboats disappeared in the 1930s as the flow of the Darling declined. In the 1950s, the Darling surged back with historic floods followed, of course, by drought in the 1960s.

Bourke peaked in the 1890s but it had arrested decline and was now a fairly steady commercial center. Cotton, Mandarin oranges, grapes, and melons joined wool as cash producing endeavors.

Bourke looked prosperous. It had a busy business street, a bowling club, a race course, a hospital, and an information center. But our only stop besides the weir was the cemetery, which held some fascinating surprises.

When camels moved into the area in the 1880s, so did Afghans to care for them. It was hard to envision the scene, Outback Dundees and bushrangers working alongside turbaned, bearded Muslims, but that was the reality of the place. Several Afghans were buried in Bourke's cemetery, easily identified because they faced Mecca.

The most fascinating grave in the cemetery, however, was Fred Hollows'. I had never heard this name until I saw it on a tombstone, but now I won't forget it. An expert in cataract removal, Fred Hollows solved the problem of trachoma, which responded to his treatment in the 1920s.

Trachoma is a severe form of conjunctivitis that, left untreated, causes loss of sight. It's the leading cause of blindness in the world, afflicting over 400,000,000 people according to something called spedex.com. It doesn't usually occur in places where sanitation, proper diet, education, and antibiotics are available. That's why it's relatively unknown in the United States.

After Hollows encountered this widespread disease among the Gurindji people of the Northern Territory, he became devoted to Aboriginal health, and his eye clinics eventually spread to Bangladesh, Nepal, and as far away as Central America. His philosophy that made this possible was, "Don't live with a problem, solve it." He did, with interocular lenses. Hollows died in 1993.

Back on the bus, my seatmate was Roger, Jan's husband. Silver hair tipped with white above a round face of serious expression, Roger cultivated a tuft of hair on his chin that bobbed when he talked. Behind his thick glasses were kind eyes that indicated a gentle nature. We found quickly that we had reading in common and were soon deeply involved in book title exchange. As we zipped through Barringun, Roger was highly recommending David Malouf's *Conversations at Curlew Creek* to me as a window into all-things Australian. He next pushed Thea Astley, whom I learned was a chain-smoking stylist who either vexed or amazed readers. While also teaching, she cranked out 15 novels between 1958 and 1999, winning more Miles

Franklin Awards, which I assumed were equivalent to Pulitzers, than any other writer.

As Roger and I discussed Australian authors, we apparently crossed the border between New South Wales and Queensland. I must have been engrossed in conversation because I didn't notice when. Had I been paying attention, I would have, at the least, recorded the information in my log. At the most, I would have demanded that we stop, taken a few dozen pictures of the welcome sign, and passed around some confetti and champagne. But I wasn't.

Roger had been an economist before retirement. He and Jan seemed less affluent then the other passengers, more like Ruth and me. They were the only couple who had never been to the United States. He said that, while they did like group touring, "camping is less expensive."

When pressed about where they had been or hoped to visit, Roger said vaguely, "Jan wants to travel more." Then he let the subject drop.

They lived for two years in Dar el Salaam, Africa, while Roger worked on a native project. "Back in Australia" he recalled, "I became involved in Aboriginal development and spent the bulk of my career handling court cases and writing about native rights, like protecting burial grounds." He went on for a bit, and a bit more candidly than I expected, about how difficult that work became and how insensitive his culture could be. He finally had enough frustration and left.

In retirement Roger had started a book-a-month club to discuss both classics and serious contemporary literature with others, and he was well up on American authors of note. He and Jan also became avid bird watchers, and no one took more photographs of flowers in The Outback than Roger. Subsequent to our time together, Jan and Roger developed a passion for China's wildflowers and its Silk Road connections and have visited there.

As we neared our destination, our casual conversation turned to politics, and Roger said, "We are watching your race with great interest and personally hoping that the Democrats can bring back voters so they have a chance of winning."

I was pleased that Roger felt comfortable enough to say this to me, but I was also a bit nonplussed. How did he learn enough about American politics to choose sides? And why *that* side? And did I respond like a good will ambassador or a partisan? Luckily enough, this decision was lifted from my shoulders because by that time we were pulling into Nardoo Station.

Dave interrupted our increasingly serious discussion with some information about Patterson's Curse. This invasive plant is native to Mediterranean lands, but the emigrant Patterson family liked its purple flower and planted some seeds in their Australian garden. "They watched," said

Dave, "as it spread in every direction to become the main weed in pastures as far away as Tasmania."

Heads were nodding vigorously up and down the bus, and I heard Jane behind me tell Ruth, "It's also called Salvation Jane. Thankfully, not after me. I wish Dave would tell us something we *don't* know."

So. Lynette, and now Jane, were overtly disenchanted with Dave. Would others follow?

"We spend millions of dollars every year trying to control it," Dave continued in his serious seminar voice. "When eaten by livestock, the Curse causes weight loss and can even kill if the animals get enough of it in their systems." He lightened up and closed with a stupid-question joke with the punch-line, "In Australia, which direction is north?"

The laughter on the bus was merely polite.

Nardoo Station turned out to be a 110,000 acre working sheep and cattle ranch. After showing us to some rustic, free standing, zero amenities cabins, Carmel, the owner, ordered us to assemble for a tour in five minutes.

Shortly thereafter we were listening to her and looking at a flat horizon in every direction. Carmel was a no-nonsense, tough as tungsten woman, because she had to be. Mother of four, three away at school and the fourth underfoot and annoyingly pre-adolescent, Carmel ran Nardoo Station by herself most of the year. Although she had earned a degree in nursing, she spoke about going back to school for another in the travel host industry to make the tours of her spread more appealing. "Right now, though, Ringo has a burr in his paw," she said stooping down to remove the offender from the limping pure kelpie that was following us around. Mission accomplished, Carmel told us about her fulfilling life on a spread the size of several recognized countries.

At one point she took us over to an outsized metal tub full of water, a makeshift Outback spa as it turned out, and encouraged us to have a soak in it at some point during the evening. "That's thermal water from the Great Artesian Basin in there," she said, pointing to her rustic tub and then dipping her hand in to gauge the temperature.

I subsequently learned that the Basin is the largest underground reservoir in the world. It formed between 100 and 250 million years ago and underlies about 20% of Australia, mostly the arid and semi-arid parts of Queensland, New South Wales, South Australia, and the Northern Territory. Water from it comes to the surface between 90 and 212 degrees Fahrenheit.

That there are any people besides subsistence Aboriginals living here in this part of Queensland is due to this reliable, underground sea. Discovered in 1878, the Great Artesian made human settlement possible. By the early 20th century, 1,500 bores had been drilled to tap it and running livestock became dependably resident.

Carmel spoke eloquently about the importance of this humongous though ultimately finite supply of water in an otherwise dry land. "The Government just made us cap our outlets, personally costing our family over a million, matched dollars," she said matter-of-factly as if this was just another irritating, out of pocket expense and not a small fortune.

Angus asked about her husband, and Carmel said that he was off watering 14,000 ewes and 1,800 head of cattle and was gone for weeks at a time.

She talked about the closest town to their spread, Cunnamulla, population 1,500. Like many interior towns, this one's Aboriginal name translated to "long stretch of water" because of the Warrego River but also inspired by the eternal quest for liquid sustenance. Cunnamulla's woolshed, Tinnenburra, was at one time the largest in the world with 101 blade stands. Carmel said about her vast domain, "It's Mitchell grass plains with lots of gidgee."

"What's gidgee?" I asked.

"A hardwood tree that gives hot heat when burned. Vegetation here must dig deep to survive drought, so our grass has 12 foot roots. On the other side, our property practically disappeared in the big flood of 1990. Everything you see here today was under water, except for the house. And again in 97, a 16 inch rainfall filled our creeks and the Warrego. But we've had almost nothing since." She kicked the desiccated, red earth to illustrate her point. "Our property's had only eight inches of rain in the past four years." Surprising me, she concluded, "I love my life."

Dinner at Nardoo was ranch food—big chunk beef stew and over-boiled potatoes—at some picnic tables that mandated closeness and camaraderie. Ruth and I sat across from Christine, a student from Dusseldorf, Germany. She was staying with Carmel's family in a financial/cultural exchange until the coming November. We quickly introduced Christine to Allan, who spoke German, and she was grateful to have someone to converse with in her native language. Allan appreciated the chance to practice and later thanked us.

After dinner conversations waned, Jane, Allan, Ruth, and I walked down the road to get away from the few, inconsequential, artificial lights and have a look at the night sky. We found the Southern Cross, something identifiable and familiar in an ocean of flickering glitter, virtual galaxies of stars and planets. In the process of sharing our awe, we were moving from acquaintances to friends.

It was cold, so everyone gathered around the gidgee fire built in a huge, rock-rimmed hole. Within minutes it became a relaxed and intimate circle of humans warmed only on one side and surrounded by total darkness. Jokes were told. After one that ended with the punch line, "Abscess makes the fart go Honda," we began telling ghost stories.

Ruth related a frightening story about a sleepwalking cousin and a loaded gun, but Karin won the most chills with her tale of a young man, very dead, who sat glumly at the end of her bed desperately trying to make contact. She subsequently found out that, besides her bedroom, he had made two other appearances in her neighborhood.

I was listening intently with my feet propped on a huge rock, part of the fire circle's enclosure, clearly forgetting Carmel's warning about gidgee's intense heat. Suddenly I realized that my shoes, the only ones I had to wear for almost three weeks while trudging around The Outback, were smoking. Shocked, I yanked my feet towards me and felt the soles. They were as hot as in-use skillet bottoms, and I realized, stupidly, that both of my feet were uncomfortably hot too. Luckily, after my shoes cooled, there was no real damage, except to my ego. After I took some gently ribbing from the crowd, I had to admit that I wouldn't last five minutes in Carmel's shoes.

A couple at a time, we headed for bed, not to the spa. Ruth went to sleep immediately. I read for a bit but quickly began to fade.

Just before turning in, I had a carpe diem moment. I pictured bubbling artesian water under a canopy of closer than ever stars and whispered to myself, "This is probably your only chance to submerge your body in the thermal splendor of the Great Artesian Basin, Harbaugh. Are you going to let this chance go by?"

"No," I whispered back. I pulled on my swim trunks, closed the door quietly, and jogged past the fire hole. The night was now bitterly cold. The big barrel full of hot artesian water that doubled as a spa seemed increasingly inviting as I sprinted. When I was close enough to see it by the splendor of lights from the heavens, I became aware that it was already occupied. At first I thought it was a jolly group of bus mates and continued my advance. But then I realized that I was hearing a single male voice. He was quietly singing to himself. It was Dave, indulging. I stopped in my tracks and began backpedaling.

Rather than subject myself to endless mate-ing and a string of late night fart jokes, I turned back, scurried into the relative warmth of our cabin, and climbed under the blankets.

Before I drifted off, it occurred to me…here I was practically in the middle of Australia on a huge ranch and I still hadn't seen any wild roos.

Chapter Four

Caught Red-handed

After serving us a hearty ranch breakfast the next morning, Carmel took us into her shearing shed to share her considerable knowledge about a very Australian topic—sheep. I knew virtually nothing about this still important part of Australia's national economy and was surprised that the Aussies also listened in rapt attention to Carmel and asked many questions, especially about current conditions. "We get $64 a head," she told us. "The market's high."

She pointed to an empty stall. "We can do 1,600 sheep a day, using all male shearers. Females check the fleece because they have more sensitive hands. After shearing, we brand."

I wanted to know why females were excluded from shearing but didn't feel exactly comfortable asking. I looked over at Jan, the most likely native female in our group to challenge the status quo, but she didn't have her angry face on.

I also knew that a large number of Carmel's sheep could end up being sent to the Middle East and ritually sacrificed during religious ceremonies. But, again, this was probably a hot-button issue best left alone, at least for now.

Nardoo Station was an unforgettable experience, and I left reluctantly, staring out the rear window of the bus until we had turned onto the main road and its cluster of buildings disappeared. It was the first destination of the trip that made me want to immediately go back to learn more. I left a bunch of questions and my e-mail address with Carmel, but she never sent the answers. Probably, make that certainly, she was too busy. I also regretted passing on my chance to soak in the thermal purity of the Great Artesian Basin and hoped for another opportunity.

Few cars were on the Mitchell Highway, also called the Matilda according to my map, and the ones that came infrequently from out of nowhere behind us usually passed our bus as a greyhound would a basset before quickly disappearing up the road.

But then we eased up to and were directly behind what appeared to be an oversized transport truck. Dave was practically bumping its mud flaps, and I had the impression that he just might honk repeatedly for this wide-load to get out of his way. But instead he got on his CB.

After he stopped talking into his mouthpiece, he asked, "Has the Yank back there seen a Road Train yet?"

I was sitting in a single seat today and conversing intermittently across the aisle with Rob. He had liked Nardoo Station too, and we were sharing our impressions.

Before I could answer, Dave dismissed me like an impatient teacher would a slow student. "Ruth?" he asked, leaning slightly toward her. She was, after all, his co-pilot. Each day a passenger was selected to take the single seat next to the driver. The view of the road ahead through the wraparound front window was great, and it was perceived as kind of an honor to be asked. Ruth was the first designated female co-pilot and Dave was treating her like teacher's pet.

As we had waited to board at Nardoo Station, Ruth had uncharacteristically begged me to take her place.

"What's the problem?" I asked.

"Dave!" she replied, joining Lynette and Jane.

We had never discussed our opinions of our driver, so I was surprised.

"What about Dave?"

"He's the male bonding type. He gets along better with men."

I hadn't noticed this and was curious to learn what she had observed that made her say this. Ruth has always been a much better judge of personalities and personal agendas than I, so I assumed she was right. But standing in the middle of a group waiting for Dave to finish stowing the suitcases had not been a good time to ask her to, as Lucy would say, splain.

"May well be true," I whispered to her, "but everyone has to take a turn up front, so you might as well get your obligation out of the way. And you have a better chance of spotting kangaroos up there."

She thought this over, mounted the steps, and climbed awkwardly into the seat, the only possible way to get into it. I could now see the back of the transport truck mere inches, it seemed, from her face.

I knew what a Road Train was but had seen them only in pictures.

Instead of watching the massive rear end of the truck, Dave was looking directly at my wife, smiling like a guy at a bar who just delivered his best pick-up line. "Ruth?" he repeated. And I could see her shaking her head *no*.

So I took the bait and called out, "What is it?"

He looked into the rear view mirror directly at me and, although I could see only his eyes, I knew that he was grinning. "It, mate, is an up to five trailer transport lorry carrying livestock, grain..." His voice trailed off as he turned and smiled again at Ruth, rather intimately. He was soon back on the CB, and I realized that he was talking to the driver of the rig just up ahead.

Off again, Dave looked back to see if I was paying attention. "They change drivers without stopping, and vehicles behind them, like us, need their help to pass."

Dave hid his mouth again with the CB to continue making arrangements.

"They're ready now, so let's have a go," he said coolly. He pulled into the right lane and slowly began to inch forward beside the behemoth. My eyes were on the road ahead, my heart racing. If anyone was speeding toward us, we were certain to have a head-on collision. There was no shoulder. No margin for error.

"It's truly well named," I called out to Dave while I was counting off the units as we crept forward. I couldn't help imagining the mayhem that would occur if these freight warehouses were allowed on busy US highways. There were five, full-sized storage units behind a massive cab, and I could clearly see why it would be impossible to pass one safely without cooperation, even on roads with few vehicles traveling in either direction.

Ruth made eye contact with the Road Train driver and waved as we continued to advance at a deliberate pace. I now understood why Dave had tailgated, and I fervently wished that he would speed up and move into the left lane ahead of the roaring train as soon as possible. My fingers gripping my book were practically numb with the kind of tension one feels when touching down on a runway in a snowstorm. Dave remained steady in his pace until he judged that he could safely ease in front of the mechanical monster. It was, I had to admit, a masterful performance.

I was greatly relieved when the entire Super Chief was behind us, and I looked around to see if the others were beginning to relax too. But no one was paying the least bit of attention to either the Road Train or Dave's commentary. I felt suddenly like the new kid in class, yet I continued, "Why didn't he slow down for us, Dave?"

"Good question, mate. In the Outback, and especially in the Northern Territory, the dirt roads are like talcum powder, and a Road Train's, say, twenty wheels churn up so much dust that it takes twenty minutes to clear the air," he explained, "so they don't brake unless it's absolutely necessary."

I looked over at Rob. He had nodded off.

Lynette was staring out the window, paying no attention to the questions or answers.

Dave was clearly on one of his favorite topics and glad to have someone, anyone, interested. Me. "They have 36 gears and it's impossible to stop on short notice. Once you hit the brakes, it takes about half a mile to stop. The roads are mostly straight out here, and any transport driver can see far enough ahead that passing shouldn't slow anybody down."

I was surprised that he used the word *miles* instead of kilometers. Probably, a slip-of-the-system since it hasn't been all that long since Australia went metric.

Lynette was one seat back from me, so I turned and asked, "Didn't Dave mean kilometers?'

She tsked. "Right-o. But we still have trouble, and some Australian women still complain endlessly about having to measure in grams instead of ounces."

Dave must have sensed, or overheard, what we were discussing. "It takes 10 kilometers to get a Road Train up to full speed, and you can only travel at 50 miles per hour despite the 500 horses you're riding."

I decided to attribute this mixed measuring to speedometers that showed both systems, and I didn't ask for further explanation.

As the Road Train slowly faded from view on the highway behind us, Dave told a bunch of hair-raising stories with very unhappy endings to illustrate his point about how difficult it was to stop a Road Train. One had to do with a young woman who stood in the middle of the road trying to wave one down only to realize too late that it couldn't stop before reaching, and swallowing, her.

Our situation had changed, but Dave wasn't done with the subject. "On long hauls when the road is hot, tires get blown, sometimes three on a typical run."

"Is there a limit to how many trailers can be towed?" I called out.

"Well, mate, a Super Road Train has seven trailers and hauls 190 tons."

Mightily impressed and still a bit intimidated, I turned to look back up the road for the colossus, but it had already receded to the size of a Tonka toy.

My eyes, like Lynette's, moved to the landscape. I scanned 360 degrees and there were no cavorting kangaroos. But as if to compensate, wild emus were often common along the roadside. There was also, but only occasionally, prickly pear, the cactus that's so common in the American Southwest. I remembered being surprised by its appearance in Italy on the Gargano Peninsula and in other exotic places. And now, here. I wondered if, thanks to global warming, I'd soon see prickly pear in Antarctica. It could be similar to Salvation Jane in its adaptability, I surmised.

I already knew that Jane, Lynette, and Jan were flora experts, and the first two were close enough to ask, "Is prickly pear a native plant?"

Jane answered. "No! It was imported and took root, menacingly so. There's a monument to it in some Queensland town. Kili something, I believe."

I later found the monument that Jane referred to, a cairn actually. But it wasn't to honor the plant. It honored a moth. On Marble Street in Dalby, Queensland, about 300 miles due east of where we were at the time, the monument was erected to recognize and thank the Cactoblastis Cactorum. A single prickly pear arrived in Australia in 1839, and its progeny quickly spread over 50,000,000 acres. It took this Argentine, egg-laying moth 10 years to completely eliminate the threat.

"What a noxious plant," Jane concluded. She always knew the answers to my questions, and it was not unusual for her to lean toward me and exclaim, "that's a desert oak!" or "do you see those birds up there with pink breasts? They're galahs. Here in Australia we say, 'Silly as a galah,'" her tone of voice telling me that she was describing very foolish behavior. "We also have grey and pink cockatoos," she would add with more than a hint of Aussie pride.

We were on our way to Charleville, the "Gateway to the West". I never, ever saw a sign that informed, "YOU ARE NOW ENTERING THE OUTBACK," but if such a sign existed, it would probably be placed just about where we were on this Monday morning. The landscape was beginning to look like the pictures in the books.

The recorded voice that Dave had selected to entertain, or subdue us, today was droning on about Banjo Patterson, 1864-1941, a bush poet dear to the hearts of doggerel loving Aussies. His verses made me cringe. Why? A sample says it all.

> When Clancy took the drover's track
> In years of long ago,
> He drifted to the outer back
> Beyond the Overflow;
> By rolling plain and rocky shelf,

> With stock whip in his hand,
> He reached at last, oh lucky elf!
> The Town of Come-and-help-yourself
> In Rough-and-ready Land.

Next Dave put on Henry Lawson, second only to Banjo Patterson in esteem and popularity. Besides poetry, Lawson was also a fiction writer who specialized in bush lives despite the fact that he had little exposure to The Outback. Born 3 years after Banjo, he lived until 1922, which amazed a lot of people. Lawson, deaf most of his life, ended up a beggar battling alcohol on Sydney's streets. Here's an example of his output from his poem, "Andy's Gone With Cattle".

> Our Andy's gone to battle now
> 'Gainst Drought, the red marauder;
> Our Andy's gone with cattle now
> Across the Queensland border.

> He's left us in dejection now;
> Our hearts with him are roving.
> It's dull on this selection now,
> Since Andy went a-droving.

The other passengers listened intently. I didn't, fearing loss of brain cells. And, more importantly, I might get sidetracked and miss a cavorting kangaroo.

Charleville is Southwest Queensland's largest and most important town. Today, as on most others I assumed, it looked sun-baked. The streets were practically deserted. I kept reminding myself that this was the Southern Hemisphere's winter and yet it looked like a Yuma, Arizona, summer out there. As we drove towards city center, I tried to imagine what it would be like to actually *be* here in mid-summer.

Dave pulled over to the curb and a woman climbed aboard. She and Dave greeted each other warmly and she turned to us with a cheery, "G-day. I'm Rachel." She commenced a colorful commentary about her hometown while Dave drove us directly to its biggest tourist attraction, a singular curiosity, the Vortex Gun. This contraption dated from the drought of 1902 and was only one of many rain-making experiments that didn't work. The Chamber of Commerce obviously found it important and had more or less pedestalized it for posterity. I didn't get a close up look because we didn't disembark. Dave kept the engine running as if a Vortex Gun might be dangerous and he might have to back away suddenly. Rachel described the weird metal construction's failure to launch.

Although Rachel displayed a great deal of earthiness and droll humor, the best word to describe the Charleville tour was, because of Charleville, *mildly entertaining.* Like the local travel literature, she spoke of the importance of Cobb and Co in the town's development. She called its plant "the largest and longest running coach making factory in Australia" as if horse drawn coaches should and would really impress frequent flying, text messaging passengers. She told us that the assembly plant burned to the ground in 1980, but that this didn't put folks out of work since the Company's horse drawn carriages hadn't been made in Charleville since 1920. I was trying to care.

We drove slowly past a typical, small town depot, and Rachel spoke of the trains from Brisbane that arrived twice a week after a 17 hour trip. She hoped that service would continue despite the fact that neither carried many passengers.

Like Carmel before her, Rachel told us about the life-sustaining Great Artesian Sea under her town. She segued into a local bilby breeding program that attempted to preserve this rare and endangered marsupial species in its natural habitat. Also called the rabbit-eared bandicoot, a bilby looked like the result of crossbreeding a rat, a rabbit, and a mole, but nevertheless kind of cute.

Rachel would drop the subject of water but then circle back to it, particularly in regards to the Great Artesian and the unpredictable Warrego River that flowed, on rare occasions, through town. "We have flooding roughly every seven years, so many houses are on stilts. Like that one." She pointed out the window at a modest dwelling, the only kind I saw in Charleville. "In 1990 was the 100 year flood," Rachel said as if reporting an event of minor consequence.

Deadpan dry, she told about a statue of Mary in the Catholic school that we were passing. "It was lifted off its pedestal and floated away, later to be found in a low lying spot popular with teenagers and returned to the school. She was the only virgin to come out of Bradley's Gulley still intact."

Rachel ended her tour with details about Charleville's once a year camel races, which were, I was learning, a fairly common phenomenon in The Outback. She made theirs sound like World Cup Finals, and maybe it was. With a hearty "Cheerio!" she stepped down from the bus in front of a local landmark, the Corones Hotel, a fading yet authentic landmark. Rachel disappeared up the street.

This was our lunch spot. Before eating and simply because it was there, I took some exterior shots of the fairly typical, main-corner Australian hotel. Then I went inside to find the men's rest...uh, loo. Because of my photo-op delay, I was in there alone. Rinsing my hands, I looked about for the soap. There was no dispenser, but perched on the windowsill just above the sink was a small round red disc. It looked very used, just a nub, but it *was* available. I took it down and began rubbing it vigorously into my palms and, curiously, it didn't lather. Its feel reminded me of old-fashioned Lava soap. After a vigorous effort, I looked down to discover that my hands were turning the color of the disc, an angry orangish-ironish red. I put the disc back on the windowsill and attempted to wash off the huge stigmatas, which just made them worse. Both hands were now literally covered, and I felt like a sleepwalking Lady Macbeth about to make her big entrance.

I couldn't stay in the john…uh, loo, any longer without creating suspicion, and Ruth was surely wondering what happened to me. I weighed my options and concluded that I had no choice other than to stick my hands in my pockets and locate the group.

They were seated at a single, long table in the dining room. A plate lunch was being served. It didn't look very good, and I had a big distraction.

As soon as I could, I discreetly showed my carmine hands to Ruth.

Her eyes widened. "How did you do that?"

"Help me," I whimpered.

"How? And how did you get air freshener all over your hands?" she asked.

"Never mind. See if there's soap in the ladies' bath…uh, loo."

I kept the napkin over my hands as best I could while I picked at the salad, and then Ruth and I excused ourselves one at a time like Trapp children at a Nazi dinner party. The self-important, very long-winded hotel manager giving an interminable speech involving the history of the Corones didn't seem to notice. As to his speech, involving it wasn't.

There was no soap in the ladies ro…loo either, so I had to resign myself to walking about with threateningly tight fists until the color began to fade, whenever that might be.

"Let's go back in and make the best of it, "Ruth suggested, but I refused to listen to the tiresome gentleman anymore. Instead, I went exploring.

At the other end of the lobby I found a huge, square Outback bar, the first I had seen not in a movie. It was wonderfully authentic. It must have looked exactly like this when the Corones, the project of an eminent Greek family, opened in 1929. A Greek concern is not unusual for Australia. Melbourne contains the third largest Greek community in the world after Athens and Thessaloniki.

I walked around the bar slowly and it could have been a movie set. This one even had a scattering of male patrons who looked like extras from *Crocodile Dundee*. I wanted to join them, but they looked rather unfriendly, maybe even a bit menacing, and I recalled Hollywood films of my youth with saloon brawls following the taunting of the Tenderfoot stranger who ordered sarsaparilla. That would be me. And how would I explain my rouged hands when I held them up to fend them off?

I headed back to the lobby but made a promise to myself to somehow, somewhere, sometime have an authentic pub/mate experience while in The Outback.

I have since learned that the Corones went into receivership, emerged from it, and was being restored. This is a good and not unexpected series of events given its condition when I was there.

I was browsing a few very tired history displays in its lobby when Allan happened by. By now he was a mate whom I knew would be discreet.

"Pssst, Allan," I began.

As he approached, I opened my palms and showed my twin stains. "Do you have any idea how I might get this off?" I asked.

"Where did you encounter air freshener?" he wondered.

"On the sill in the men's loo. I thought it was manly Outback soap."

"That's going to be on there for a bit," he advised, doing a very good job of not appearing amused.

"Allan. Would you mind doing something for me?"

"As I said, I have no idea how to remove it."

"No. I want to go into a real Aussie pub some evening and have a beer or two. Talk about crocodiles. Will you go with me?"

Allan was a reserved, dignified lawyer, a government service veteran with *Who's Who* credentials. But he also had a twinkle in his eye and a robust sense of adventure. I knew this from his now frequent and delightfully told stories. He hesitated as if gauging the risk. "They can be kind of rough, Hank," he began.

"We don't have to."

"No, no. We'll do it. We just have to choose a bit carefully."

"You're on."

As we left Charleville, I was flipping absent-mindedly through a local travel booklet and came upon this quote. "The first thing we hear from visitors in our area is 'I had no idea there was so much to do.'" Well, that says a lot about human perspective, and I wondered how locals who found the Vortex gun way cool would react to Times Square.

I also read a few Outback traveling tips. "Ensure that your vehicle is mechanically sound and carry ample water and spares such as tyres, radiator hoses and fan belts, together with a good tool-kit. Two-way radios or satellite phones are recommended as normal mobile phones do not work in remote areas."

Hmmmm. Did I really want to experience a pub filled with drinking men who needed serious survival skills just to live here and carried heavy-duty tool kits in their pickups?

We reached Tambo, our overnighter, by four p.m., and co-pilot Ruth asked me, "Did you see all those dead kangaroos?"

"Where?"

"All along the road. Hundreds of them!"

"Must have been hit by Road Trains," I surmised and then added, "At least we now have hard evidence that they do exist. Or did."

We quickly exhausted the ambiance of the Tambo Mill Motel, which was for sale but not tempting, and decided to have a walkabout. About a block into it, an excited Jane approached us from the opposite direction.

"There!" she said, gesticulating wildly toward the direction from which she had come. "Roos! A large number of them!"

"Where?" Ruth and I asked simultaneously.

"Beyond the gazebo in the park. You can't miss them!"

But we did. We ended up crossing a bridge and following the Barcoo River without seeing so much as a kookaburra, the Australian bird with a raucous, human-like laugh. While I did have an authentic bush experience along a rough river bank dotted with gum trees, Ruth wandered off to visit with a woman in a caravan, what we would call a camper or RV in the United States. Aussies take them into remote areas like this, park in some isolated spot, and "go bush", whatever *that* entails.

We finally realized our mistake, re-crossed the bridge, and found the gazebo. There were zero roos in this well maintained, little park.

"I suppose they bounded away," I said to Ruth.

She slowly turned to face me and her eyes widened.

"Hank! Turn around!" she said breathlessly.

I did and was confronted with a mustering of motionless grey roos on a vast plain, so many it would have been impossible to count them.

I did the predictable, jumping up and down like a fool to see if they would move. They didn't even blink. So I attempted to ease closer to authenticate my first-live-wild-roo sighting with photographs. For every step I took, the whole herd hopped. It was as if they calculated my stride to keep me at just this exact distance from them. We finally had to give up on everything but the sheer thrill of having an unprecedented experience in a remote place.

At dinner we got stuck sitting with Dave—alone. Some of the others were beginning to avoid him whenever possible. He, of course, didn't want to hear about a herd of kangaroos, so I went into reporter mode and asked him a series of interview-type questions about fishing, his favorite topic. His stories moved on to crocodiles, a subject that Dave knew well from first hand experience.

Much later in a letter after visiting The Kimberley Region of Northwest Australia, Allan wrote to me, "You wouldn't believe how far out of the water such a big animal can project itself. Two-thirds of its body, including all four legs, is above the water. Incredibly, there are some people out on the rivers in small boats, quite unprotected, who try to tempt crocodiles into jumping."

I thought of my cavorting while surrounded by kangaroos that can really kick and decided I wouldn't do that again.

Over dessert, Dave told Ruth and me some riveting true tales about his personal encounters with crocs, and all of a sudden I realized I was enjoying his company.

Chapter Five

The Real Australia

I've been to Sydney six times. Melbourne the same. Brisbane, three visits. Etc. But it wasn't until I traveled from Tambo to Longreach that I really began to understand the basic Australian character that I had read about in books. Being around Aussies all day, every day helped.

Sydney, great as it is, is just another big city with all of the pluses and fewer of the minuses. Ruth and I loved to explore a new neighborhood each time we visited, and we knew and appreciated the differences between, say, Darlinghurst and King's Cross. But to say that Sydney truly represents the real Australia is like saying that New York City represents the real America. It just isn't that easy to define us, although many try—the blue state/red state debate, for example. International travelers who see only our east and west coast cities like Miami and Los Angeles, and they are legion, end up with blurred vision.

We were now in the morning of our fourth day and on the Landsborough Highway, also known as the Matilda according to my map. For most of this trip, Michael was my seatmate. He regaled me with stories of his 16th century Irish ancestors, the complex history of Australian flags, and what not to miss in the Kimberley region of Western Australia.

Although it may have seemed so, Michael was not in any way self-involved. He peppered the conversation with frequent questions about my life and interests. The only reason he spoke of The Kimberley, for example, was in response to his question, "Where are you going on your next trip to our country, Hank?"

When the conversation turned to politics, which it so often did with the men aboard, Michael made careful observations about United States politics but did not bait me to see how I viewed events.

Michael did have a tendency to belabor a subject, but no one could be as interestingly pedantic as he. This paragraph from a subsequent letter says it all about Michael, who is passionate about flags of any kind. When he wrote this, he was responding to a particular flag that I was taking pictures of outside the Australian Stockman's Hall of Fame in Longreach while in his presence. "The Star beneath the Union Jack started off as a 6 pointed star (six for the number of colonies) and was changed to Seven in 1908 in order to incorporate the Territory of Papua which Queensland was 'forced' to transfer to the Commonwealth—and thereafter was regarded (the extra point) as representing all the Territories of the Commonwealth, now a total of two internal Territories, The A.C.T. and the Northern Territory and seven external Territories: Norfolk Island, Heard Island, Christmas Island, the Cocos (Keeling) Islands, Australian Antarctic Territory, the Coral Sea Islands and the Ashmore and Cartier Islands."

The above was followed by the sentence, "Here ends the geography lesson." This was typical Michael, as in self-awareness and self-deprecating humor, universal Australian character traits.

Australians, the men especially, are fascinated by American politics and our elected leaders. All but Michael probed for my understanding of and reactions to the 8-year Bush administration and our never-ending, typically messy election campaigns that begin, seemingly, the day after swearing in ceremonies. If I were to say something, anything leaning toward one side or the other to test a reaction, the men would often become agitated and mildly argumentative. They were certainly informed, much more so than I was about their political system and current elected officials.

Early on, I shared an e-mail that I had just received from a cousin. It poked fun at a pompous candidate. I found it abrasive, partisan, yet very funny. I shared it with Brian, who was highly offended. I learned to avoid the subject of politics with him whenever possible.

Our first major stop of the day was Blackall, "Home of the Original Black Stump." As I write this, I still don't understand the Aussie fascination with this original Astro Station. Its relevance escapes me the way our national obsession with blonde, boob-exposing female celebrities must addle Muslims.

Nevertheless, I'll try to explain "The Black Stump," as regards its literal meaning, as opposed to its mythic importance. Way back in 1887 surveyors were busy sectioning off Queensland. Here at the town of Blackall, they placed their theodolites, angle measuring tools, on an anonymous tree stump to observe longitude and latitude. The tree stump gave their instruments stability. As a result of these efforts, Queensland was measured accurately from Brisbane to Boulia. Over time, anything beyond this exact point in Blackall was considered "beyond the Black Stump." I suppose it's like our Mason-Dixon Line, which divided the North and the South in the United States and became controversial when differences on either side flared into conflict. But, then again, The Black Stump didn't divide a nation. It just marked a spot and became part of the Australian mythos. Get it? Neither did I.

The Aussies in our group loved this stop, and we lingered and lingered as each couple, and then the men alone, posed for pictures before the Stump like Asian tourists at Disneyland.

When I later probed for cultural insight, the men had definite stars in their eyes as they attempted to explain the Stump's epic, culturally significant meaning. I questioned whether or not it had to do with ethnic separation, as in Anglos vs. Aboriginals, and they became genuinely confused. Their denial seemed sincere. No matter how I approached the subject, the Stump's true import always got lost in translation like the discussion following the question, "What is love?"

One Queensland Heritage website tried to explain it to outsiders this way, "It basically means beyond the back blocks, far off in the backcountry, far from civilization." So I gather that it's a "galaxy far, far away" kind of thing for Australians having something to do with personal freedom out beyond the reach of the law and authority. These are, after all, independent people with a lot of empty space who like to "go bush".

Directly across the street from the Black Stump was something far more understandable, an easy insight into Australian character. It was a statue of Jackie Howe. Jackie was grasping a plump sheep about the midsection with a look of smug satisfaction on his face. Jackie's, not the sheep's.

Jackie had reason to be self-satisfied. The bronze statue captured the time he sheared 321 sheep with blade shears in 7 hours and 40 minutes—a record. Of course, a record. Think about this feat. I have watched shearing in Australia three times now, and it took, on the average, about ten minutes per sheep. Do the math. Jackie also mastered machine shears.

Add its historically livestock-based economy to the humble roots of the vast majority of its immigrants, mostly poor and troubled Europeans, and Australia's adulation of Jackie Howe certainly becomes logical. Many societies, including our own, celebrate the mythic accomplishments of otherwise ordinary citizens—Babe Ruth, Paul Revere, Thomas Edison.

Father of 10, Jackie was also a gold prospector, a singer, and a union activist. He lived most of his life in Blackall and died there in 1920, age 59. He was buried in the local cemetery. After his retirement from shearing at age 39, he basically became a publican, the Aussie term for innkeeper and, almost always, barkeeper.

The Universal Hotel behind the statue was not really as it had been when Jackie ran it on this very spot. That building was demolished in 1950. The replacement we went into was a garden center selling plants, trinkets, and tickets to a small museum dedicated to all things Jackie. Every Aussie paid the fee and then talked at great length about their hero with the proprietors. Ruth and I didn't, not because of the modest entry fee but because we felt we had learned all we needed to know about Jackie without seeing his favorite chair, eyeglasses, etc.

We went from there to the Blackall Wool Scour for a guided tour. At the time I was rather fascinated by both the process and the economic and social import of sheep shearing, but later when I transcribed my notes, I fell asleep in a sitting position with my fingers on the keyboard.

So I believe it wise *not* to describe the tour in detail. Suffice it to say that the Blackall Wool Scour was another historically significant place—the only substantially intact steam driven wool scour incorporating a wool shearing shed surviving in Australia. Built in 1908, it was in operation until 1978.

All of Blackall's water supply was from the Great Artesian Basin. In fact, it was the first town to drill an artesian bore way back in 1885. Water rises to the surface here between 58°C and 62°C year round. This is easily misunderstood information to the average Fahrenheit mind. To me it sounded kind of tepid until our female tour guide, whose name is somewhere in that sleep-inducing recording, said, "If you haven't got a cooling tank, you run your bath about lunchtime and hope you can sit in it by 7."

A wool scour would not have been possible here without a large and dependable water supply since 200,000 gallons a day were needed to wash the wool after it had been sheared from the sheep in the 20-stand shearing shed.

My attention wandered freely as I followed the group around the Scour. I tried to imagine this empty, barn-like building bustling with activity and noise, but that proved relatively hard because the huge machines were silent and there were no Jackie Howes about. The guide occasionally re-engaged my attention with details such as, "This little beauty here is a Harkin saw, also called the widow maker for its really bad habit of tipping." Ouch.

One Blackall tourist brochure proclaimed about this Scour, "It is unique, totally authentic, full of history, culture, and great educational and social values." From the local writer's perspective, this was, I'm sure, not overstatement. But, really.

The town itself was very proud of its three attractions—a stump, a champ, and a scour—and presented them well, but I was quickly ready to move on. A local legend said that anyone who crossed the Barcoo River at Blackall ten times was "here to stay." So I was careful to count my crossings, and had it gotten anywhere near ten, I would have turned back toward Canberra. The thought of Ruth and me moving here and making its population 2,202 was beyond the Stump.

There were an abundance of National Parks in the area, but Dave passed them all. I studied their remoteness on the map and read warnings about the roads to and through these parks and decided that this was a good thing, especially when they had names like Hell Hole Gorge and Snake Range. Some of their names made them sound downright charming, like Lark Quarry. Other were enigmas. Mazeppa? Australia, I noted as I poured over maps, seemed to have devoted more land to a national park system than any other country on the planet. There were more than 500. By contrast, the United States has slightly under 60.

Our next major and purely Aussie experience was in Barcaldine—the Australian Workers Heritage Centre where the displays focused on national labor issues through the stories of ordinary citizens. It was a bit more interesting than it sounded, but only a bit.

Before we visited the Centre, Dave dropped Jan at the house of a friend who had moved here from Canberra. Because of the distance, Jan seldom had the chance to visit with her and appreciated both the opportunity and the to-the-door service.

Our picnic lunch without Jan seemed a bit strange since we were getting used to functioning as a group.

Barcaldine, a railroad town, was named after a castle in Scotland, the ancestral home of a mid-nineteenth century immigrant.

The only one remotely interested, I wandered down the street to a traffic circle without traffic to check out the town's World War I memorial. If you walk in a straight line for a time anywhere in Australia, you'll bump into one of these. I suppose it's because 8,709 Aussies died and another 19,000 were wounded at Gallipoli, a battle that forever haunts Australians. Just under 62,000 died overall between 1914 and the end of the conflict. This was a devastating sacrifice for a country with a total population of less than 5 million.

The Workers" Heritage Centre looked like a miniature World's Fair Site. Several architecturally diverse buildings surrounded an artesian bore billabong, in this case not a scruffy brackish water hole but a shaped and tended pond.

The dominant structure was Celebration Theatre, or The Tent, a canvas covered structure that looked temporary both inside and out, as if the displays were put up by itinerant workers or restless gypsies always ready to move on. The premises were once the home of the Barcaldine State School, and some of the buildings on exhibit—a railway station, a one room school—had been relocated here.

The Centre paid tribute to the lives of ordinary people who built this Nation—nurses, sheep herders, teachers, construction workers. The problem with such a thrust was that the curators were dealing basically with ordinary men and women doing ordinary jobs. Not that their stories couldn't be made interesting, and the Centre really tried to show the hardscrabble backgrounds and grit of ordinary Australians. They succeeded in what they set out to do, but it was kind of like looking at old family albums full of blue collar strangers.

I sampled some areas—The Workers' Wall, Women in the Work Force, and the Queensland Teachers' Union—and skipped others.

The most interesting display to me was a thorough study of the most critical labor disruption in Australian history—the 1891 shearers' strike that led to the Australian Labor Movement.

A lot of the first union meetings and strike action occurred under an ancient ghost gum, a type of eucalyptus tree, right here in Barcaldine. Like the Black Stump, the tree had assumed deep-rooted status, a silent-witness-to-history sort of thing, like Plymouth Rock. It was also called the Tree of Knowledge or the Alleluia Tree, and it had "emergency surgery" on three occasions and yet survived.

Until recently. Vandals poisoned it with Glyphosate in 2006 and it was declared dead and removed in 2007. What was left has been preserved, however, and it survives in yet another way because cuttings from it were planted all over Barcaldine and they're now mostly thriving.

The Labor Movement began when shearers refused to sign an agreement. Camps of unionized shearers sprang up all over the region with Barcaldine at its center. Owners tried, of course, to bring in non-union workers, called "black legs". Police and the Queensland Defense Force were recruited to ensure their safety.

Unrest came to a head on February 28 when 700 shearers organized a march, held a mock trial, and burned effigies of the Premier, Sir Samuel Griffiths. This led to arrests, charges of conspiracy, and real trials. George Taylor, for example, endured a 17 day trial, a guilty verdict on 13 of 24 counts, and was given a 3 year, hard labor sentence at St. Helena, not a nice place. He served 2 ½ years in gaol, the word I know as jail.

This and some other displays read a lot like the history of the American Labor Movement, and this made me feel both at home and in touch. The differences were mainly in the work—sheep shearers instead of coal miners.

By the time I had had enough, the others of our group, including Ruth, were already in the restaurant having drinks and chatting. Less than an hour among the anonymous workers had clearly satisfied everybody, and, unlike our visit to the Jackie Howe shrine, there was no follow-up discussion on the bus about the Heritage Centre.

We picked up Jan, who was close enough on the bus for me to ask, "How's your friend?"

She thought for a moment and said, "Oh, she had a bit of an adjustment problem at first, but now she's fine." Jan didn't need to explain further.

The only town between Barcaldine and Longreach was Ilfracombe, a burg of fewer than 200 people with an over-developed love of old machinery. Stretched along the road through the entire town were angle-parked antique tractors, earthmoving equipment, and obsolete industrial conveyances. It mostly looked like a rusty, used truck lot from one end of town to the other. The whole thing was called the Machinery and Heritage Museum or the Great Machinery Mile. No one was around in the entire town to wave and beckon us to stop.

I considered it a blessing that we didn't pull over. Dave didn't even slow down, and no one shouted, "Stop the bus!" I also didn't get to see the nearby bottle display amassed by Hilton Jackson who seriously needed to get a life. The Outback Holiday booklet that I was thumbing through on my way to Longreach described it as, "A spectacular collection of rare bottles of all shapes, sizes, ages and colors which he has gathered over many years."

Here again we have the Vortex Gun phenomenon—one person's delight is another's tedium. I was certain that any Aussies who stopped at Ilfracombe and lingered would love the world's largest ball of string in Kansas.

The rest of the day involved travel to the Longreach Motor Inn, our first two night accommodation in a very interesting, very characteristic Outback town with some exceptional attractions.

The standard buffet dinners we had so far had been passable, but they had become more about bonding with the other couples than enjoying food, which was always out of cans and freezers and cold by the time we stood in line, selected a table, and sat down. Fresh fruit and vegetables didn't usually appear during these buffets in places where shipping costs and distance made them as precious as caviar.

By this time, arriving in any town where we'd overnight meant three activities for Ruth and me. A walk to loosen up and search for an exercise facility after being cooped up in the bus, a hunt for a place to get on the Internet to check our mail, and a stop in a grocery store for bananas and apples, far more desired than Kobe steaks at this time.

In Longreach we found the middle one first, and I left Ruth happily writing a note to our daughter Lisa while I tried to locate number one. The Motor Inn's staff had given me directions to the only private gym in town. It turned out to be a few pieces of dilapidated, dangerous looking equipment in an old warehouse, and I decided two things. Small town people in Australia, as in the United States, either aren't interested in toning and sweating, or they are active enough in their Outback routines not to need treadmills and the like. I made some vague promise to the lonely teenager manning it to return in workout gear with ten dollars, but I never made it back.

We never foraged in a grocery store on this trip without running into another couple from our group doing the same thing. This time we met John and Jenny in the IGA and exchanged casual yet formal greetings. This was the couple that was proving hardest to get to know. John wore the perpetual smile of a good will ambassador, and Jenny had the demeanor of a deeply respected if not well love teacher. They were reserved and stand-offish with Ruth and me. Oh, they were pleasant enough, I suppose, but they kept up an invisible barrier. While by this time all of the others rotated seatmates regularly, John and Jenny always sat together, perfectly groomed and in matching outfits. They didn't even seem to attract flies like the rest of us, and in The Outback these annoying pests are as common as snowflakes in Siberia.

The biggest social crime in Australia is self-promotion. As soon as someone starts to brag or show any kind of supposed superiority, Aussies are turned off. Donald Trump and Madonna would make lousy goodwill ambassadors to this culture. This makes it tough on natives who *are* superior, like John and Jenny. I suspect that they learned while young to keep others at bay by being very buttoned up so as to fit in and not offend.

Ruth and I continued to work on this relationship while on the trip and beyond, and we have become better friends since the tour ended. In one letter, among other milestones, Jenny reported, "Steve graduated from the Australia National University last week with a PhD in Finance. He is lecturing in finance and Jenni is also on the faculty staff while she completes her PhD." What's not to admire?

By the way, due to social custom, most Australian couples, or at least those of our acquaintance, sign both names on a letter even when only one writes it. This gets kind of awkward when you have a specific message for either letter receiver, but it somewhat reduces "I" and "my" in the text and makes one less likely to focus on events of the self.

Speaking of self, after dinner that evening I took a walk alone. I strolled up Longreach's main street and looked in many store windows. The town was clearly thriving. I passed a bowling club and saw many couples sitting at outdoor tables. All towns of any reasonable size in Oz have gathering places like this, and bowling clubs seem to me to be popular middle class country clubs where lawn bowls, limited gambling, buffet dinners, and social interaction are the attractions.

Having drinks, these Longreachers were loud and laughing. Peering over the fence, I felt like a fringe dweller.

On my way back to the motel, I pressed my nose to the window of yet another real Aussie pub where hard-muscled Outback men in wide-brimmed hats were bonding. Their voices rose over the percussive sounds of typical bar music. Aware of my outsider status, I decided to hunt up Allan to see if this was the time and place to have that golden pint and talk about fishing and fists. But it was getting late and I wasn't sure which room he was in. So, again, I didn't get my dandy Dundee experience.

However, the day before I had seen kangaroos leaping with abandon on a vast plain where the land met the sky very, very far away from home.

Chapter Six

Longreach

A late-winter day in The Outback is a beautiful thing. So is a day of freedom in a sunny, no humidity, 80° setting.

Longreach was our first two night stay, and we had a free Wednesday to explore local attractions, three of which sounded, and were, excellent. The fourth sounded like fun in the itinerary's description, but it proved to be a thudding dud that engendered a host of apologies over the next several days from our embarrassed companions.

Longreach had the look of a west Kansas town spreading out on flat, tough Mitchell grass covered prairie. However, it didn't have Kansas' typical winter climate. The mid 40s is as cold as it ever gets in Longreach, and that's in eternally rainless July.

In looking over the Longreach Visitor's Guide, I discovered that there was an attraction back in Barcaldine called Mad Micks Funny Farm, and I was certain from its description that I should not be sorry that I missed it. On the other hand, where else in the world might I have seen a relocated 1886 slab hut, a 1939 one-room golf clubhouse, and a night horse shed? I decided to add Mick's to my list of Outback regrets, which also included the Paroo Lizard Race Track in Eulo.

The local tourist literature described the nearby Thomson River as "mighty" and this area of Queensland as "amazing". A good number of the descriptions of Longreach's attractions were littered with exclamation marks. And each brochure made it sound like most of its 4,500 residents were "award winning" tourist guides who just couldn't wait to show visitors around! Well, Aussies *are* friendly. The only place Ruth and I have been in our travels with more unexpected people contact was New Zealand where strangers regularly invited us into their homes for tea and cookies, uh, biscuits. One Longreach tourist brochure suggested, "Now is the time to roll up your swag and go bush!" But I never once asked myself, "Should I?"

Our first voluntary stop of the day, the School of Distance Education, was one of four scheduled but not mandatory events. Pauline, our host, worked in its busy office and began the tour by telling us their motto, "Effort Conquer Distance."

Once called The School of the Air, now an outdated name in the PC age, this educational institution still existed because there weren't enough Outback families with children to support local schools. At the time of our visit, the Longreach branch of The School of Distance Education, operating here just since 1987, served only 200 students in a 402,712 square kilometer area that stretched all the way to South Australia. Levels ranged from pre-school to year ten. From this base in Longreach, each teacher worked daily with 12 students who lived on isolated spreads.

The School was at the end of a big transition. High frequency radio communication had been phased out and telephone and computer linkage was being phased in. PCs were supplied by the school, up to $250 granted to each family for their purchase.

Teaching wasn't easy in The Outback. LSODE instructors were required to drive to the very distant properties each year and to stay overnight so as to gauge academic performance in the home environment.

Textbooks, library materials, and homework used to be sent by mail but assignment books were digitized in 2003 so now work and feedback took a day or two instead of a month. Half-hour direct-link classes occurred daily, and we were allowed to listen in on one, a fairly typical English grammar lesson. Rigorous testing in major subjects was done after years 3, 5, and 7.

Curiously but understandably, Japanese was being taught to all 5 to 7 year students in weekly lessons. Japan is relatively close compared to Europe and the US, and it has become a major trading partner, a role quickly being overtaken by China.

Bulletin boards were littered with examples of student effort. It seemed like a very normal school, except for the fact that few students were around.

Enrollees weren't charged for services, but parents paid for most activities, like special projects, one being something called the Thinker's Club. Most students went to boarding school after year seven. When I heard this, it clicked. So that's why Carmel's three teenaged children weren't at Nardoo Station during our stay.

Each year students were given the opportunity to come to Longreach for a week of on-campus instruction. They attended regular classes with their teachers and lived on the premises. Most mothers accompanied them since Outback footy moms do 90% of the home instruction.

The facility had a purposeful atmosphere and a make-the-most-of-a-tough-situation attitude. I concluded that they should change their motto to "Making the Impossible Work."

Despite the fact that it was a semi-day-off for him, Dave picked us up outside LSODE and took us directly to a local attraction on the outskirts of town that genuinely earned its exclamation mark—the Australian Stockman's Hall of Fame & Outback Heritage Centre!

From the outside it looked like the project had three architects who couldn't agree on a single design detail, thereby yielding the kind of building that would be described as *interesting* by those reluctant to criticize and *brilliant!* by the 4,500 local tourist guides.

Inside, however, was a different matter. Expecting to learn yet more about cattle and shearing, I was immediately fascinated from the first display, a complete guide to Aboriginal weapons. Of course, everyone knows about the boomerang. They're for sale in every souvenir shop in Australia. But I didn't know that there was a non-returning type. It's lethal in warfare because it cleverly catches an opponent's shield and swings behind, striking with great force. Your enemy's out before he can say, "Shi_!" or whatever it is that natives say when painfully surprised. It sounded like a primitive guided missile and gave me new respect for Aboriginal inventiveness.

I had never heard of the woomera, a streamlined throwing stick, either.

I pored over a huge map showing the native tribes as they existed in 1940. I found this serious focus on the indigenous fascinating stuff in a society where many of the citizens, descendants of hardscrabble immigrants who pulled themselves up to respectability through hard work, seemed to be annoyed and/or felt guilty about anyone on the dole. They especially resented those who were dependent on the State by choice or as the result of treatable dysfunction like alcohol dependence. Many, I gathered, would not be upset if the original inhabitants would simply disappear.

Aboriginals almost did. Perhaps as many as 3,000,000 were living in what was called Terres Australes, or Terra Australis Incognita, or the Great Southland, or New Holland when the British sailed into Botany Bay in 1788. That number was down to 50,000 by most estimates at the beginning of the 20th century. Tasmania's native population was absolute zero. Apparently through decimation, resettlement, and then benign neglect, the last full-blooded Tasmanian Aboriginal died before the 20th century arrived.

I have probably read more about Australia's history than most Americans. By the way, *American* is the Aussies' most common label for a US citizen, but they don't call Canadians or Mexicans *Americans* even though they are. Specifically, North Americans. Why is that? Don't know. I also don't know why we're the only North American residents to call ourselves Americans. Over fifty of our movies begin with the word *American*, like *American Pie*. I guess it's because United Statian or some other variation is awkward.

Anyway, the best, most readable book about Australia's convict and émigré history is, in my opinion, Aussie/*American* Robert Hughes's *The Fatal Shore*.

In the Outback Heritage Centre I learned, or re-learned, a lot from a "European Exploration Timeline".

The first Westerner to set foot on Australian soil was not peripatetic James Cook, who was first on the beach almost everywhere else in this part of the world. It was, appropriately enough, a man looking for water—William Dampier. I didn't know, or had forgotten, that the territory-minded Dutch way back in 1753 considered this unexplored place part of their empire, Nouvelle Hollande.

Explorers like Brit buccaneer Dampier skulked along Australia's western coastline but couldn't get across the reef in places to land and explore. It's no wonder that early maps of Australia are unusually vague and ships' logs often wrong. For example, as they sailed along the coast, Dampier and his men could see The Pinnacles, some natural limestone pillars, but they figured these were an abandoned civilization's gravestones.

I was familiar with Burke and Wills. No one who visits Australia can avoid learning about these two adventurers. In 1860 they set out from Melbourne hoping to become the first explorers to go north to land's end and back again. They made it to the Gulf of Carpentaria, but misconnection on the way back caused both men to starve to death. Ironically, they didn't find the food that had been left for them. Several books tell their tale and a dozen movies have been made. To my knowledge, only one made its way to the United States with an actual release, *Burke & Wills*, in 1985.

But John McDouall Stuart? I knew nothing about him, the first European to cross the Red Centre from Darwin to Adelaide and return alive, before I visited TASHOFAOHC!

Here I also learned that Captain Graham James Bond aboard the HMAS Flinders discovered a new shipping route through the Great Barrier Reef. This surprised me for two reasons. It had never occurred to me that the famous Reef was so continuous that ships couldn't get through it and, as a result, was a severe navigational problem. Secondly, Bond's barrier breakthrough happened in 1982. Yes, that's not a typo for 1882.

Jane came by to ask, "What do you think of this place, Hank?"

"I think it's terrific. Bloody marvelous!" I said with real enthusiasm. "But I haven't learned anything about stockmen yet."

"Oh, you will," she promised, pointing vaguely behind her. "Michael and I have already been in that section. You have lots to see and record." This sounded like a warning.

I was beginning to gain a reputation for being the slowest of the group at every stop, forever taking notes and always the last one on the bus. On the upside, no one ever complained, and everyone but John and Jenny began to search me out to tell me about items of special interest to look for, like Jane did. "Have you seen the furphy?"

"The what, Jane?" I asked, thinking I had misunderstood her.

"The old furphy around there on the other side."

By this time Jane was my main source of Australianisms. She knew of my fascination with our language differences, especially as they have created new words, and she steadily fed my beast. "I'll check it out," I promised.

The Centre's layout was a system of clever ramps that led from display to display, and I found myself out of formal history and into Outback life. It was immediately engrossing. Not just about bushrangers, the displays explored the experiences of ordinary people for whom life here was often dangerous, even tragic.

For some inexplicable reason, one story said it all for me. In 1894 John Goggins was working at Portland station when his brother got typhoid fever. John nursed him for fifty miles on horseback to the nearest railhead, then 17 miles by train to a hospital where his brother died. John got it too but survived. He returned to droving but got typhoid again five years later. He died on the 23rd of May, 1899, age 24.

So far the displays had been off-beat, original, or at least they seemed so to an outsider like me. I truly knew their worth when Allan passed by and said, "I've read a lot about my country but am learning still. Such exhibits!"

"Yes, I agree. Cowboy equipment, circuses, Wild West shows, boxing troupes, bush crafts, carved emu eggs," I enumerated while he and Barbara, who had come up behind him as we spoke, bobbed their heads in agreement.

"Have you seen something called a fur piece?" I inquired.

"A what?" they asked in unison.

"Jane told me not to miss it. I guess I'll have to find her and ask."

I did just that. "What did you tell me to look for?"

"You're getting close to it," said Jane enthusiastically. "It's just down those steps."

"What is it again? And how will I recognize it?"

"You can't miss it! It's an army issue water cart that inspired a pure Australian word."

Barbara, lover of music, tracked me down again to ask, "Did you see the Smoky Dawson display?"

"No," I replied. "Who's that?"

"One of *our* cowboys who had a varied career," she said pointing toward it.

She was certainly being modest. Dawson—whip cracker, songwriter, radio host, soldier, author, musician, knife thrower—made a two year tour of the United States in the 1950s. After reading his biography, I tried to think of someone comparable in our celebrity worshiping culture and could think of no one with such a diverse background, expect maybe Clint Eastwood.

Also impressive was James Barrington Mulvaney, who competed in countless rodeos and was seldom bested by man or beast. He had enough ribbons to have a bedspread made of them.

I came across a display of agricultural shows and now understood the cultural richness of the movie *Babe*, some pig!, for the first time.

I was looking at all of the equipment needed by a drovers' party when Jane came by yet again.

"You're so close! It's just there, next to the Dava Singh General Merchant cart."

"I don't see a fur piece."

"Furphy. Let's go see." For a second, I thought that she was going to take my hand.

Right next to a colorful hawker's wagon, the itinerant cart that Jane had repeatedly mentioned turned out to be a simple silver-colored tank mounted on wagon wheels. I tried to look impressed.

"A man would pull this around a battlefield, going from soldier to soldier and giving them water," Jane explained. "In peacetime it became a water carrier on a farm. Now you only see them in museums, but the name survives. Today, a 'furphy' is a rumor."

"A person living in a boarding house?"

"No. r-u-m-o-r."

I must have looked puzzled because she said, "Someone giving out water would have been about the battlefield and would have the latest news, the most current information, true or not in all that confusion. So Australians now say, when they have reason to doubt what they're hearing, 'That's a bit of a furphy.'"

"Got it," I said and thanked her. "What else should I see?"

"I think you're about out of time!" she warned, heading up the ramp toward the exit.

Jane by now had unofficially become my surrogate mother and officially my personal dispenser of language news—my very own reliable furphy since I could trust her information implicitly.

I looked at my watch and despaired. It was time to find Ruth and leave even though I was far from done.

She was just inside the entrance tapping her foot.

"It's a free day," I said in self-defense.

"Yes, but…"

"Can I have more time here?"

"No!" she said with finality as she pulled me through the door, where we found only Jane and Michael left from our group. Michael was hung up on an imposing ring of flags and was checking them for authenticity. I joined him, briefly, before we followed our wives across the busy road to the third big Longreach attraction, the Qantas Founders' Outback Museum.

We found the others having lunch, except for John and Jenny, in the on-the-premises McGuinness' Restaurant. Ruth joined them, but I was anxious to get to the displays.

Perhaps because they already knew the story, the others ultimately paid scant attention to this museum. Not me. I was fascinated by Qantas.

Dave approached me as I began to browse and challenged, "I'll bet you don't know what Qantas stands for."

"Queensland and Northern Territory Aerial Service," I said rotely since this had been my fifth or so test.

"Good on ya'!" Dave exclaimed as if I had passed some kind of citizenship exam.

This airline's story *is* rather one-of-a-kind. Registered on November 16, 1920, Qantas is the oldest continually operating airline in the world. Passenger service began in 1922. For a time it manufactured its own planes, seven DH50s, because it had to. Qantas was the first airline outside the US to operate Boeing jets. The black box was their idea.

Exactly why is this museum here as opposed to, say, in Brisbane? I asked myself. To save time, I replied, *you could find someone to ask instead of scanning all the display descriptions.*

Dave.

I spotted him over by the entrance desk visiting with the staff and I wondered, suddenly, how many times he had been here. Often enough to be friends with everyone who worked here it seemed. People like Dave who give tours must become really bored by even a worthy attraction about the fiftieth time they bring folks to it. He looked like he was having a good time, though, and I hated to interrupt.

I looked down to realize that I had poked a Museum brochure in my notebook. I checked and it explained succinctly, "Qantas was conceived in Cloncurry, born in Winton, grew up in Longreach, came of age in Brisbane and reached maturity in Sydney and the world."

I read on and discovered that The Founders' Museum was the only place in the world where civilians like me can enter a 747 jumbo jet, but I had just missed the last tour of the day that began at 3 p.m. Damn!

The original 1922 Qantas hangar was also on the premises. I missed that too because I became so caught up in a display of 1950s and 1960s advertising posters. Ruth came by and joined me in admiring them, but then she said, "Do you realize we're the only ones left?"

"Where are the others?"

"They went back to the motel with Dave. We'll have to walk."

It's not far," I reminded her. "Give me just fifteen minutes more."

Ruth sighed. "I'll be outside enjoying the beautiful weather." This was not the first time, nor would it be the last, that she indulged me by waiting patiently.

I had bought some time to hunt for a major unknown piece of the Qantas story—its founders.

Qantas was the creation of two men. Paul McGuinness' memorial described him as having "a restless intelligence, energy, and resolve." But the actual founder, who had one of Western Culture's great names, was Wilmot Hudson Fysh. He was said to be shy and known for natural caution and reserve. This sounded like the Australian Odd Couple to me, but the combo apparently worked.

In the late 1930s Qantas' "Kangaroo Route" to London took 9 days since there was no night flying. Passengers stayed in Darwin, Singapore, Rangoon, Karachi, Bahrain, Cairo, Athens, and Marseilles. My imagination, maybe even my brain, expanded as I tried to envision such a romantic, exotic trip.

The original kangaroo used as the airline's logo, I learned, was adapted from the one on the back of the Australian one penny coin. The current familiar leaping roo with tail deployed like a sail has been around since 1984.

During World War II, some of Qantas' planes were pressed into service by the RAAF, or Royal Australian Air Force. Others were operated in support duties. A number of them were lost in enemy action, but they kept the mail lines opened to England. Two Flying Boats were shot down and another lost in the bombing of Broome, a northwest Australia town. Darwin was also bombed and its hangars destroyed. This Country saw more domestic War action than the US, which, to my knowledge, only had "native soil" invasion in the Aleutians and two incidents in Oregon. On a Sunday night in June,

1942, a Japanese submarine lobbed 9 high velocity shells onto the Oregon coast near Fort Stevens, their first attack in the continental US on a primary military objective. No damage or deaths resulted. The following September a sub launched a float plane that flew over Brookings and dropped a few incendiary bombs in the forest nearby. The enemy was hoping to start a forest fire, but recent rain had occurred and the citizens had no trouble putting out the ineffectual flames. Twenty days later the Japanese tried again. These bombs have never been found. However, the situation grew so desperate in Australia that the Government drew the Brisbane Line across the Continent. Above was the territory it would surrender if necessary and below the land it would defend to the death.

Over time, Qantas absorbed six airlines, like Air Queensland. And I had finally absorbed all that I could by 4 p.m., so Ruth and I walked back toward the Longreach Motor Inn, which in the daylight looked like a 1950s, Route 66 creation.

On the way we stopped in the local public library and checked our e-mail. At all the other stations were intent grade and high school kids, like the youth of China and Chile, surfing the world outside Longreach.

Outside the library, the trees were alive with hundreds of chattering cockatoos, but we couldn't stop to delight in them for long. It was almost time to get ready for a much anticipated evening. Our itinerary described the entertainment as, "A Paddlesteamer cruise/dinner on the Thomson River."

This sounded wonderful.

It was dreadful.

The crew lined us up close together on uncomfortable wooden seats around the perimeter of the Thomson Belle, the steamer, handed out plastic wine glasses, and poured cheap champagne into them. From above in the wheel room, the Captain announced, "The Thomson is one of the world's cleanest rivers!" I guess so. It's out here where there are no towns, no fertilizer run-off, few people, fewer industrial polluters. I had learned before embarking that it's really not a river. It's more like a series of connected waterholes, this one tainted only by the effusions of the Thomson Belle, and its companion, the charmingly named Yellowbelly Express, which gave dinner cruises.

Would we have to disembark and board the Yellowbelly for dinner? I wondered as it sailed by. I would have been happy, at this point, to be taken back to town, but it was about 15 miles away, a bit too far to walk. Oh, well. I looked down into the waterhole's depths and reminded myself, *Go with the flow, literally and figuratively.* Then I looked around the boat for a diversion.

"These waterholes flow into the Barcoo River," the Captain announced, "and a strange thing happens! These two free-flowing rivers become a creek named Cooper, which empties into Lake Eyre North near Moomba."

"Tell me about Moomba," I said to Angus, who was sitting across from me and staring into space as I was.

"It's Australia's natural gas center, very remote."

"...and the creek completely disappears!" said the Captain from the deck above like a ring master describing a circus act.

"It's a weird kind of headwater to delta reversal then?" I asked Angus, who nodded.

"See the whistling kite in that tree?" the Captain asked. "It builds *big* nests!"

No heads turned. Either ennui or bargain-basement champagne had by now numbed his captives.

I decided to climb up the ladder for a chat with the skipper.

"How you enjoying the cruise so far?" he began.

"Interesting," I lied and backed down the stairs.

The promised awesome sunset from the middle of the Thomson was a non-event, and I have the pictures to prove it.

Back at the dock, we were greeted by the scruffiest bearded fiddler I had ever averted my eyes from. He and his backup rube made the Beverly Hillbillies look like members of Great Britain's Royal Family. Unfortunately, his crude fiddling was a foretaste of the evening.

At just past sunset we were led to a circle of lawn chairs about a giant fire. "We'll have live entertainment after dinner with our billy tea and damper around this campfire at the...Sheraton on the Thomson!" exclaimed our scraggly master of ceremonies, who paused for applause as if he had uttered the cleverest joke ever cracked.

Suddenly Allan was at my shoulder. "Pssst."

I turned to see him holding a paper bag and two wine glasses.

"Here, this will help."

Ruth and I took the glasses and Allan poured red wine from the brown bag's opening. "It's called The Cover Drive," he whispered.

It turned out to be a way delicious South Australian cabernet sauvignon.

Allan slipped away, then returned with yet more. The wine really helped. But then the hundred or so passengers from the Thomson Belle were ordered to line up for dinner. The Cover Drive had been wonderful, but unfortunately, it was gone by the time we sat with plates of beef stew, at least I *think* it was beef, on our laps. Damper, which I had heard about in song and poem, turned out to be tasteless, coarse bread. That was dinner.

I passed on the suspicious looking dessert but felt obligated to try the billy tea, an Outback tradition. At the first opportunity I tossed it over my shoulder into the bush under the cover of night.

The entertainment was genuinely embarrassing—hillbilly jokes that were too dumb to be offensive, lugubrious doggerel passing for bush poetry, and raucous music.

Now that the sun had gone down, it was bone-chillingly cold despite the roaring fire.

As soon as Ruth and I could do it without attracting attention, we slipped away.

On the path, we ran into Michael and Jane, who had also escaped.

"Quite chilly tonight," Michael, always a gentleman, observed as the four of us groped our way through the inky bush under a universe of stars.

It proved a bit hard to find our veteran bus, but we finally succeeded. Luckily, Dave was aboard and it was already warm. Even he, avid collector of the lamest jokes, expressed no surprise that we had left the entertainment before it was over.

We climbed in to find Allan and Barbara already aboard.

Within minutes, Dave was opening the door for Rob, Lynette, Angus, and Gwen. They made no comment as they passed.

Ruth and I were mum about the evening, but Jane turned to Barbara and commented, "Wasn't that the worst?"

Barbara rolled her eyes.

Jane turned to us. "I'm embarrassed and must apologize for...." Her voice trailed off. Word-wise Jane was unable to describe the experience.

"No need," I assured her. "Let's call it revenge. You get plenty of American television."

She laughed.

One by one the others joined us. Jan and Roger, great supporters of Australian culture, seemed especially glum. John and Jenny were as close to culture shock as I had seen them.

Karin and Brian were back at the motel. They had opted not to go. How had they known?

We could all still hear the music in the distance as the bus slipped away. No one spoke, not even Dave, as we returned to Longreach.

Chapter Seven

Waltzing Matilda

This chapter could just as easily have been named "The Romance of the Swag", a phrase which I saw often in Outback Queensland. *Lonely Planet Australia* defined a swag as a "canvas-covered bed roll used in the Outback." However it's defined, this humble traveling bag has taken on iconic status all over Australia, and the Waltzing Matilda Centre in Winton, an important livestock shipping center, did a pretty good job of explaining why.

I had a single seat on the bus that Thursday morning and enjoyed my time with Alan Marshall, a fine writer best known for *I Can Jump Puddles*, a recounting of his childhood struggle with polio. When I finished his book of essays about Outback Australians that morning, I held it up and asked, "Is anyone interested in reading this?"

"I am!" I heard from behind me. Barbara took it and soon I could hear her laughing. Over the next couple of days she told me how much she was enjoying it and thanked me again and again. She subsequently convinced others to read it. By the time we returned to Canberra, it had passed through several hands and I had the extreme pleasure of sharing a first-class Australian storyteller with...Australians. Hoping to keep him alive for the next generation, I left Alan Marshall's book with Rob's grandson Robert in Canberra.

I had bought this book of essays, an Australian publication, in the United States at Powell's in Portland, which has an impressive Oz section. So I also felt a bit like I was bringing it home where it belonged.

We made it to Winton on the Capricorn Highway by mid-morning. For the last 20 or so miles before entering town, we paralleled a mesa that Dave said was the Forsythe Range. It was the first land uplift we had seen for days. Beneath us, way, way down below, the Great Artesian bubbled away at 99.9° Centigrade, making it the hottest spot in the Basin. That's 210° Fahrenheit.

Winton, population about 1,100, had four claims to fame. Nearby was the only recorded dinosaur stampede in the world. Even though it happened 93 million years ago, the impressions that the fleeing herd made in the earth as they ran still exist. Locals claim that Steven Spielberg based the thundering dinosaurs in *Jurassic Park* on these footprints. I didn't know whether this was true or a bit of local wishful thinking, and Steven wasn't around to ask.

By this time I had learned that Dave wasn't the go-to person for information, unless the answer I wanted had to do with sports and other male bonding activities.

The Chamber of Commerce was definitely taking advantage of this long ago phenomenon, though, and among other reminders, public trash bins scattered about Winton were plastic dinosaur feet.

The largest dinosaur found in Australia so far was a Sauropod, the biggest land animal ever to have lived. Someone gave the one found near Winton the rather bookish, nerdish name of Elliot, again for no reason I could easily determine.

"Elliot's bones are displayed in the Lark Quarry Dinosaur Trackways," Dave told us, "but we don't have time to see them."

Great! Now I'd never know if Elliot was a spot on name for a Sauropod, a creature with an incredibly long neck.

Winton was the first opal town we visited, but it certainly wasn't *the* opal town. That would be Coober Pedy in South Australia. There were enough opals around Winton, however, that I did see ads for fossicking tours. The Quilpie Opal Field with the hamlet of Opalton in its northern quadrant is south of town.

Without consulting Jane, I figured that fossicking was the Aussie term for digging in the earth in the pursuit of gems. And I was right as my dog-eared Webster later confirmed: "to prospect or search, as for gold," it informed. The word's origin?—Australia.

Tours leaving from Winton prospected for unusual Boulder opals that were said to be common in the area. The Boulder variety formed in veins inside actual boulders made of ironstone, causing them to have low water content and exceptional durability. Queensland opals are mined with bulldozers using an open-cutting process.

Opals, the silica gemstones that gave English speakers the word *opalescent* and most visitors to Australia credit card debt, ranged in value from completely worthless to extremely valuable. 95% of the opals used in jewelry throughout the world come from Australia, but I didn't see too many retail outlets in Winton.

Opal stores were so common Down Under that I wondered how they all survived. Buyers in general must beware, but women like Ruth had an advantage. She had access to seven savvy, female opal owners *not* connected to the opal industry. She could, and repeatedly did, shop with trusted Australians, all of whom already had prized opals stashed somewhere.

Opals were enough of a force in Winton that the town held an Opal Expo each year. Signs about town hawked the Sunset Opal Factory and caused a considerable buzz among the women aboard, including Ruth, who had resisted buying opals on every previous trip to Australia because she was confused by the many varieties and suspicious during sales pitches. This time was different. Here in Winton, she was already asking questions of the other women, and I knew that an opal purchase on this trip was inevitable. But not here. For some reason, the women did not demand time to shop for opals in Winton as they would elsewhere.

Two firsts occurred in Winton, Qantas Airlines was registered here as a company in 1920, and the Winton Club was the site of Qantas's first board meeting one year later. Secondly, it was the scene of the world's first performance of the song *Waltzing Matilda* in 1895, making this the logical place for a memorial.

Our tour of the Waltzing Matilda Centre in the center of town on Elderslie Street began at an indoor, re-created billabong, a pool of trapped water. As I stared into its stillness, a face appeared in an eerie holographic effect. It was a grizzled man, or Swaggie, who told me about a squadron of troopers who confronted him, setting the stage for what he called "the peoples' national anthem".

In the 19th century when this part of Queensland was being overrun by settlers, poor squatters were hired to check fences or move stock. Dubbed swaggies, these hapless men traveled by foot, and eleven names—among them shiralee, willy wag, and matilda—were coined for the simple bag they used to carry their portable beds and meager possessions.

We hadn't been here too long before Allan came by and said, "It's quite unusual to have a museum dedicated to a song, isn't it?"

"This is the only one I've heard of," I agreed.

"I'm wondering about the origin of the name Matilda in what must be… can only be called our national song," he continued.

"Maybe Matilda was a dance teacher," I suggested helpfully.

"Doubtful. But I don't know for certain. I wonder what she actually had to do with waltzing?"

I was surprised that Allan, a learned man who had lived his entire life in Australia, didn't know the source meanings of this anthemic song's lyrics. But then again, I didn't exactly know what *so proudly we hail* was hailing the first several times I heard our anthem.

He and I both lingered over the displays, never straying too far from each other and exchanging details that sometimes explained but more often resulted in even more puzzling, unanswered, perhaps unanswerable questions for both of us.

As I worked my way through the Centre I found myself trying to gauge where truth and accuracy ended and folklore began. Among the men, Allan was the only one especially intrigued and thoughtful. The rest simply waltzed through the displays.

What is true without question is the fact that in 1877 "professional" swagmen formed their own union with Rule #1 being, "No member to be over 100 years old." Whether this was a bit of swaggie humor or something else was as mysterious as why Matilda waltzed. And who was she? The Centre simply didn't explain adequately. Or at least Allan and I didn't find the answers to our questions.

My deep interest in the song at that time waned as soon as I left the Waltzing Matilda Centre, unlike Allan, who continued to regale me with e-mailed information long afterwards as he dug for Matilda's true roots. "As far as "waltzing" is concerned," he wrote, "my German-English Dictionary shows the verb "walzen" as meaning 'to roll'. It suggests that "waltzing comes from the German expression "auf der Walz' (on the tramp), thus connoting an itinerant worker on the lookout for work." That would certainly explain the dancing half of the title.

Allan also explored Matilda and concluded, "Most of the websites that I scanned claimed that the word *Matilda* was a name or word of Teutonic origin meaning 'Mighty Battle Maiden'. (This sounds faintly Wagnerian). It is said that this word came to be used to describe the women who accompanied soldiers into battle in former times as 'camp followers', and has evolved to apply to the trench coat carried by soldiers in a roll on their backpacks (In the absence of any female company, the rolled trench coat may have been the only comfort to the soldier when times were hard." Thus Allan concluded that immigrants applied that name to the swagman's bundle.

Allan, having a scholarly legal background, ended his research with this observation, "I am prepared to assume that the Winton Museum did its homework before making the claims that it has, but I remain slightly skeptical."

The enduring song's creators, however, were well documented in the Centre. Lyricist Andrew Barton was born in Narambla, New South Wales, in

1864. He went on to become a lawyer, war correspondent, social commentator, and beloved bush poet. By the time he wrote the words to *Waltzing Matilda* in Winton, stranded by a flood and staying with the Macpherson family, he was familiar with the eruptive disputes between shearers and pastoralists in this part of Queensland.

Parallel events were occurring at the same time between ranchers and farmers in Texas, Oklahoma, and other settlement locales in the frontier United States as barbed wire stretched across range land and tempers flared.

Matilda's melody was influenced by an old Scottish tune named "Craigielee". By the time Barton wrote the lyrics to fit this tune, he was already using the name A.B. Patterson, the B standing for Banjo.

This haunting song with underlying cultural significance had gone on to national acclaim and wide international recognition. Winston Churchill once exclaimed to General Charles de Gaulle, "That's one of the finest songs in the world." Marjorie Lawrence, opera singer and polio victim, helped introduce it to United States audiences where most people, like me, recognize it and can sing a few bars especially if we're *in* a bar at the time.

The 20th century also seems to have produced an iconic song that might one day be considered as enduring as *Waltzing Matilda—I Still Call Australia Home.* Every time he speaks of it, Rob can't help but get emotional. And I've seen others choke up too when it's discussed or sung. Academy Award winning Aussie composer Peter Allen, whose life and career was celebrated in *The Boy from Oz,* grew up in Tenterfield, a New South Wales town just south of the Queensland border. But he moved to New York and found another home—Radio City Music Hall.

The Winton Museum provided different musical interpretations of *Waltzing Matilda* at listening stations, including the Queensland version that had a completely different tune from the familiar one.

I listened attentively to Slim Dusty's recording. He sounded kind of familiar and I soon realized why. Dusty sang *Waltzing Matilda* to the entire world at the closing ceremony of the Sydney 2000 Olympic Games.

I suddenly sensed that I was alone. I circled the entire display area and discovered that I truly was. Yesterday when left behind at the Qantas museum, I could walk to the motel. Today, our destination was Mount Isa, far to the Northwest, and Ruth and I were not sitting together on the bus, so as it departed she might not see that I was not aboard. Or, after yesterday, she might be eager to teach me a lesson. I began to sweat like a swaggie when I realized that I was alone in a remote place and I bolted.

I found Ruth and the others ready to board the bus, and I did learn two lessons—constantly look around at every attraction, especially the riveting ones, for familiar faces and never be the last person to board. I abided by these rules for the rest of the trip. Well, mostly.

Knowing that the song has been buzzing around in your head as you read this just like it did in mine as I toured the Waltzing Matilda Centre, it's now time to sing…

> Once a jolly swagman camped by a billabong,
> Under the shade of a coolibah tree,
> And he sang as he watched and waited 'til his billy boiled
> "Who'll come a-waltzing Matilda with me?"

Almost everyone from Bombay to Baltimore knows at least some of this song, but few people, even Australians, know the story behind the words.

Roughly, an itinerant shearer was waiting for his tea to steep when a sheep came down to the water to drink. The swaggie shoved the animal into his traveling bag for later use when times, and perhaps something else, were hard. Alas, three troopers showed up shortly and asked him what was in his swag, and rather than be arrested, the swagman jumped into the waterhole and drowned. According to legend, the swagman's ghost still sang his song to people who passed by the billabong.

The fact that he exclaimed, "You'll never catch me alive!" in the process of dying appeals to those of independent spirit and pokes seriously at Australian mistrust of authority figures. Remember, many of the current citizens' ancestors of not all that long ago were sent here initially on trumped up criminal charges or simply because they were poor and underfoot.

I listened for the swagman's ghost when we stopped for lunch at the Combo Waterhole on the Landsborough Highway, the inspiration for Banjo Patterson's lyrics. This billabong was the color of coffee with real cream and, indeed, it was surrounded by coolibah trees, a type of gum or eucalypt. The scene swarmed with highly annoying flies that could easily have drowned out a singing ghost.

I made it a point to ask Karin, our resident ghost expert, if she could hear the Swaggie. But she laughed and said, "No."

The Combo was near Kynuna. This once thriving community was down to one pub, the Blue Heeler, where Banjo once drank with squatters and swagmen, the inspirations for his still popular poetry.

The landscape from Combo to Kynuna and beyond became increasingly treeless, and the narrow, two-lane road was as flat as a central Nebraska Interstate.

Our next stop was the Walkabout Creek Hotel in McKinlay, home to five more people than Kynuna, 30 to be exact.

As we approached this Outback outpost, Dave said, "This is the pub used in *Crocodile Dundee*. The movie was shot here, and they used some of the other buildings in town too."

As I made a mental note to rent it again when I returned home to see where I had been, I overheard some of the ladies behind me, led by Barbara, talking themselves into having lemon squashes on this hot afternoon.

"What's that?" I asked her.

"It's a traditional British drink made with lemon juice, sugar, and carbonated water."

"Any good?"

"Well, I like it," she said.

I was mildly curious. And thirsty. This was, after all, a sweat inducing day in the middle of not much and requiring a thirst quencher. XXXX, Queensland's popular beer? No, a frosty Foster's.

The other men either stayed on the bus or wandered off to the loo as I followed the women into Walkabout Creek. It looked vaguely familiar but there were no patrons shoving each other and applying fists to each others' midsections and chins so it was hard to tell.

It was, beyond a doubt, a real, I mean really, really authentic Outback drinking pub. I had seen enough of them by this time to know. I sidled up to the empty bar with Foster's on my lips, and the rough-hewn bartender sauntered over and asked what I'd have.

"A lemon squash please," I replied to my utter shock and humiliation.

The bartender hesitated for a split second of condescension, said, "Right, Mate," went over to the cooler, grabbed a pretty little bottle, slammed it down on the bar in front of me, and popped the cap.

I paid sheepishly and drank it outside while trying to convince myself that I had done the right thing. I'd had Foster's but never a lemon squash, a popular refreshment in Masterpiece Theatre type entertainments about prim, effete Englishmen who drank it at garden parties or while watching formal sporting events. Gossiping women in big flowery hats who disdained alcohol or were beginning to feel their Pimm's would ask bowing waiters for lemon squashes. At the time I stood at its bar, the Walkabout was deserted, except for the Trust ladies and me. No laddies. I would have been the only one drinking beer…in the middle of the afternoon. And lastly, this was not the rowdy, back-slapping experience that Allan and I still planned to have some evening in a brink-of-mayhem pub.

Road Train traffic increased on either side of McKinlay because we were close to the BHPCannington Mine, said to be the world's richest lode of silver. Australia was also home to the world's largest open pit gold mine, Kalgoorlie's Golden Mile.

"BHP merged with a British mining company called Billiton in 2001," Dave informed us while passing an especially long Road Train. "But it's still a dead set."

"What's a dead set?" I asked Allan.

"A very successful Australian concern."

Dave didn't seem like the type who would follow business, so I was impressed with both his knowledge and his interest. I, like most, underestimate people.

Dave's BHP's evaluation was no exaggeration. I later read in *The Australian*, the national newspaper owned by dead set local boy Rupert Murdoch, that BHP-Billiton delivered the biggest profit ever achieved by an Australian company up to that time—4.73 billion Australian dollars. This was a remarkable 78% gain over the previous year and the result of China's insatiable demand for commodities. PHP-Billiton had become the biggest company listed on the Australian stock market. By now, its profits are probably measured in gajillions and it owns half the planet. Mining in general and PHP-Billiton in particular are making Australia increasingly prosperous and its dollar stronger.

Trees returned to the landscape with mini-mountains behind them just before Dave took a left turn into Cloncurry. I glimpsed a sign that said, "Australia's highest temperature." Passing it quickly, I had no time to learn the intriguing details, but I had to find out. Later, I did research and found that on January 13, 1889, the temperature reached 53° Celsius here, that's 128° Fahrenheit and just 8° under the world's record.

I had read that Cloncurry was a mining town and major transportation hub of abut 4,000 people, and I envisioned a tough, dug in, dusty community. I was, therefore, unprepared for Cloncurry's cultured reality of bougainvillea, bowling clubs, and saddlers. But the wash hanging on lines in yards around town must dry quickly and have to be removed promptly to avoid spontaneous combustion during the hot season.

Qantas was conceived here, and the aircraft hangar where it was born still stood at the Shire Airport.

The Royal Flying Doctor Service also took-off for the first time from Cloncurry in 1928 when a man named John Flynn initiated medical services to the vast Outback. Just one year after Charles Lindbergh crossed the Atlantic, Flynn sent a doctor aloft in a DH 50 to make the Service's first-long-distance house call.

We crossed the Cloncurry River just west of town and the road became curvy as it twisted through some hills. Termite mounds, those curious monoliths of The Outback, appeared for the first time. Since the landscape looked a lot like Arizona, the mounds seemed like positioned props on a small scale Monument Valley movie set.

I hadn't seen termite mounds since our trip to the Northern Territory several years previously. They can grow up to 20 feet high, and the size has something to do with ventilating the termites' tunnels. Fortunately, these insects have no interest in tourists like me who stop to prod and kick their towers. I have, gratefully, never actually seen them swarm as I admired their impressive architecture.

As evening approached, we arrived in Mount Isa, home to one of the largest mines in the world, the company logically named Mt Isa Mines. One sign to welcome visitors said, "Now you're a real Aussie." That sounded about right.

Dave took us to City Outlook and we stared down into the commercial district. Like Cloncurry, Isa was a surprise. It had the feel of a bustling city with traffic lights and shopping centers, our first real urban experience since leaving Canberra. From the park-like promontory, one could easily see that the city hunkered down on the floor of a cramped valley surrounded by respectable mountains. The mine was down there too, right in the action and dominating the place like an industrial Emerald City. As I stood looking about panoramically on this dying day, Angus sidled over and observed, "It looks a bit better than it did sixteen years ago."

"Were you here on business?" I asked.

"No. Gwen and I took a driving trip." He went on to describe the difficulties involved in taking one's vacation in The Outback with great distances to be covered and so few services.

It had been our second longest day, and we arrived at the Mercure Outback Mt Isa Motel gratefully. We would leave the next morning even more gratefully, and it had nothing to do with the fact that Lynette was beginning to show early signs of serious illness. She was coughing frequently and suffering respiratory distress. But she didn't want to talk about it.

Rob was stoical.

Ruth and I were very concerned.

On a major trip a few years previously, Lynette came down with what she and Rob thought was a viral infection while on a European excursion. By the time they reached the very top of Norway, she was seriously ill. An ambulance took her to Hammerfest followed by an airlift to London where she was stabilized. An Australian doctor was summoned and arrived from Sydney to take her home. Testing resulted in treatment that saved her life but couldn't determine the cause, so the reason for her illness remained speculative. Lynette's recovery was slow and her overall health impacted.

And now, on the way to Mount Isa similar symptoms began to beleaguer Lynette, and she reported having trouble sleeping. She was once again, as she had been in Lapland, in a place where treatment was limited. And further on down the sometimes unpaved, narrow roads of the Red Center, emergency help would become virtually non-existent, except for the flying doctors.

Chapter Eight

Rough Roads and Spinifex

Mount Isa sits atop Australia's largest copper field, and Mt Isa Mines also produces silver, lead, and zinc. At the time of our visit, it was the world's largest producer of all four minerals.

Most huge mines of my experience were discreetly outside of town, but not Isa. It was a gargantuan industrial complex with venting smokestacks surrounded by homes and businesses just across the Leichhardt River from town center. Oddly, it looked like it belonged. It was even kind of picturesque, with the Selwyn Ranges for a backdrop. The Selwyns also provided Isa with the mountaintop overlook that we had experienced the previous evening.

The Isa, as the town was called here, was a bit of a megalomaniac. All of the local tourist literature reported that it was one of the largest cities in the world. *Discover Guide* trumpeted that the city was "covering an area the size of Switzerland and with a main street 180 km long!" However, the claim had more to do with zoning than with reality. The *Guide* also called a visit to The Isa and the area around it "crammed with exhilarating, mystical and wild adventures not found anywhere else in the world."

We truly weren't there long enough to test these claims, but I don't recall ever feeling *exhilarated*.

Harold Bell Lasseter was. In 1897 this American-born explorer claimed to have found a fabulously rich gold reef somewhere in the Petermann Ranges in the southwest corner of the Northern Territory. For years he sought financial backing and followers for an expedition to relocate it. Finally in

1930 he got it, the Central Australian Gold Exploration Company. But, alas, crashes and desertions ensued.

Lasseter's dead body was found the next year in a cave, his diary stuffed in a sardine can. He had failed to find, or if he was telling the truth, re-find the gold vein.

John Campbell Miles was luckier than Lasseter. He discovered local minerals in 1923, and the current mine went into operation the following year.

The Isa also called itself "Birthplace of Champions!" Well, I suppose most people who follow sports do recognize the names of golf's Greg Norman and tennis' Patrick Rafter.

In addition to its claim to be huge, the Isa also described itself a *cosmopolitan,* and this was a somewhat justifiable claim thanks to the mining engineers, executives, and residents from more than 50 different nations who, at least when we were there, were calling Mount Isa home. They scurried about town in their Holdens wearing ties and talking on cell phones. At 22,000 inhabitants, this was Queensland's largest provincial city west of the Great Dividing Range.

The Isa had seen its share of ranchers too, and it still honored its hell-west-and-crooked roots by being home to "this nation's largest rodeo!" in July/August. Cooler writers of travel guides called it *one* of the largest.

The Isa was, understandably, a School of Distance Education base, and since 1964 it had been the operational headquarters for The Royal Flying Doctor Service, which oversaw what was described as "a 500,000 square mile treatment center." That's pretty accurately what it was. RFDS claimed that no one in Australia was more than two hours flight time from medical help thanks to its services. It called itself, "the largest civilian aeromedical organisation (Australian spelling) in the world." From 22 bases deploying 45 planes, it provided both routine health care and emergency help 24 hours a day, seven days a week to 190,000 people.

I wanted to visit its service base here. It was opened to visitors on weekdays and this was Friday, so I asked Dave if we could afford an hour.

He continued to load suitcases in the little trailer behind the bus as he said, "Sorry, mate. We have a long day ahead."

He must have noted my disappointment. As we pulled out of the Mercure's parking lot at 8 sharp, he attempted to mollify me. I was, as usual, in the very back of the bus, so he grabbed his microphone and said, "For those stroppy that we didn't get to the flying doctors, we'll have more time in Alice Springs, and there's a Flying Doctors' base there open to the public. We need our time today for Camooweal." Through voice inflection, he made The Cam sound irresistible.

So we didn't linger in The Isa to experience RFDS or its unusual Underground Hospital. We also didn't get to visit 12 million dollar Outback at Isa which *TRAVEL ACTION*, yet another local tourist publication, described as "a mine-blowing experience." It did sound interesting with its Hard Times Mine Tour and Riversleigh Fossil Centre. Oh. Excuse me. "Award-winning, bone-chilling Riversleigh Fossil Centre!"

Would I return to Isa? Yes. Would I bring my hype-remover? Definitely.

We were on the road early, and while the passengers yawned, Dave went on and on about Camooweal. "It's an old droving camp and the Gateway to the Northern Territory," he said. But then he stopped talking as if he'd suddenly become unplugged. But from past experience I knew it was only a pause and, sure enough, he soon repeated what he had already said about Camooweal, making it sound unmissable.

I was skeptical. Dave was clearly overselling and I couldn't understand why. Perhaps it was simply to justify our leaving Isa, a stellar stop that had been not much more than an overnighter.

I also couldn't understand why the tour planner booked the Mercure Inn, also called the Burke and Wills Mt Isa. It was centrally located but, in my generous opinion, a half-a-star accommodation despite its slick-paper promises. The reality of the room was a rusted, stained teapot, the pervasive odor of stale cigarette smoke, dim mine-tunnel lights, an uncomfortable bed, and rattling pipes which didn't quite drown out the sound of Lynette coughing in the next room. This was not, I want to assure everyone, an annoyance like the accommodation. It was a growing concern.

Ah, the joys of travel! In truth, I had experienced far worse accommodations. In Amsterdam, I slept on the floor with my son Matthew's feet in my face because the bed was too tiny for two. The room itself was so small that there was barely enough room to stretch out on the floor. The bathtub was a bizarre, high-lipped trough. In San Francisco, a major chain hotel turned out to be in the red light district. Patrons signed in on a clipboard, and I was solicited the minute I stepped outside. At the other extreme was that convent in Rome with the boot camp beds, a single 25 watt light bulb, and an 11 p.m. curfew. If you arrived later than that, you literally couldn't get in because the nuns locked the door and, apparently, went deaf until dawn. In New Brunswick, Canada, our children were severely bitten by bedbugs one long-ago summer. Etc. So the Mercure had been endurable if not pleasant.

Oh, oh. Dave was hyping Camooweal again. But at least I had a big distraction, The Outback. Amazed at its ever changing landscape, I made notes about the Barkly Highway in my notebook. It was also called the

Overlander's Way, and we and the Road Trains were following the original route of early stockmen across the Barkly Tablelands where tree dotted mountains fronted by cattle skirting termite mounds continued for miles to the west. I wondered if cattle ever backed into these pillars, knocking them over with disastrous results.

"Is this the first time you've seen termite mounds, mate?" Dave asked, and I realized that he was talking to me.

"No," I replied.

"Know anything about them?"

"No," I said, playing along.

"Termite colonies can extend to several million, but the termites, or white ants as they're sometimes called, are well below ground," said naturalist Dave. He told us that there were six types of termites in Australia. The Great Northern devour any plant material in their path, and the Magnetic build the largest mounds on a north/south alignment because "they have some sense of the Earth's magnetic field," Dave informed.

For some unknown reason on this, our 7th day, Dave began calling himself our "ground pilot". Each time he said it, he paused to see if we appreciated his wit and laughed. After about the tenth time, he said, "Did I mention, mates, that I did some racing in the US?"

I looked up and saw his eyes staring at me again in the rearview mirror to see if I was paying attention. "Daytona, Fort Wayne, Franklin. Know where that is, mate?"

"The one in Tennessee?" I responded.

"Tennessee! Right on ya," he said, like a game show host with a refrigerator to give away. He went on, of course, to tell about the wild parties he had attended and his frequent Daytona Beach drives.

When he ran down, I was able to return my gaze to the Tablelands. But the land had flattened out again, and we were crossing desert. I couldn't help but notice an abundance of plants that looked like a children's book version of Little Miss Muffet's tuffet. Interspersed like checkers on a half completed game, they stretched to the horizon. I asked my seatmate, Rob for the first time, what they were.

"Spinifex, the most common plant in the Simpson Desert."

"Is that where we are?"

"More or less. It's to the south and west of us."

"Is spinifex a cacti?"

"No, it's compacted grass and easily recognized by its green, or grey, tufts."

I nodded in understanding. Rob had been my patient, inexhaustible teacher of everything Australian except for birds and flowers, Lynette's specialties, for more than ten years. He was quietly but fiercely proud of his homeland.

Ruth and I met him and Lynette on a Great Barrier Reef cruise on our second visit to Australia, and we have been friends practically ever since.

We had parted after the cruise with no plan or intent to see each other again. In fact, when Ruth asked Lynette for their address in Canberra, Lynette said, "We have so many friends all over the world that Rob and I have stopped giving out our address. We simply can't take on any more social obligations." Travel veteran Ruth certainly understood.

But while Lynette was saying this to Ruth as we approached Townsville's harbor, our final port-of-call, Rob was dictating a list of books about Australia for me to read. I found a few, like Mary Durack's epic *Kings in Grass Castles,* in Sydney and read them avidly over the next several months, and I wanted to thank him.

Canberra was on the itinerary on our next trip, and I checked the ACT's phone book. There were three men with his name, and I randomly dialed the third number. Rob answered, invited us to tea, gave us a brief tour of his city, and a lasting friendship began.

Rob and Lynette had ties to the United States. They lived in Washington, DC from 1977 until 1982 after Rob accepted an ambassadorial type appointment. Lynette told great stories about these years that included attending a pregnant-with-twins Laura Bush's baby shower. They remained very fond of the Carters. Lynette and Rob's grandson Andrew lives, teaches, and works on a music career near New York City.

While on a trip to The States to explore a few of the places they hadn't previously experienced, like Chicago, Rob and Lynette visited Andrew and then spent some time with us in St. Louis. So we had a chance to reciprocate their hospitality. On another solo trip to New York, Rob came to our new home in Washington State, and Ruth and I had an opportunity to show him the grandeur of the Northwest and be *his* teacher for a change. This was just after Lynette's Nordic scare, so she was reluctant to travel internationally.

And now, here we were on this Outback trip together. Lynette had been fine for the first few days, but then raspy coughing began. Lynette had not been well for the last two days, and Rob, in his concern for her, was preoccupied and not very talkative as a seatmate.

I had purposely avoided sitting next to him until today. It was as if we had tacitly made an agreement not to constantly seek out each others' company. Social exclusivity is just not Australian, and Ruth and I had many couples to get to know. But I had missed Rob's delightful company, so I treasured this rare opportunity to sit with him.

"Spinifex looks tough," I prompted. "Is it an out-of-control import like Salvation Jane?"

"No, they're native plants. Survivors in a harsh environment. If you look closely at one you'll see that it's impenetrable, compacted grass."

"I'll check one out," I promised.

"It provides a home for any number of animals. So be careful," he warned. "They burrow underneath."

As soon as I was near one, I kicked and pummeled it and found it tough and unyielding. I was somewhat dismayed to learn, far too late, that the animals Rob referred to included the venomous mulga snake and the well named desert death adder.

Spinifex is a fascinating survivor. Highly flammable, it thrives with almost no moisture and is abundant throughout The Outback. In addition to killers with fangs, it shelters the Australian hobby, the spotted harrier, and budgerigars. This information in a brochure sent me straight to the dictionary. Not an elf, a vertical take-off plane, and dishonest accountants, they're all birds. There's even a spinifex dove, which sounds a bit like an oxymoron similar to tough love.

Eucalypts continued to prosper along the road too, especially ghost gums. According to my *Lonely Planet*, "Of the 700 species of the genus eucalyptus, 95% occur naturally in Australia." One of Lynette's favorites, the ghost gum, was both common in The Outback and quite beautiful with pale white bark and green leaves that contrasted nicely with the red soil.

The landscape became less hospitable looking as we traveled mostly west and I saw only an occasional cow or car, or their remnants in the form of a rusting metal hulk or desiccated bones beside the road. The pavement narrowed and deteriorated as we traveled atop the burnt sienna of the Barkly Tablelands. The bus trembled, teeth rattled.

We stopped at Camooweal for tea. As I looked about, Dave's morning fixation on this town escaped me. Its 300 people lived in one-story boxes perched precariously atop a system of 500 million-year-old caves and sinkholes.

Camooweal was already here and considered the gateway to the Northern Territory long before Mount Isa sprang forth. Its Great Artesian bore went down in 1897. Due to a quirky law, this frontier-looking town had, allegedly, the longest Main Street in the world. Camooweal, it seemed, was included in Mount Isa's city limits despite the fact that The Isa was 115 miles away. Local travel literature effused, "Visitors experienced in serious caving will discover a whole new world beneath Camooweal."

We stayed up on the surface, however, and visited only Freckleton's Store, rebuilt in 1922. Yes, not constructed but rebuilt. The sign above the door read "Freckleton General Storekeepers" and inside the keeper on duty looked as though he was old enough to have been on the original construction crew.

The store had the authentic look of a frontier emporium, and it and the town seriously reminded me of the paintings of Russell Drysdale, a prominent Australian artist whose Outback scenes are a cross between Andrew Wyeth and David Hockney.

Above the doorframe was something labeled "poison box". I didn't ask because the proprietor was crotchety, but I hoped it was for death adders.

Seven miles west of Camooweal we crossed into the Northern Territory, Oz's barren and, except for Darwin and Alice Springs, almost townless non-state. Because only about 1% of the Australian population lives here, it will probably remain a Territory instead of becoming a State for an indefinite time.

About one-fifth of Territorians are Aboriginal, and their land is carved up into many Land Trusts with names like Karlantupa and Murranji.

The Northern Territory is often and aptly called "The Red Centre" since that color brilliantly predominates in the landscape, especially at sunrise and sunset.

The NT is bisected by the north/south Stuart Highway, which stretches from Adelaide to Darwin, in other words from temperate to tropics with a vast stretch of arid desert in between.

As I saw signs of the Stuart Highway's approach, I recalled climbing out of a rental car just south of Darwin several years previously to take a picture of a sign that announced, "Alice Springs—1443 km." Alice was on our itinerary this time, a little less than half the Stuart's total distance from Darwin to Adelaide. At the time I photographed the sign, Ruth and I were on our way to Litchfield National Park, and I had to restrain myself from continuing on the Stuart when we reached the turnoff. Ever since, I had wanted to travel more of it, and, at last, here was my chance.

But we weren't there quite yet. First, we had to cross a bit more than 100 miles of ocher desert. Our lunch stop was at Barkly Homestead, a sprawling, full service pit stop in the middle of a desert next to another desert, etc. In fact, this was the *only* service center *on* the Barkly Highway. Our road side table covered with sandwich makings attracted any number of flies and birds, giving a lie to the expression "lifeless desert".

For the rest of the afternoon I stared out of the window at a spinifex covered panorama that was equal parts fascinating and mind-numbing. I stopped taking notes, mesmerized by the total lack of any evidence of civilization.

We turned left onto the Stuart at the Three Ways Roadhouse but didn't stop at the John Flynn Memorial. Too bad. I was interested. Dave didn't even mention it.

We pulled into the Tennant Creek Telegraph Station, only seven miles north of our destination for the night. This was the first of three such outposts that we would explore. A fourth, Powell Creek, still stood about 120 miles north of Tennant Creek. TCTS was a series of empty stone buildings, mere shells of what they had been when telegraph was the state-of-the-art link between Darwin and Port Augusta in 1872. Tennant Creek was one of 11 repeater stations connected by 36,000 wire-strung poles. Repeaters were necessary because the signal traveled down bare steel wire and the original transmission became so weak after 300 kilometers or so that it needed a boost to keep going. Since it cost the equivalent of $50 today to send a message along the wire, businesses and newspapers were its main customers.

According to the Guide Map available in the Visitors Centre, this particular Station became, in its time, "a haven for travelers, a post office, and a ration depot for Aboriginal people."

There was no one manning the Station, but a self-guided walking tour pamphlet described the life of an operator, who had to maintain equipment 24-7, keep a garden, tend sheep and cattle, assist the native population, provide medical services, and repair and make tools in the blacksmith shop. And no 401K.

This particular facility ceased its main function in 1935. As gold mining and Tennant Creek grew, post office and telegraph services moved south to town.

After seeing the forlorn, abandoned station, we traveled to the north end of Tennant Creek, arriving at our motel at 4 o'clock in the afternoon. Freed from the cramped, jostling beast, Ruth and I needed a walk.

We strolled from one end of town to the other, meeting Allan and Barbara just past a not so prosperous downtown's store strip. They were already done with The Tennant in record time and were heading back to the motel.

Tenant Creek seemed smaller than it was, a town of 4,000, and it appeared to be, by far, the poorest community we had visited up to this point. One local information source called it Australia's third largest producer of gold, but the quantity must be small or the owners living elsewhere if the town's apparent lack of maintenance was any indication of its wealth.

My well-used *Lonely Planet* reported, "To the Warumungu people, Tennant Creek is Jurnkurakurr, the intersection of a number of dreaming tracks." I had been reading about Dreamtime for many years, and here it was a way of life. Since I still didn't grasp this belief system, I hoped for greater understanding while I was in the Northern Territory as we moved south to explore Uluru and other significant Aboriginal sites. I was also eager to meet and talk to the first Australians, who were clearly a real presence in Tenant Creek.

Outsiders were lured to their area by lust for gold, not in the 19th century when it was happening everywhere else but in the 1930s. Most of the unkempt buildings in town were of this era, and most of them looked like they needed serious attention, or a wrecking ball.

Tennant Creek was named in 1860 after a narrow trickle of water 7 miles north of town. Explorer John McDouall Stuart was credited with coming up with the name. I suppose he didn't think to ask the locals what they called their river and use their name despite the fact that it had been the somewhat reliable source of their water for millennia.

The town and river, instead, honored Andrew Tennant, a South Australian politician with interests in gold, steamships, cattle and sheep stations, and race horses.

Tourist literature boasted about 16.6 inches of rain per year, but I suspected that it came all at once in horrifying torrents. The most common road sign in this parched part of the world warned, "Floodway."

We found a grocery store at the other end of town, but there was little to tempt us. Jan and Roger were inside talking to the staff as if they were long-term residents. I was envious of their ease and the smiles they were inducing.

On the way back to the motel, Ruth and I followed the narrow sidewalk on the other side of the street for variety. An Aboriginal couple about our age approached, so I stepped behind Ruth to make room for them to pass. As the woman came into close range, she said with a touch of acidic judgment, "Don't worry, children. We won't hurt you."

I became immediately defensive and replied with a smile, "We know that. How *are* you?"

She passed and didn't answer.

I was stunned by an obvious misperception in our very first real encounter with native people. At first I didn't understand what I had done to incite such hostility, but then I decided that by stepping back I had shown…what…fear? Maybe I had unknowingly breached some social custom I knew nothing about, and I would only escalate the situation by turning around and forcing contact. Or perhaps my stepping back was interpreted as a desire to avoid contact. Not the case. I wanted to turn around and pursue to explain, but I didn't.

The wildly misnamed Eldorado Motor Inn where we were staying smelled as if its septic system was near crisis, and the buffet in its dining room was awful.

I haven't said much about the meals we were having in The Outback because most were nondescript affairs. Barely warm and in huge serving trays, the entrees and sides were always cold by the time they reached the table. And food that sat out, in my opinion, tended to get unappetizing in a hurry.

Australian cuisine doesn't differ much from basic US restaurant food expect for two national passions—pumpkins and Vegemite. Pumpkin soup is on most menus and pasty, salty Vegemite can be found in almost every grocery store and jelly caddy. It's basically a yeast extract that's, admittedly, a rich source of the vitamin B group. However, the first time I tasted it, and there won't be a second, it lingered on my tongue for three days. Vegemite is, to say the least, an acquired taste.

Our evening meals were at best passable, but the company was consistently exceptional. Our Eldorado dinner companions were Jane and Michael and Jan and Roger. Jane spoke of her love for Cyprus where she was born.

Michael related yet more tales of his illustrious ancestors. Several of them participated in The Crusades. Some served under William the Conqueror before and during the 1066 Norman invasion. One married the daughter of the Earl of Ulster and brought the family name to Ireland for the first time. As I listened to Michael relate concrete details stretching back more than a thousands years, I mused that I didn't even know my paternal grandfather's occupation or the names of his parents.

Roger told us about the local wildflowers we were likely to see in the next few days.

Since Jan had just talked to local Aboriginals in the grocery store, she was eloquent about their concerns, the limitation of native title rights and the need for reconciliation.

Every meal, without fail, was a delightful education for Ruth and me, and we listened more than talked. We didn't, for example, tell anyone about our unfortunate afternoon encounter with the Aboriginal couple. We hoped that it was just an isolated incident that we'd laugh about, or at the very least understand, later. Was it a forecast of future hostility?

I deeply regretted that we didn't have a decent conversation with local Aboriginals, who, like the couple on the sidewalk, seemed to avoid contact with people like us. Feeling like an intruder, I vowed to watch Roger and Jan to see how the chasm might be bridged.

Ruth and I were also distracted and worried at dinner. Lynette was coughing more and more and having greater difficult breathing with each passing hour. Claiming tiredness, she was participating less and less in activities. Today as we stopped to investigate roadside attractions, she stayed on the bus after saying, "Rob, you go on." He continued to join the group although clearly reluctant to leave her side. But when Ruth or I probed for more information about her condition, he would shrug his shoulders and say, "She wants no fuss made." And we had no choice but to honor her privacy.

Chapter Nine

In the Middle

Outback roads, even the paved ones, were hard on the spine. And we were covering great distances each sunrise to sunset. For a few days now I had lingered over breakfast because of some fascinating conversation, or I dawdled about getting our suitcases down to the trailer, or I had to take some last minute photos. The result was that Ruth, if she didn't sit with Jane or Lynette or Barbara, and I often ended up in the most uncomfortable seats with the worst view on the bus, the ones in the very back over the jouncing wheel.

So today for our cruise down the Stuart Highway to Alice Springs, I was determined to claim the best seats for us. It was Day 8 and more than our turn. I paid attention to the time so as to board early. As I approached the bus, I saw not a single face in any window or anyone lurking about. I congratulated myself on my wiliness and boarded, juggling Ruth's bag along with my increasingly heavy carry-on. My goal was to plop them on the best seats, the ones directly behind Dave. We had never sat in them, the equivalent to about 8th row center for a Broadway show.

To my surprise, there were bags already on this pair, and as I moved to the rear of the bus looking for the first available space, surprise turned to anger. Every seat, except for the two in the back over the wheel, had personal possessions already on them. Unobtrusively, my traveling companions had already boarded and claimed all of the other seats. Then they skulked off. I had no choice but to put our stuff in the usual cramped space without adequate leg room and prepare to bounce all day. And I thought that Australia was a democracy. "Make that a monarchy with dynastic intentions," I told myself, hot under and above the collar.

I thought it over and resolved to say something to Dave, but he headed me off. As we pulled away from the Eldorado, he said, "Mornin', mates. I see you're all in the same spots as yesterday. Keep in mind that we need to rotate so that everyone has a chance to sit in the more desirable seats."

Perhaps he had been watching when I stomped down the steps with a scowl on my face and smoke coming out of my ears.

He paused and looked in the rear view mirror to see if his point had been made and there was complete silence. So from that day forward he kept the bus locked until everyone had assembled, making it at least a public event if someone insisted on being selfish.

This day, like the ones that had preceded it, was sunny. Cool, crisp Outback mornings so far segued into almost hot afternoons, and then it became downright cold after sunset. We had not seen rain, or even a cloud, since our first day on the road.

The first stop this morning was The Devil's Marbles. Well named, they were huge, almost perfectly round boulders of varying sizes scattered about on both sides of a sealed, the Oz term for *paved*, road just off the Stuart. Some marbles were piled atop others haphazardly as if some bellicose giant was stockpiling for war.

"They're granite," Dave told us. "Formed around 60 million years ago. What happened was that over time a rock as big as Uluru cracked and divided. Then wind and water shaped these boulders. You can't tell, but they're wearin' down and will one day be just sand, bits of quartz, feldspar, and mica blowin' in the wind."

As he stopped and opened the door, I thought he might break into song. But instead he lowered his voice and added, "Just to warn you, it's considered very unlucky to take anything away from here. The Abos consider this a sacred place. One chap took a few pebbles and he…had some serious problems." Dave didn't elaborate further.

I supposed he was trying to tell us that there *is* something to Aboriginal lore, and that those who pay heed to their beliefs and practices don't consider them mere primitive superstition. According to natives, some entity they call the Rainbow Serpent placed these boulders here, and, if he or she was still hanging around, who wanted to tangle with…it? The Aboriginals who claimed this area, the Warumungu, believed that these spherical oddities were the Serpent's eggs.

With time to explore, everyone scattered. There were paths completely circling the Marbles on both sides of the road. I watched Roger, camera ready, disappear behind a condo-sized rock on the side where Dave had parked.

There was what appeared to be a slightly larger configuration of Marbles on the other side. So I followed Ruth over there to where the path divided, and she went off with Jane and Barbara. The three, chatting about the wild flowers in profusion everywhere, went counter-clockwise. Left to hike alone, I decided to head in the opposite direction.

The Marbles were so enormous that at times I was alone on the trail and the view ahead was blocked. I came around one pile of rocks and saw two young guys. They were shouting at each other in German as they blithely climbed, ever higher, from boulder to boulder, and I wondered if I should warn them about the Rainbow Serpent. But they seemed totally self-involved, at least to the extent of ignoring my presence, so I walked on. I didn't want to witness the Serpent's wrath heaped on these trespassers. Or did I?

Around the next bend I looked down and spied in the middle of the path just in front of me the evilest looking insect I had ever seen. It was black as onyx and had pincers and feelers and all sorts of other nasty appurtenances. As I came closer, it scuttled back and forth as if trying to prevent me from proceeding. As I stood above it immobilized by curiosity, it moved about menacingly as if drawing a line for me not to cross. I knew that Australia had the most dangerous snakes in the world, so wasn't it logical to assume the same for its arachnids and insects? I gauged the bug's ability to leap or fly and the personal risk involved if it did either as I poked and prodded it with my shoe. As I did, it just became more agitated. I thought about scooping it into my hat and seeking an Australian to identify it, or should I simple stomp on it and rid the world of a potential menace? I wasn't even supposed to pocket a pebble. And, especially here, wasn't it foolish to tempt the unknown? What if this combat-ready bug was one of the Serpent's protectors? Or, could Rainbow morph into other entities? And was it environmentally fair to squash an insect simply because it was ugly and looked dangerous? After all, this was its home, not mine.

Filled with repulsion and wonder, I strode the circle faster looking for an Aussie to walk back with me to identify this fierce looking creature. I figured that Roger would know, but he had chosen to explore and photograph the Marbles on the other side, as had Rob and Lynette, walking hand in hand. Michael was nearby but he probably wouldn't know since it wasn't a flag or a historical footnote.

I finally spied Ruth, Jane, and Barbara coming from the opposite direction. "Quick, follow me!" I shouted.

But by the time I hustled them back to the spot, the insect was gone. Either it had scuttled away looking for a baby to ingest or I was wrong about its exact location.

I later checked websites looking for information about native bugs and, according to the staff of the Australian Museum, folks who would know, "The majority of insects in Australia are not harmful to humans." Hah! Notice how they slip the word *majority* into their disclaimer. And they go on to further qualify, "It is best to avoid touching them if you want to avoid being stung or bitten."

The Devil's Marbles were a remarkable attraction, and all too soon we were on The Stuart again, heading south to the not very distant Barrow Creek Telegraph Station. It was Like Tennant Creek but with more historical significance. Barrow Creek was, for example, a staging camp for army convoys during World War II.

In 1874 Aboriginals from the Katish tribe attacked the Station and two men, the station master and a linesman, were killed. A news cable sent to Adelaide by some anonymous someone said, "Civilized Native Boy has had three spear wounds. Mr. Flint, assistant operator one spear wound in leg, not serious." A large police hunt ensued.

As we stood in the cemetery together reading about the victims, Jan became perturbed. "Why is there no mention of the Katish who were killed defending their land? Where are *their* names?"

This comment didn't surprise me because Jan often and heatedly spoke about the mistreatment of Aboriginals and the denial of their basic rights. And, at least in this case, she was definitely right. Many more than two tribal members were killed after being hunted down, and there was zero mention of their fate. What did surprise me, however, was what Jan added, "I have a male descendant who had two families. One was white, the branch from which I came."

"And the other side?" I prompted.

"He had a relationship with a native woman."

"So, you have Aboriginal kin?" I asked.

"Yes, I do," she said as if still adjusting to the news. "I recently met a cousin from the other branch for the first time, and we got on quite well."

Jan continued to describe the meeting with animation, but then she abruptly changed the subject as if deciding she had said too much. I didn't press again for details but I now understood her a little better.

Roger went off to study and photograph plants, so I followed him because the Station buildings weren't all that thrilling. I never regretted hanging out with him and always learned something by doing so. He seemed glad for the company. "This land was once under the Larapintine, a tropical sea teaming with life," he told me.

"How far back in time?" I asked.

"Water covered most of central Australia 600 million years ago."

Roger scuffed the red soil with his shoe and added, "The landscape is still eroding and revealing fossils."

Near us was a tree that I had now seen many times but still couldn't readily identify. "What kind of tree is that, Roger?" I asked, figuring he would know.

It's a mulga."

"Oh, sure. Jane and Lynette already told me about them."

"They're survivors, those. They collect their own water by making swirls like the ones in fingerprints that channel rainwater to their roots. Clever adaptation in a flat landscape, that. It's a hard wood. The first Australians made spears from mulgas. See those flowers over there that look like upside down brollies?"

I nodded.

"Parakeelya."

While he photographed this flower, I studied this curious and vivid purple plant's five-petal silky bloom that looked like it needed to be in a hothouse but was thriving instead in extreme conditions.

I left Roger avidly snapping close-ups and went back to study what was left of Barrow Creek Station. The entire telegraph system was quite a remarkable feat of 19th century engineering. On October 21, 1872, a submarine telecable linked Australia with the rest of the world via the island of Java for the first time. This cable connected Aussies to the entire British telegraph system. The British Empire, then at or near its height, was in the process of creating the first international information age.

The heat and Dave's insistence that we had a long way to go eventually got Roger and me back on the bus. I took my seat atop the wheel for the relatively short bounce to Ti-Tree. Or maybe it just seemed short since there were no speed limits in the Northern Territory.

"That's the Barrow Creek, a fair dinkum pub," Dave said as we passed a Roadhouse without stopping for a lemon squash.

On our way south again, we passed the Central Mount Stuart Historical Reserve, the mathematical central point of Australia. Dave didn't slow down, but I glimpsed what looked like a memorial of some kind as he rambled on about the John McDouall Stuart expedition that passed through here in 1860.

The nearby mountain named for Stuart was said to be the geographic middle of this Continent/Country that is almost 3,000 miles wide, similar to the United States. The drive from Sydney to Perth is almost exactly equal to the one from Atlanta to Reno. *Approximate* seemed the best word to describe Central Mount Stuart's claim to be the middle according to the literature I was reading.

Ti-Tree, pronounced Tea Tree, was off the road and we didn't turn.

"This area is the home of the Anmatjere people," Dave said. "Ti-Tree is a base that serves a number of Abo communities." He made it clear in a very carefully worded way that the land had been given back to the original inhabitants for an experiment in self-rule.

Later, a few of the men in our group took me aside and privately grumbled about what a failure Ti Tree was since the Aboriginal power structure had proved incapable of self-government for various reasons. I couldn't tell if this was ethnic superiority rearing its ugly head or fact-based analysis of the self-rule results.

Back home, I found an Anmatjere Library website that quoted the Honorable John Ah Kit, a smiling minister for Regional Development who wrote, "By 2012, people living in the Anmatjere (Ti-Tree) region will be enjoying the fruits of both a strong economy and a vibrant and harmonious community." He spoke about the citizens and the native government shaping "the Masterplan" together. He mentioned setting clear goals and taking control, fairly typical words for a man in his position. He warned about passivity and forecast an economy based on "pastoralism, tourism, and horticulture." So, the experiment was on-going and, I suppose, the jury should still be in the listening-to-testimony stage.

It's hard for me to envision any kind of Eden in Ah Kit's harsh environment. But Icelanders grow flowers and Israelis fruit.

And I still wondered why, if the Anmatjere wanted and needed tourism, we didn't visit Ti-Tree. When I asked Dave why, he told me that the township was in the Ahakeye Aboriginal Land Trust and that access to Aboriginal land was prohibited without a permit. Perhaps that's why we stopped only at the Red Sands Gallery.

This proved to be a very fine seller of what appeared to be exceptional native art. In one room, an Aboriginal woman sat on the floor delicately dabbing paint speckles on a canvas with a primitive twig brush. She was creating a wonderful swirling design and I longed to talk to her, ask her about her inspiration, and compliment her. But she never looked up, never acknowledged the presence of the many other potential customers circling her work. It was as if she toiled behind an invisible glass wall.

The only salesperson I saw was a clearly Caucasian gentleman who was busy showing expensive art works to clearly interested couples. I wondered where these well dressed, twenty-and thirty-somethings came from. They certainly weren't day-tripping from Perth or Sydney.

Or maybe they were. I recalled seeing on a previous trip an impressively large private airport just outside Adelaide, the nearest real metropolis to Ti-Tree. It was at least 700 miles south, but the affluent can and do hop about the world pursuing their passions, so maybe these browsing customers were from distant places.

Barbara, who could afford to buy, circled by me and exclaimed, "Such prices!"

Many of the others in our group then and later expressed regret that they hadn't bought native art a few years before when such works could have been had very cheaply.

I suspected that, baring a global depression, prices of Aboriginal paintings and crafts would not be going down. The native works sold here at Red Sands and in other places are in the Vatican and Holmes a Court Collections. The new Denver Art Museum designed by Daniel Libeskind has a notable collection on display. In truth, Aboriginal art works belong there and elsewhere.

I was atypically tempted to buy something too, but I had no means to carry even a small memento, and shipping from Australia would require a chunk of cash. My single bag was already swelling alarmingly with gathered materials. But this was my first chance, and perhaps last, to acquire what appeared to be exceptional native art.

Teetering between rationality and desire, I recalled *Lonely Planet*'s warning, "Much of the so-called Aboriginal art sold as souvenirs is either ripped-off from Aboriginal people or is just plain fake." Naïve natives sell their works for small amounts to sellers who put big prices on them in city galleries. The writers recommended buying directly from communities, but we weren't going into Ti-Tree. This remote gallery certainly had plenty of business. But could I trust the answer were I to ask the salesperson, "Are the locals reaping fair rewards from your gallery's sales?"

Reason won. I left empty handed.

Heading south again we passed a huge vineyard on the right side of the road. It looked lush but completely out of place, like a palm tree in The Arctic. I silently wished the Anmatjere people well.

"Camels!" Karin shouted, as if someone was surreptitiously trying to light up on the bus and she had caught them. "There. Just over there!" she said to many bobbing heads, including my own.

I looked where she pointed and saw three wild camels running across the landscape parallel to the road. It was such an unusual and exciting sight that I spent the rest of the day idly looking for more. I scanned non-stop until the MacDonnell Ranges loomed before us.

Reaching the foothills, the road began to twist upward as we neared Alice Springs, the city that began as a repeater station and grew to become the undeclared capital of The Outback.

Before we saw The Alice, as it was fondly called here, we pulled into one of its finest attractions, the Alice Springs Telegraph Station. Lovingly maintained, this was reportedly the best preserved of the original 11 telegraphers that reduced the transfer of news from London to Adelaide from 3 months to 3 hours.

Dave introduced us to a tour guide, an elderly Aboriginal gentleman, and then Dave eased outside the ring to listen. Odd, I thought, since he usually disappeared.

"Hello, my name is Alec," the gentleman began in a crisp somewhat British accent. "At one time 130 mixed blood children lived here at the Historical Reserve. I was one of them. My Mother was a full blooded Aborigine and my Father was Scottish."

Our group and the other visitors stepped closer, sensing that we were about to get a true insider's view of local history.

Dave, who clearly knew and respected Alec, was hanging on every word as if he had never heard Alec's presentation before.

"This was a children's home from 1932 to 1942. I was a young boy, so it was just another home for me. The missionaries looked after us. There were no records kept back then, so I don't know my birth day. What I do know is that my mother gave me to the missionaries when I was about 4 years old. After 1942, this became an Aboriginal Reserve for the Arrernte people." Alec would know. He was there. He was not then, nor had he ever been, bitter, and his gentle demeanor supported his claim of kind treatment.

Before 1932, this Telegraph Station was the first "white" settlement in central Australia, and 94 Europeans lived here at the Alice Springs Post Office/Morse Code interpreter.

The nearby town didn't become Alice Springs until 1933. At first called Stuart, it was primarily a service provider for ranchers, miners, and Afghan camel drivers. When folks celebrated the new century in 1900, there were 12 residents in Stuart staffing and/or supporting a store, a boarding house, and, of course, a pub. By the time it became Alice Springs, the population was around 2,000. It was 27,000 and growing at the time of our visit.

In 1871 British soldiers started building a telegraph repeater station at what was now the Reserve. It was named for Alice Todd. A resident of Adelaide and the wife of the Telegraph's Superintendent, Alice never visited, and there was no actual spring. The almost always dry Todd River had a depression here at the Reserve that trapped water atop some granite. The result was a relatively stable pool of water. I learned later that this so-called spring was not Alice's water source. She derived her water from bores driven down 200 feet. Alec told us, "I have never seen water restrictions in Alice Springs."

Alec remembered that resident soldiers left in 1945, and The Barracks they abandoned was still around, now the oldest building in Central Australia. He charmed me when he spoke of how the staff kept goats for milk on the surprisingly grassy, gum tree covered hillside that I was now eyeing. But he lost me when he said, "This hill is the site of Corkwood Dreaming, a part of the Aborigine explanation of creation." He went on to elaborate, and the crowd gathered around him listened respectfully. But I suspected that I wasn't the only one who didn't fully comprehend. But at least I now understood that dreaming had something to do with explaining the long-ago creation of the landscape, and I assumed that Aboriginals had been just as confused when some Protestant missionary told them the story of creation in Genesis. Some of Alec's guests asked questions which showed unusually deep involvement in his story, and they led to a genuine cross cultural discussion.

Alec took us through the telegraph office, the stables, and the station master's residence. In other words, he gave us a complete tour of his home. As he thanked us for visiting, he told us that his last name was Ross. I found his autobiography for sale in the gift shop, but I didn't buy the slender volume because I had met and listened to the author.

We boarded the bus and headed into town, which, like The Isa, we saw dramatically from a promontory, the top of Anzac Hill. This was a memorial to all the Aussies lost in any war, not just World War I. One sign mentioned that this was also a site of Corkwood Dreaming to local natives. Another cross-cultural coming together, I noted.

The bus pulled up to our well-situated motel on the edge of downtown at 6 p.m. We could finally unpack for a while since we were spending three nights here in Alice. I didn't know it then, but one evening and two days wasn't nearly enough time for a love affair.

Chapter Ten

Alice Springs Ahead

The Mercure Inn Oasis was our best accommodation yet, and it was right across the street from a large hospital. So Ruth and I encouraged Lynette to at least have a check up. But she refused, certain that her congestion and coughing were the result of overdoing it, not some sinister disease.

I reminded her that our next three or four destinations had no hospitals and only limited-service clinics, if that, so wouldn't it be better to be sure?

Not wanting to be fawned over or a bother, she claimed she would get proper treatment by staying in her room at the Oasis and simply resting.

But first she had to go to Desert Park.

Everyone was going to Desert Park. This was a free day, and we could have chosen any number of options, but the buzz about this local theme park for all ages was so loud that the bus was full long before departure time. In fact, I had to run back to the room for my hat and was the last to board. I almost missed the ride.

West of town and just outside Alice's growing urban sprawl, Desert Park's approach was spectacular. It huddled at the base of flat-topped Mount Gillen, a soaring vertical cliff.

Alice Springs is truly in the mountains. The MacDonnell Ranges extend for about 250 miles east and west of town, and The Alice's high perch is totally encircled by waterless desert. The MacDonnell's crevices had been known for eons as sources of both semi and permanent water. Deep pockets of trapped rain shaded by red river gum trees were infrequent but life-sustaining for desert dwellers.

And yet. As was true of every other city, town, and village in Australia, in 1974 Alice Springs became an island in a sea of flood water during a genuine Old Testament deluge.

Desert Park's guides, mostly looking as though they had just graduated from a university and were really enjoying their first day on the job, enthusiastically provided us with a "What's on Today?" handout as we entered. On this Sunday morning we had our choice of four guided presentations— desert bush foods, wild figs, a wander through the woodland, and Living Lollipops. This last one turned out to be edible honeyants. Yum.

We had to juggle these tours with visits to permanent habitats and a movie, *The Changing Heart,* which was shown frequently in the Exhibition Centre Cinema.

Ruth and I studied our options, but almost everyone was headed for the 10 a.m. Birds of Prey Show in Nature Theatre, so we joined the parade. I judged it a singularly exciting attraction right away because a wedge-tailed eagle, Australia's largest bird of prey, swooped down and landed near a Park guide. It was close enough for me to feel a rush of air on the top of my head and to experience, like a small rodent, a frisson of fear. The guide fed the eagle a tidbit of something and told us about the daily lives of these magnificent creatures.

Adult Wedgies, the world's most common eagles, can have a slightly more than 8-foot wingspan. They can soar at 6,000 feet and above for hours without landing. They are assiduous predators and have been known to team up to kill red kangaroos.

Black kites and kestrels circled overhead looking for handouts too. These were not tame birds, mind you. They came sweeping down from Mount Gillen's crevices when they saw the crowd gather and were truly wild. The guides didn't know at any given demonstration which birds would be lured down the mountain with the promise of food. Among other things, I learned that the brown falcon and black kite were the most common indigenous birds.

This was the first truly hot day of the trip, and most of the Desert Park attractions were outside, so Ruth and I were worried about Lynette's tolerance level. Happily, we ran into her and Rob several times and she was beaming and animated each time, her health issues at bay and ignored for a few hours. In her natural habitat, a place full of unusual flora and fauna, Lynette, peering through her big glasses, had something new to report, some *must* for us to see, at every encounter. "Did you see the kowari?" she would ask, or, "Did you notice that cassia over there?"

"What's that?" I would reply so that I might get a chance to see the natural twinkle in her eyes as she explained.

"Those yellow flowers. Cass ee ya."

"Are they native trees?"

"No, they come from China and their bark is dried and used as a cinnamon substitute."

"Is a kowari a tree too?"

"No, it's a rodent."

Since I had missed them, I tracked kowaris down to discover that they were also called brush-tailed marsupial rats, an imposing, somewhat negative sounding name for the cute little critters. Grey with a white underbelly, the nocturnal kowari had a face like a Chihuahua and a tail that reminded me of a lint remover. I didn't get to see this behavior, but they can reportedly leap more than a foot into the air when startled.

At one point Lynette, Rob, Ruth, and I headed for the cool interior of the Cinema, which was already practically full. *The Changing Heart* was the only ho hum experience of the day, one of those films that wowed an audience with multi-screen, flashing images but didn't have much depth. Ironically, in its attempt to constantly stimulate my senses, it put me to sleep instead. After the movie, Ruth and I headed for the Desert Rivers Habitat, a bush forest of river red gum trees with places to sit silently and wait for cockatoos and barn owls to fly into view.

The Sand Country Habitat was like a microcosm of the land we had been driving through for several days, but labeled. The spinifex was described as "lush green spiky vegetation." That was apt.

Since Australia has the world's richest lizard population, it was fun to look for them on Desert Park's red rocks. Basking in the sun, they looked as though they were posing for a Discovery Channel or Animal Planet documentary.

We ran into small but mighty Lynette again in the Nocturnal House, which was a cool wonder. *Lonely Planet* called it "a great assortment of creatures you wouldn't have a hope of seeing otherwise," getting it exactly right. Where else in my lifetime might I have seen a gidgee skink, a blistered pyrgomorph, and a red tailed phascogale? Nowhere that I knew, but they were resident and active here.

The phascogale was a climbing marsupial with a second name, Wambenger, and I wondered if this nickname was a crude commentary on the male's bizarre sexual behavior. After only one year of life, he mated in a frenzy and died. Coming in two varieties, the Brush-tailed and Red-tailed, they looked like a cross between a fox and a feral cat.

Pyrgomorphs were grasshoppers covered with lines of spots that looked like miniature runway lights. They were known to display bright red or orange wings in defensive mode, but I didn't get to see this behavior. I nevertheless came to the conclusion that, due to its isolation, Australia had produced the strangest creatures on the planet.

While looking for an insect that resembled the one I had encountered at The Devil's Marbles, I learned that there were more ants in Australia than any other place in the world. I never, however, found the Rainbow Serpent's aggressive guardian among the creepy crawlies.

I carefully examined one of the most unusual plants I had ever seen, the blue mallee, a eucalypt with stems passing through its leaves as if speared.

Ruth and I lingered in the Woodlands, which was a large enclosed forest with close up views of native birds, like the splendid fairy-wren, a brilliant blue charmer. We followed the erratic path of a masked wood swallow for an insane length of time and I understood, for the first time, the obsessive behavior of bird watchers.

The Living Woodlands allowed us into a pen where we could chase emus and red roos.

We were offered witchetty grubs, a dining delicacy for locals which I personally didn't sample.

Rob and Lynette came by and took us down a path to closely examine yet another mulga tree. A few strands of Lynette's grey hair had gained release from the sweep of mane held tightly behind her head in a bun.

Dave was always going on about mulgas and, looking out of the window of a fast moving bus, I still could never be sure I was seeing the trees he was talking about. Earlier in the day, I had asked Rob to again point one out to me so I could finally do a close-up study where they were thriving and plentiful. Rob produced a fine example and Lynette provided commentary. "They provide seed, insect galls, and honey for Aboriginal families," she said, amazing me yet again with her depth of knowledge.

Desert Park was truly a stellar attraction that focused attention on the tough plants and strange fauna of Australia's interior with great skill by creating realistic, fairly natural habitats. It showed how animals and humans actually lived in a desert. No wonder Sir David Attenborough said about Desert Park, "There is no museum or wildlife park in the world that could match it."

By now it was afternoon. It was still technically winter in The Outback, but the day was very, very hot. Our group had scattered. The couples we still saw were waiting for the bus to take them back to the Oasis. Ruth and I asked the driver, not Dave who was enjoying a day off, if we might be dropped near the Cultural Precinct.

We were the only ones from our group who were interested, and I'm sorry that the others didn't get to experience this cluster of high culture with an ethnic thrust and eight attractions. By late afternoon Ruth and I had seen them all.

Our favorite was the Albert Namatjira Gallery. I was having great difficulty understanding the Aboriginals' belief system, but not its art. It simply yet deeply reflected a profound understanding of their natural environment. And Albert Namatjira was the Winslow Homer of the Outback. He lived from 1902 to 1959 during which time he became the first Aboriginal artist to gain an international reputation.

He was honored everywhere in the world and at home in Australia too. When I later tried to tell Rob about this artist, Rob replied, "Oh, we have two Namatjira's at home. I'll show you when we return to Canberra."

I was amazed and impressed.

Like the Wyeths of Pennsylvania, the Namatjiras of the Northern Territory became a cottage industry. Albert's sons and even some grandsons all became excellent painters. In fact, sons Oscar, Enos, Ewald, Keith, and Maurice accompanied Albert on painting expeditions.

The eponymous gallery in the Cultural Precinct called Namatjira a realist watercolor artist who "captured the true essence of the central Australian landscape." Well put.

One of the Aranda people and educated at a Lutheran mission, Namatjira was a blacksmith, carpenter, stockman, and camel driver who didn't become an artist until he was in his thirties. Approaching mid-life, he met Rex Battarbee, a self-taught Victorian watercolorist who had ended up in Alice as the result of a coin toss. Albert persuaded Rex to teach him, and Albert showed an instant flare for the water color medium and soon began to exhibit his work. A relatively short 25 year career followed. Early critics who had not seen The Outback called his reds "irritating" and his purples "dangerous." I called them "true." Because of his acceptance and fame, Namatjira became the first Aboriginal person to be granted Australian citizenship in 1957.

He was buried in the Memorial Cemetery, another of the Cultural Precinct's attractions on the other side of Big Sister Hill, and we found his grave and paid our respects.

The other cultural institutions included the Museum of Central Australia which displayed natural history artifacts. I was most fascinated by yet another Australian anomaly. It was, for reasons unknown, a meteor magnet. One interesting map showed the locations of the 21 known direct hits, coded for "crater only" and "crater with meteorite." The display was labeled astrogeology, a term I had never heard but that fit perfectly. It explored the affects of these comets' impacts on Oz topography. For example, in the Alice Springs area, meteors had altered the composition of the sandstone.

Two attractions in the Precinct had to do with aircraft. The Kookaburra Memorial had what was left of a plane that crashed in the Tanami Desert in 1929 while many searchers were looking for aviator Charles Kingsford-Smith, who had disappeared while attempting a round-the-world flight. The two men aboard the Kookaburra died when it was forced to make an emergency landing, but Kingsford Smith was found alive. Also called The Westland Widgeon, the Kookaburra was not recovered until 1978.

The other was a very small aviation museum. Its most interesting plane, at least to me, was a Royal Flying Doctor Service Connair that saw service between 1939 and 1973 while making over 5,000 emergency flights. I was certainly looking forward to visiting the Service's local facility in The Alice the next day.

After walking through a gigantic Yeperenye Caterpillar sculpture, a significant Arrernte totem, Ruth and I made our own flight.

Back at the hotel, Ruth needed rest.

I was pumped, so I took a walk alone along the Todd Mall, a wide pedestrian-only strip with stores continuing for two long blocks. I passed shops selling Outback gear, opals, didgeridoos, and native art. Noting outdoor cafes populated with relaxing end-of-the-roaders like me, I had one of my *I'm here in an exotic place and I "realize" it* moments. Long ago, I made a promise to myself that while traveling I would pay attention to special, irreplaceable times like this and immerse myself in the experience. Now!

At the end of the Mall was a liquor store, one of the drive-in varieties so common in Queensland and the Northern Territory. These stores usually had cases of beer stacked to the ceiling, row upon row of hard liquors, and busy windows, like fast food joints for sots.

They mostly had tiny and not too specialized wine selections. I wandered in and perused what they stocked, and, damn, there it was—the cricket player on the label. The Cover Drive! This was the exact wine, even the same year, as the one Allan served us out of a paper bag around the campfire at the corroboree four days previously. I could now return his kindness.

From there I wandered a few other commercial streets and found a Coles, Australia's Safeways, and in this case a busy, full service supermarket. I loaded up on snacks and fruit and headed back to the Mercure.

Something was wrong.

About two blocks from the store, I still felt uneasy. I reached into my pocket for the receipt and change.

So that was it. The checker had shorted me by $40. Her line had been long and she was clearly new at the job.

What to do? $40 wasn't a fortune, yet it wasn't small change either. Reluctantly, I walked back to Coles, deciding as I neared it that I would tell her gently, not at all accusatorily, and if she demurred, I would just walk away and forget it. I didn't want to have to wait while she counted the drawer and discovered her mistake. And I also didn't want her, a local girl struggling with her first job, to get into trouble for an honest mistake.

I recalled the time a male checker gave me change for $100. The problem was, I had given him a fifty dollar bill. My daughter once worked in a supermarket like the one that employed him, and I knew that the manager would dock this teenager for the difference. $50 represented several hours of hard work.

So I told him.

To my surprise he was surly. He insisted that he had made the correct change. I encouraged him to look in his cash drawer, but he didn't want to be bothered.

I finally prevailed. He discovered his error and, again to my surprise, he took the money back as if I had tried to steal it and he didn't thank me. I hoped history would not repeat in Coles.

But this was Australia, land of integrity. So when I told the girl she owed me $40, she simply opened the till and gave me 2 twenties, followed by a smile and an apology.

The evening was so balmy and the hotel's outdoor patio so Hollywood perfect that a good portion of our group decided to join in impromptu games after dinner.

At one table Lynette and I sat across from each other with Ruth and Rob on either side of us. Ruth and I considered ourselves lucky not to have been asked to join the serious contract bridge players at the adjoining table.

Since we played bridge for the first time and for some inexplicable reason, Lynette and I are magical together. We are dealt marvelous hands and play them like masters. We never lose. Since we only get to play as partners about once every other year, I savor each moment. Instead of saying "pass", Lynette says "No" in that characteristic Aussie way that adds about 5 syllables to the word. She never fails to say "Thank You" when I, the dummy, put my hand down, no matter how weak it is. Her eyes sparkle when she makes a great bid or plays a hand especially well.

That night was no exception and so, for the second time in one day, I experienced the full realization of where I was and how unbelievably lucky I am.

Chapter Eleven

The MacDonnells

"You can see why it's called the Red Centre," said Dave. "The colors just come alive."

We had taken Namatjira Drive west and were standing together on Chalet Ridge at 9 o'clock on a perfect morning. Dave and I were looking out over a vast mountain landscape like nothing I had ever seen before. It looked ancient, like an area of the planet frozen in time since the Jurassic Era. Or before.

Dave's love of The Outback was apparent as he pointed expansively to bare outcroppings along a ridge and acres of gum trees below to be sure I hadn't missed anything. Sharing this spectacular scene caused me to appreciate him. He had, after all, brought me here to a special place that I would not otherwise have found on my own.

Chalet Ridge was, as it turned out, only one of several memorable places in West MacDonnell National Park where we would spend most of this hot winter day.

Then the traditional Dave spoke. "There's a famous race here. In The Alice. The drivers go 120 miles in one direction and then they race back the next day. It's called the Finke Desert Race."

"Cars?" I asked.

"Modified. Cycles. Buggies. Off-road. Multi terrain." His eyes gleamed. "It's been a big event for about thirty years now. You have to be recklessly fast to participate."

101

"Have you?"

"Not yet, mate. And it has an opposite, The Henley-on-Todd Regatta." he added, assuming a twee British accent.

"Oh, sure. Some of our cable TV channels dote on that one," I told him.

"It's wild. A bunch of blokes drink a lot of beer and run down the dry riverbed in bottomless boats."

"Homer Simpson would love it," I surmised.

Dave knew this enduring character and laughed.

I left him to reminisce about races past and future and walked to a precipice to admire the view all by myself.

But Michael came over and asked, "Do you know why Lynette isn't with us?"

"She decided to have a day of complete rest to try to shake off that nasty virus."

"Is that what it is?"

"I hope it's nothing more."

Michael thought this over and switched gears. "When you get to Melbourne and go to the museums, Hank, look for a painter by the name of John Glover. He came here to record this marvelous land."

"It is indeed marvelous," I agreed.

"Actually, he came to Van Diemen's Land." He hesitated before adding, "Tasmania."

I did as he said and found Glover to be an excellent early 19th century artist whose work reminded me a lot of JMW Turner, the ground-breaking English landscape painter who, in my opinion, was the first Impressionist. Glover was from England too, but he followed three sons to Tasmania, arriving on his 64th birthday. There he raised sheep and became the first artist to try to capture on canvas what was surely a strange place to him. But it became home. He went back to England only to sell his creations, which now hang in museums from San Francisco to London.

I wondered why he was so little known and never found out exactly why. Perhaps his prolific output was deemed a bit too academic, a shade too ordinary. Despite his popularity, he was never elected a member of the Royal Academy. The Tasmanian landscape and its people gave him a fresh subject and a late career, and he finished his most esteemed painting at the age of 79.

Not close enough to walk but near Chalet Ridge was an ochre pit. Aborigines had come here for thousands of years to collect colorful clay that contained varying degrees of iron oxide. This common mineral made intense color stripes ranging through shades of yellow, red, and brown spilling kaleidoscopically down a lofty cliff side. This particular ochre bearing, still-life waterfall had been mined for so long and so much clay was exposed that the tumble of color looked like an explosion in an Estee Lauder research lab. Mixed with water or animal fat, ochre was used to paint bodies for ceremonies, or it was employed to decorate crevice walls to illustrate the Arrernte peoples' surroundings. They also used it to treat ailments such as head colds and aching muscles.

There were many, many gorges in the West MacDonnell highlands and we visited several. MacDonnell, by the way, was spelled Macdonnell on a lot of Australian maps for reasons I never discovered. Each gorge appeared to have been made by a giant with an axe who pounded rocky cliffs down to a V. The sheer walls on either side of the V always soared to cloudless sky. Water usually accumulated in the depressions.

Some of these water holes were semi-permanent. Three of the largest were fed by springs. Extremely cold and deep, they were treacherous for swimmers. If hypothermia didn't get them first, a submerged rock or log could become an ugly surprise to divers unfamiliar with the territory.

As we visited each water hole, a few young Australians were almost always there and choosing to ignore the warnings. Another of which was, "No suntan oil due to animal usage."

Some water holes in the MacDonnells were Emu Dreaming Places to Aboriginals, but certainly no rain gatherers. Ten inches was not uncommon for the entire year. And yet water could almost always be found somewhere.

The hole at Ormiston Gorge was estimated to be 46 feet deep. No sunlight penetrated to that depth. This natural pool was ringed by red river gums, and we stood beside the shaded pool and studied Ormiston's green depths and soaring rock wall reflections in the placid water.

Ormiston Creek, a tributary of the Finke River that Dave poetically called, "a dry river of sand," ran through this Gorge when the rains came.

The Finke was said to be the oldest river in the world. Eons ago it carved a gorge that was now in remote Finke Gorge National Park. I regretted not seeing it since Natalie Kruger wrote in my old, well-thumbed *Frommer's* about its Palm Valley, "Groves of rare Livistona mariae cabbage palms have survived since central Australia was a jungle millions of years ago." These were, as far as anyone knew, the oldest trees in the world, and they continued to thrive in Palm Valley. The entire range of this incredibly ancient palm was in Finke Gorge National Park.

The Aborigines called Finke a place of many lizard stories, and black-footed rock wallabies were said to leap about with abandon. Alas, four-wheel-drive was needed to explore this Park, or a damn-the-torpedoes spirit. And our careful driver, Dave, who only had one nearly disastrous lapse while pulling out into oncoming traffic in Alice Springs, lacked the former. Moreover, we simply didn't have the time. This pre-history enticement, though, could lure me back to Alice and her charms.

We went from one strangely unique place in West MacDonnell to another, the next being a one man graveyard. Hendrik Gerrit Guth's remains, by choice apparently, lay right at the turnoff to Ormiston Gorge. His epitaph read, "Creator of Panorama Guth—19-10-21 to 20-7-2003." I asked around and learned that Panorama Guth was the largest circular painting in Oz. It showed the natural landscape around Alice Springs and could be found in a museum on Har Street. A recent community effort had saved it for posterity.

Beyond Ormiston, the road was unpaved, so we turned back and headed for Ellery Gorge Big Hole, which was spring fed and accompanied by a mile and a half walkabout. Either Rod or Carole, earlier visitors, commented in Ellery's guest book, "Only a lack of a full moon stopped me joining in the dingo chorus." These dogs, domesticated by natives beginning about 6,000 years ago, howl but don't bark. Since they attack livestock when food is scarce, they are not loved by ranchers. Apparently they had found a home in these isolated gorges.

Ellery was a spring and one of the largest permanent water holes in this National Park. The water here was so cold that swimmers were urged to use a flotation device just in case they experienced a cramp. There weren't many taking a dip.

Heading back toward Alice in mid-afternoon we stopped at Standley Chasm. There were more people here than at any other place in the Park. The walk up into this crevice began gently but ended in serious rock climbing before vertical walls made further progress impossible without climbing equipment. The deck at the end of the trail overlooked a dry, boulder strewn river bed and it was crowded with sightseers.

On the way back down Ruth and I dutifully trekked past some not-so-impressive waterholes left in a dry creek. Despite experiencing a bit of burn out, we looked up the sheer walls of the mini-canyon to where two mesas tilted and merged at 262 feet.

I joined Roger for a bit as he took abundant photos of wildflowers, which were in profusion all along the walkway. Standley was also a place of lacy ferns, tall gums, and timeless cycads. It would have been better to be here at sunrise or sunset when the walls were said to glow orange. But this was a time of hot glare, and I was done with Standley and with gorges in general, at least for today.

It wasn't that they weren't fascinating. They were. But I was anxious to get back to town and visit the Royal Flying Doctor Service. Given its isolation, Alice had been a major base since 1939. And this day would be my last opportunity to learn first hand about this unique organization directly from its staff. Local tourist literature and my guidebooks spoke of a museum, personally guided tours, and the chance to listen in on conversations between doctors and patients. I anticipated raw reality, the inevitable tensions of emergency treatment, the human drama.

But instead of entering town Dave skirted Alice and headed up another highway.

"This is the Ross, named for the Ross River Homestead at the end of the sealed part of the road," Dave informed us.

I was just about to ask if I could possibly be dropped in town when he added, "I thought you'd like to see a bit of the East MacDonnells while it's still light."

I looked at my watch and it was just past 3 p.m. I looked around to see if anyone else's face registered protest but I saw only meekness, so I held my tongue. And that's the thing about group travel. It has its advantages, but personal choice is not one of them. Oh, well. Maybe the East MacDonnells would be unforgettable. There were no other vehicles on the road, however, so the East was apparently not exactly Outback Disneyworld.

We pulled into the parking area at Corroboree Rock and the flies greeted us as we stepped off the bus. They were clearly delighted to see so many to irritate and swarmed as if we were the first humans to visit their home in quite some time. Corroboree proved to be a naturally rounded rocky outcrop with two gaping holes near its summit. Despite the fact that there was no water for a great distance, this was known to be a gathering place for local Aboriginals, hence its name—Corroboree. Migrating westerners adopted the locals' name for a festive get-together, changing *korobra* to *corroboree* and thereby coining yet another purely Aussie word. The natives allegedly gathered here to exchange information, dance to celebrate a victory, or get in tune with spirits. This was, after all, a place for caterpillar dreams. They would also store sacred objects up in these rocks. Probably fly swatters among them. And I imagined that they used the two gaping holes in the Rock for any number of games and rituals. If someone remembered to bring water, that is.

The trail went completely around the outcrop, so Ruth and Barbara, as had become our habit, headed one way and I the other. I had plenty of company in the form of a festive swarm of flies, and I frequently gave them the Australian salute, a hand vigorously waving like a windshield wiper before my face.

The most interesting sign at the Rock listed the locals' food staples, and it sounded downright gourmet. "Wild fig, bush coconut, wild orange, native truffle, witchetty grubs, puffball perentia, wild passion fruit, mulga apples and seeds."

Experiencing my own dream time, I envisioned an Arrernte waiter approaching me and saying, "I'll be your server tonight, whitefella. Let's begin with wild fig infused with bush coconut and delicately dusted with mulga seeds."

I smacked my lips and asked, "Is the puffball parentia fresh tonight?"

"Indeed, it is. Our chef just caught it a few minutes ago out back." He chortled. "Get it? Outback?"

"I'll have that then," I replied, envisioning a succulent fillet. This was, after all, the second largest lizard in the world.

Ruth and Barbara approached from the other direction and I told them about my meal.

Barbara gasped and said, "I'd be a bit crook after that."

"Crook?" I asked.

"Ill. Somewhat under the weather but not seriously. It's a common expression here in Australia, as in 'I'm feeling a bit crook today.'"

The sun over Corroboree was hot and the flies annoying, so we hurried around the rest of the Rock together and boarded the bus.

Instead of turning left toward the Homestead, which one source called a "fair dinkum place to stay" making me highly suspicious, Dave turned right and I silently celebrated the *maybe* opportunity to visit the flying doctors before they closed up for the day. I might still have an hour if Dave hustled.

Alas, he pulled into the parking area at both Emily and Jessie Gaps. All of the gaps in the East MacDonnells were important spiritual sites. The Emily Gap waterhole, a popular swimming place after a rain, actually had quite a bit of water in it that day. The only way to see the Aboriginal art on the Gap's walls was to swim across, so we had to content ourselves with a profusion of wildflowers.

The fact sheet provided by the Parks and Wildlife Service here informed, "Emily Gap is probably the most significant as this is where the caterpillar beings of Mparntwe originated. These caterpillars formed Emily Gap and many of the topographic features around Alice Springs, then radiated out to the edge of the Simpson Desert." Again, I didn't completely understand, but I could clearly see that this interpretation was an attempt to explain a completely natural phenomenon. Emily, a registered sacred site, was not seen by anyone other than natives before 1871. Emily and Jessie were thought to be Sir Charles Todd's daughters, but the sheet added, "The basis on which the names are derived is unknown."

Jessie Gap was apparently a bit less sacred and was now a popular picnic and barbie spot, not the statuesque Barbie playmate in the United States, but a casual barbecue, an Aussie passion. We did, however, get to see a faded caterpillar dreaming rock painting on a cliff wall that looked like an endless maze designed to frustrate crawling insects whose only way out would be to metamorphose and fly.

We returned to Alice just as the Flying Doctors were locking their doors for the day. Ruth and I had to content ourselves with a visit to a busy Internet café where hordes of young backpackers were busy e-mailing their parents, probably asking for more money. We found an available keyboard and sent messages to relatives and friends literally on the other side of the world but about one second away.

Each evening before dinner our group of sixteen would meet for wine and conversation. This day's gathering was on a palm tree shaded patio next to a lovely, lit-from-the-bottom swimming pool. I made sure that Allan sat next to me and, when I could, I discreetly showed him the wine bottle peaking out from the top of a paper bag. He grinned and went along with the clandestine party.

The Cover Drive coupled with wine at dinner sent Ruth and me to our room early. Climbing about the MacDonnell's gaps had made us tired, and we had to think about tomorrow. After two days in Alice Springs, we were hitting The Stuart again, very early. Our itinerary said, "Depending on weather and road conditions we will travel today to Kings Canyon via either Hermannsburg or Rainbow Valley arriving in time to do a late afternoon Rim Walk at this spectacular Canyon."

The Outback, we were learning, was not a barren wasteland with nothing to see. Quite the contrary, there was considerable variety. We were constantly forced to make choices that, alas, didn't include flying doctors. At least, not yet.

Chapter Twelve

Unfit for a King

We left Alice Springs earlier than usual the next morning, and Ruth and I blew it. We lingered over breakfast conversation and ended up in the very back of the bus...again. Not being able to see the road ahead, I brooded over my book and tried to doze periodically. This wasn't easy, kind of like trying to take a nap on a roller coaster.

Dave said something about road conditions making it necessary to take the long way around, but I really wasn't paying attention until I realized that he was saying something about Albert Namatjira, which I missed. "It's too bad that we can't visit Hermannsburg. It's a real Abo settlement."

"Then why is it called Hermannsburg?" I asked from the back, half-innocently.

"Don't know, mate. Do know that Germans came in the 1880s. Some Lutheran pastors on a mission to help the Arrernte. About 50 years later Albert Namatjira was born there." Dave popped some candy into his mouth, flipped through his entertainment stash, and said, "I have a book on tape here that I think you'll enjoy—*Kings in Grass Castles* by Mary Durack." I couldn't tell if this was to quickly forestall further questions about a sensitive issue involving Aboriginals or the need for a break.

He raised the volume and the bus became silent. I didn't know if this was the result of ennui on the part of Australians already too familiar with the story or intent listening.

Rob had recommended this book to me the first time we met, so I had read this epic of the Outback, Australia's *Giant*, but without the melodrama.

I went into Zen mode and watched the landscape. There wasn't much to see out of the already dirty bus window for the roughly 400 kilometer trip to Kings Canyon except for an occasional Roadhouse or Road Train. In some info sources, it was *Kings* Canyon and in others *King's*, so I wasn't sure about possession. In any event, As soon as we were out of the MacDonnells the landscape went back to scrub, but the earth continued to be a vivid ochre color. Straight stretches were interrupted by occasional undulating hills, like ocean swells to sail through.

There were no billboards, no cattle, no houses, no towns, zero signs of civilization.

But just when I decided that this part of The Outback was unvarying, it changed. All of a sudden there were trees along the road, taller and more varied than what I had seen up until now. They were also strikingly similar and rather close together, like a cultish timber community. Here and there, the land looked more park-like, downright usable.

The most interesting trees looked like green cotton candy from the distance. I went right to the source who was seated directly in front of me. "Lynette, what are those trees called?"

"Which ones, Hank?"

"The ones that look like giant cheerleader pompons."

"Oh, those are Casurinas. They look like they're growing feathers instead of leaves, don't they?" She stopped to cough and then couldn't get her breath.

Ruth and I looked at each other with concern. Lynette had claimed at breakfast that, after a quiet day in bed, she was feeling much better. It didn't sound like it.

The mountains disappeared, but then some thickly forested hills emerged. *Monotonous* was certainly not the word to describe Australia's Red Centre.

Signs announced "Ron Ellis's Bush Safari Company, since 1965." Another promoted The Outback Camel Company—"we invite travelers to stop by for a trek, say, a sunset or sunrise camel ride for $50 each." The billboard mentioned a *camel train,* and I envisioned all of us roped together on a string of camels crossing the Simpson Desert. The unfamiliar female voice on the tape was saying, "The Fitzroy, the mighty river of the western plains…" I tuned her out.

The Stuart Highway seemed endless. In planning previous trips to Australia, I had always considered The Outback. I dreamed of flying into Alice Springs and renting a car to drive to Uluru, or Ayers Rock for the uniformed or insensitive. They were both in the center of the Outback, I

111 Harold Harbaugh 111

reasoned. When I looked at available maps in travel books, they didn't look all that far apart. But I always talked myself out of adding The Outback to an already crowded itinerary, and we'd end up on islands like Heron or in cities like Adelaide or Darwin. They're all coastal. Canberra, which is still relatively small, is the largest inland city in Australia.

I'm glad now that I didn't attempt this crazy Outback scheme. In reality, Alice and Uluru aren't close to each other at all. It's just under 300 miles from one to the other, and then 300 miles back if you drive. And there are potential hazards along the way.

Kings Canyon, today's destination, was 25% closer to Alice than Uluru yet seemed farther away due to its remoteness.

Dave turned off the tape. "Sorry we won't have time for Rainbow Valley," Dave continued as if picking up where he left off an hour before.

"What are we missing?" I called out from the back.

"Well, blokey, some very brilliant sandstone cliffs way back in the bush." He didn't elaborate.

After the Erldunda Roadhouse, a typical oasis—camping, Internet, restaurant, laundry, emus—we turned right onto the Lasseter Highway, and I figured we were getting closer to Kings Canyon. I checked my Northern Territory map to learn that we were only half way there.

The only difference between the Stuart and the Lasseter was an increase in tourist busses heading for Uluru, The Outback's biggest attraction.

We stopped for lunch at busy Kings Creek Station, as close to an Outback Amusement Park as I had experienced. One of its signs called it "The Stock Camp." I assumed that that had to do with animals and provisioning. These oases serviced incredibly large areas. Kings Creek looked hunkered down, as if it had been around for 100 years. But that proved a false impression. Ian and Lyn Conway came here only in 1981 to build their business and live among the desert oaks.

"Going to try a camel burger?" Dave asked as I stepped down from the bus.

"No, I think I'll pass," I replied. "I'm not very hungry and need a stretch more than an exotic food experience."

He looked at me as if I were a wimp.

Everyone but me headed inside for cold drinks and souvenirs. I wandered over to a huge pen and climbed up some stairs which turned out to be a platform for getting onto a camel for a ride.

Camels are big here. On this Station's website a few weeks later, I learned that it called itself "the largest exporter of wild camels in Australia." It sold them for "live export, live domestic sales and meat." So I now knew where to go when I needed any kind of camel product or experience.

Watching the camels in the pen placidly watch me, I wondered. Do they become like gigantic pets to their owners? Do they become fairly domesticated, like horses, and almost members of the family, like dogs? I flashed on countless *National Geographic* articles featuring pictures of sunburned men wearing keffiyehs and holding the reins of a camel. Their faces and the camels' were invariably close together, and the camel always seemed to be smiling too. I studied the camels in my range of vision and wondered what to look for in a good one. They all seemed the same to me, a form of animal stereotyping on my part probably. The ones closest to the platform were looking in my direction but totally without curiosity. None came over to nudge my hand into a petting situation. I recalled hearing that they could be temperamental spitters and was glad that they kept their distance.

A helicopter took off and passed over my head. Since we were now closer to Kings Canyon than when I checked the map, I figured that it was taking tourists for a look-down into the Canyon's depths. I casually checked a board to see the rates for a scenic flight or camel ride, not because I wanted the experiences but more out of mild curiosity. I wouldn't have been interested even if I had the time, which I didn't.

I was looking for the camel train group rate when Ruth came over and joined me. We watched some somnolent kangaroos, by now a very familiar sight, in a separate pen.

"We've been in the Outback for some time now. Know which ones those are?" she asked.

"Reds?" I ventured.

"No. Greys. The reds are bigger. In fact, they're the biggest kangaroos of all. But the greys are more prolific. Roos adapt very well to their environment. In very dry times an egg that's already been produced doesn't hatch until conditions improve."

"Where did you learn that bit of trivia?" I asked, impressed.

"Anyone on our bus can educate you, but Jane has the best stories." She began to laugh.

"So tell me."

"Ask her about Herbert. You won't be disappointed."

Since it was a breach of etiquette to change seats on the bus during the day, I immediately went and found Jane to inquire about Herbert.

Over time, Jane had become my favorite storyteller. She began, "Herbert's mother was killed in a road accident when he was quite small."

"How tragic!" I exclaimed. "I hope his father was around to raise him."

"Males don't do that," she said.

"Australian men don't raise their own children when the mother dies?" I asked, surprised.

"Herbert was a roo!"

"Oh," I said.

"He was a small royal joey. We created our own formula to feed him."

"I'm surprised the authorities let you keep him."

"Quite. The ACT RSPCA does forbid the practice of keeping and raising a wild, native animal without a permit."

"Which you obtained."

"Yes, because of the circumstances the Royal Society agreed to let Michael and me care for Herbert."

"What was it like living with a kangaroo?" I asked, already knowing that they could be aggressive and dangerous.

"Herbert was a dear. He slept in a wicker baby basket, and he'd follow me around the garden hanging onto my skirt. He took a bottle and ate dog food."

"Is he fully grown now?"

"Oh, yes!"

"Is that difficult?"

"Is what difficult?"

"Caring for an adult kangaroo."

She laughed. "That would be impossible! We don't have Herbert anymore. One night he hopped onto the bed between Michael and me and we knew it was time to let him go. Or more accurately, set him free. He was 15 months old at the time. I took him to a farm that cared for roos and released him."

"Did you see Herbert again?"

"Yes. The next time I visited, I called his name and he came bounding over. But then the next time, he didn't come when I called. He had become wild."

"Did the experience prevent you from further adoptions?"

"Oh, no! We had another named Fred. And then there was Wally the Wombat. He would roll onto his back for a tummy tickle."

Because it was time to board the bus, I never found out if Wally was a common or a Northern or a Southern hairy nose wombat, the three varieties of this vegetarian marsupial that looks like a creature created by a God with a sense of humor. But I did learn that Jane was a first-rate humanitarian, or would that be faunatarian?

It was only a short ride now to Watarrka National Park, home to Kings Canyon. Dave checked us in to Kings Canyon Resort, a huge low-slung facility on the top of the gorge, which couldn't be seen from the premises.

We hurriedly dumped our bags in a row of adjoining rooms and headed for the bottom and the Creek Walk, one of three available Canyon walkabouts.

Despite its remoteness, Kings Canyon was a much visited natural attraction that employed all of the usual clichés to advertise itself—Garden of Eden! Australia's Grand Canyon! Etc. It was a pretty spectacular place with some totally unique features, which I didn't get to see.

I used to get upset if I didn't experience every major aspect of a destination, especially foreign ones that would be difficult to return to. But over time I have relaxed on this and have now developed a healthier *whatever* attitude. I always tell myself, "So you missed it. So what? You have a valid excuse to go back." Although I must admit that a return to remote Kings Canyon is a diminishing possibility.

Kings consisted of chunks of Mereenie sandstone that had tumbled down from a couple of sheer cliffs for untold eons. The last major fall was in the 1930s. Canyon recesses were strewn with boulders and alive with desert oaks, which only grew in this part of Australia. With broomstick trunks and voluminous, frilly leaves, they looked forever young.

My walking companion as we followed a mostly dry creek into the Canyon was Jan. Her usual line of conversation swung from wildflowers and birds always back to native mistreatment when some sign or landmark provoked her. But today, for some inexplicable reason, she began talking about her personal writing projects and segued into reminiscences of her childhood. She mentioned a brother named Colin.

"Are you close?" I asked.

"No, not at all," Jan replied as if somewhat but not entirely regretful. "He's a composer attached to the University of Queensland. I don't see him very often."

"What's his surname?" I asked.

"Brumby. Colin Brumby. He plays the contrabass."

"Our daughter Jocelyn plays in the Canberra Symphony Orchestra," she added as if there was family competition to be dealt with.

"Has Colin recorded?" I asked, trying to picture what sounded like a far from mainstream instrument and wondering if contrabass was yet another example of an Aussie term that was different from US English.

"Yes, quite a few times actually."

"I'll try to track down a CD before I leave for home," I promised.

Jan seemed flustered, abashed. "I suspect you'll have a bit of trouble there."

"That never stopped me before," I assured her. And as soon as I returned home I went straight to Amazon and found "What a Wonderful Contrabass World!" But I hesitated to buy it since I couldn't imagine a party or quiet reading time for which a solo bass viol background would be welcomed. And I was a bit put-off by the overwrought title besides.

Jan changed the subject, and I wondered if she disliked her brother's music, or him, and regretted promoting his career.

By this time Ruth and I had experienced many opportunities to talk to the ten people in our group whom we had known for less than two weeks, and we were having more intimate conversations about families, attitudes and beliefs. The possible exception was Jenny and John. Virtually all I knew about them so far after 11 days of intermittent but regular contact was that she laundered his expensive silk shirts in shampoo each night and that he was an economist.

Jan was clearly uncomfortable talking about her brother, so I changed the subject to our surroundings. We were in an impressive gorge with soaring domed outcrops topping out at 300 feet and intersecting where a lofty bridge spanned the distance between them. I thought I saw people on the walkway, but I couldn't be sure because it was so far away. "I wonder how one gets up there?" I asked.

"That's the rim walk," Jan replied.

"Are you and Roger taking it?"

"I don't think we have time."

The creek walk ended in the center of the canyon at a busy viewpoint surrounded by huge boulders that had apparently rained down from the top during some pre-historic cataclysm.

All of our bus mates minus two converged on the platform at about the same time, so we sauntered back to the parking area in a jolly group, picking up Michael as we passed. Feeling a bit crook, he had chosen not to take the long hike up into the King. Lynette wasn't even there, having chosen to stay in her room to rest after the long bus ride. After a bit of a rally in Alice Springs, her wracking cough was definitely back, worse than ever, and she seemed sapped of energy.

By 3 p.m. we were back at the resort and I was campaigning to get a group together for a Rim Walk. I wanted to see the view from the soaring bridge. But everyone declined my invitation for various reasons. Some begged tiredness after the early start and long ride. Others claimed they didn't want to run the risk of missing what everyone comes to Kings Canyon to do—watch the sun set.

Our room was, at best, ordinary, and the septic failure smell reminded me of Tennant Creek. It was not the kind of inviting motel room atmosphere that encouraged lingering. "Let's get out of here and find a place where we can breathe more easily," I suggested.

The Resort was huge, several one-story buildings that attempted to blend into the environment with minimal impact. Ruth and I strolled about the anonymous box buildings and stepped from the heat into its store to look for strictly local souvenirs, but I was not content. I wondered what I was missing.

I found some information about the Rim Walk in a Watarrka National Park guide and began reading. It took a minimum of four hours to complete and was arduous in places, but the apparent rewards made it worth the effort. It passed through what was described as "a maze of weathered sandstone domes" called The Lost City which "resemble the ruins of some ancient Aztec city carved over time by water and wind erosion." After crossing the bridge that I had glimpsed from far below, hikers descended a staircase into the Garden of Eden, which sounded wonderful—"A fern-fringed pocket of water holes" and "luxuriant cycads around the permanent water-hole" and "a real rain forest appearance" and "a bewildering array of fauna and flora." Finally, "more than 600 plant species and 100 bird species."

I *had* to see this!

However, there were frequent warnings. "Steep, strenuous sections... only recommended for reasonably fit and healthy walkers...not for those who suffer from vertigo...designed to deter all but the most committed walkers." I was fit and free of head-spinning, but then I began reading about those who had had heart attacks on the trail.

I decided that it was well worth the risk, even if Ruth and I only partially completed the walk. But I made the mistake of telling her everything that I had found out.

She said candidly, "It sounds like too much risk and too late to me. But you go on."

So I did. But once I got outside to the road I quickly talked myself out of taking the Rim Walk alone. Ruth was right. I truly didn't have the time, unless I skipped the legendary sunset. And once darkness descended in The Outback, I didn't want to be alone under a thrilling canopy of stars, my only lights on a steep trail where a misstep would mean a long, long drop.

So instead I headed down the Mereenie Loop Road, the one that Dave said was a sometimes difficult shortcut between Alice and the King. I passed what looked like a delightful caravan park with picnic tables, lots of campers, and a roadhouse full of noisy beer drinkers this late afternoon. Then, farther off the road, there was what appeared to be a native community center. Perhaps a health clinic. There was no one around to ask.

The sealed road became gravel and ran straight into a distant vanishing point of nothingness. Dave had been vague about the reason for not taking this route. Was that on purpose? I recalled reading that the Mereenie passed through Aboriginal land and required a bought tour pass from the Central Land Council. I wondered if that rule also applied to walkers because here I was, unexpectedly hiking steadily back towards Alice at the other end of a mysterious road that I might have taken. I wondered as I trekked how long it would take me to cover the distance to her. The maps I had seen up until now were vague about the distance, making it seem perhaps unexplored in places. One section had been clearly marked "restricted access."

I turned around to discover that I could not see any sign of the resort. Cool. It was a thrill to be in this vast expanse of Outback alone in late afternoon. The silence was total. The signs of a human presence were nonexistent. The empty road stretched before me as if continuing to expand as I walked.

Suddenly a vehicle appeared in a cloud of dust in the great distance. I imagined a battered, dirt encrusted four-wheeler with a single, wild-eyed driver who would stop and jabber with relief and gratitude to the first human being he had seen for what seemed like forever. Me. Instead it turned out to be a Holden. Inside was a family behind rolled up windows in air-conditioned comfort. They passed without acknowledging my presence. When the next vehicle proved to be a sporty convertible with a young couple who looked like they had just left the country club, I turned back and headed for our room.

I had walked farther than I realized. By the time I gathered Ruth and we headed for the raised boardwalk that took viewers to the rim of Kings Canyon, it was sunset. Halfway to the viewpoint, groups of people including our tour friends, approached from the other direction.

"You missed it!" Barbara said ruefully.

"Do you mean it's already over?" I asked, carefully avoiding to look at what I knew would be Ruth's disappointed face.

"Completely. There's just a wee bit of faded light left. So if you hurry…"

"How was it?"

"Spectacular!" Everyone in the cluster nodded in agreement.

Ruth and I turned back. We had now not experienced the two reasons why people come to Kings Canyon—the sunset and the Garden of Eden.

Although our room was a dark disappointment, the buffet dinner was not. It was held in a huge, brightly lit dining room near the Resort's inviting swimming pool. Brian and Karin, an uncommon treat, and Lynette were my dinner companions. The food choices were varied and well prepared. Kangaroo was the meat specialty. I passed on it.

I had only been offered kangaroo once before at a barbecue on a beach at the Great Barrier Reef. Lynette, sitting across the picnic table from me at the time, had just bit into her kangaroo steak. I waited a while and then asked her, "How is it?"

She continued to chew and chew. "Kind of gamey," she finally answered.

"How often have you had it before, Lynette?" I inquired, genuinely interested.

"This is the first time," she responded, surprising me greatly.

Lynette had little on her plate this time, and everything she put into her mouth was treated like that long-ago kangaroo fillet, tough-going.

Brian said, "The kangaroo is delicious, exceptionally well prepared."

He looked down at my plate and asked, "Aren't you going to try it?"

It sounded more like disappointment than a challenge.

As I had learned how to travel, I had also learned to sample everything offered to eat, no matter how bizarre. This wasn't like me. So, not knowing when or if I would have the opportunity again, I cajoled myself into trying the kangaroo.

I went back to the buffet and skewered a big chunk. Back at the table I sliced off a reasonable bite and everyone stopped to watch me chew. It seemed rather innocuous, like reindeer or any other large grazing animal.

"Bravo!" said Brian. "It goes especially well with a hearty shiraz."

Brian and Karin regaled us with the details of running a vineyard with lots of stories about water rights, battling plant diseases, and the painstaking care that was needed to produce prized vintages.

The only thing that negatively impacted this great good time was Lynette. Eating almost nothing and coughing a lot, she seemed determined to show a brave face no matter how rotten she felt. We were in a very remote place. I wondered where the nearest hospital was but didn't ask the question because I feared the answer.

Chapter Thirteen

Uluru

"No matter how many pictures you've seen, nothing will quite prepare you for your first view of Uluru/Ayers Rock," said the page that I had ripped out of a local travel magazine the night before.

To save space, I had been collecting materials every day and culling at night by ripping out only those pages that I might need later on. I now had a bulging file of loose paper in the front compartment of my suitcase. When I unzipped it to add more, loose pages always spilled out. It was a growing menace.

I read this one again, savoring the thought. My anticipation was building. And I had a great view of the road ahead.

On some travel days, everything goes wrong no matter how much you struggle. Tickets get misplaced, flights are delayed, drinks spill, bowels lock, or loosen. On others, everything works, even when you make stupid choices. I call this *Hank's Law.* This day was proving to be one of the latter. Despite being late down to the bus, Ruth and I had up-front, single seats for the long drive back down Luritja Road to the Lasseter Highway, where we lurched to the right. The first sign after the turn announced, "Uluru…157 km."

Brian, sitting across the aisle from me and reading something called *The Bulletin*, poked me on the arm and said, "You can sometimes see the rock from here." He pointed out of the window due left, and I became even more focused.

I later browsed his magazine to learn that *The Bulletin* was Australia's *Time*. First published in 1880, *The Bulletin*, a weekly, was influential politically and culturally. Many found its political commentary, which ridiculed everyone, and its sometimes racist cartoons offensive. It became less controversial in the early 1960s when Sir Frank Packer bought it and actually modeled it on *Time*. Circulation steadily decreased to 57,000 and it ceased publication in 2008.

But when I saw it for the first time on the bus and Brian thoughtfully offered to lend it to me, I didn't want to bury my nose in anything printed. I was afraid I would miss Uluru's first sighting.

About ten miles further down the Lasseter, there appeared on the distant horizon, a purple, blue, and dusty rose monolith. It rose importantly, imposingly from near desert far, far away but already so big that it was clearly visible. A thrilling sight to say the least.

"There's Uluru!" I exclaimed, and many eyes followed my finger to the rock. There were appreciative *ohs* and *ahs* behind me and to the side.

Looking like all the mesas in Arizona merged into one, it continued to grow in size and me in awe as we neared. The very sight of it hushed the passengers. Uluru was proving to be everything I had been told to expect, maybe even more.

"And there's Mount Connor over there," Dave announced, nodding towards the monolith. "859 meters high and called Artula by the natives."

I craned my neck looking for this second vision.

"Connor is often mistaken for Ayers Rock," he went on, and I realized that he was talking about the monolith that had been the total focus of my attention for several miles.

Indeed, as it got closer, it didn't look at all like the familiar pictures of Uluru that I had seen all my adult life. It looked, in fact, more impressive. Connor, I learned later, is three times larger, and many visitors prefer it. It certainly wowed the passengers on our bus, and I took comfort in the fact that these well-traveled Australian citizens were also fooled.

Then I realized that this massive outcrop was sometimes spelled "Conner" in the literature. So even some of the Outbackers who live in its shadow are either not sure what to call Artula or are poor spellers.

We stopped at ten sharp for morning tea, and Rob and a few others for no apparent reason crossed the highway and scrambled up a red, rising path.

Ruth and I spent our time watching a local bird that was hanging around hoping for a handout. It looked like a quail or maybe a pheasant with red eyes, grey feathers, a long tail and a pointed crest atop its head. For the first time, no one could identify it.

"I wonder what's up that rise?" I asked Ruth idly.

"Let's find out," she replied. "What to come with us, Lynette?"

"No, you go. I don't want to risk it," Lynette said, so far cough free this morning.

We headed across the road and, as we climbed, Rob was coming back down the steep incline. "You're in for a surprise up there," he said with a big smile.

Rob was always great at understatement. It was the second most awesome scene of the entire trip. And the first wasn't Uluru. It wasn't Connor/er either. #2 was a stunning wasteland vista stretching in every direction for an incredible distance, and in its midsection was a salt pan, the first I had seen in Australia. There was a small isle rising from the middle of this incredible dryness, and I wondered how often it actually became an island surrounded by water. The salt pan's perimeter disappeared into the horizon making it seem the size of an average New England State, and I tried the impossible— to take a panoramic photograph.

Kicking myself for not investing more in photographic equipment, I had captured less than half of the vista after several clicks. And like most dramatic views, it didn't translate into a great photo. The stitched together finished print looked like an unfocused, horizontal white streak, a bit of laughable, minimal art.

"What's the salt pan's name?" I asked Roger who was up there ignoring the view and photographing the abundant wild flowers.

"I don't know. It's a small one."

"A small one!" I yelped. And he was right. When I later studied my maps I realized that it was not even a contender. And the winner? Lake Eyre, the world's largest expanse of salt. It was on our itinerary further on down the road in Outback South Australia.

Back in my comfortable bus seat with the great, panoramic view, I noted a passing sign that trumpeted, "Camel Safaris…10 km, Curtin Springs." Now jaded, I yawned and said to no one in particular, "Another roadhouse, more camels." This had become an all too familiar sight in this part of the Northern Territory, its southern border now about 40 miles away.

Ruth didn't respond to my observation. She seemed lost in thought, and a few minutes later she tapped me on the shoulder and asked, "Have you noticed how much weight Lynette has lost?"

"No," I replied but then I recalled that Lynette had eaten virtually nothing the previous night at dinner. I had sat across from her and she looked at her plate as if the pathetically small portions were poisoned. They looked as miniscule as that island in the salt pan. Lynette had just refused half of a health cookie that I had pressed on her during tea.

"She wore those slacks the first day, and now they're loose on her," Ruth continued. I could hear concern in her voice. She considered Lynette a true and lasting friend who was spiraling from vigorous to frail before her eyes.

"You're right. I hadn't noticed," I said as I recalled last night's conversation when Brian asked me, "Why do you return so often to Oz?"

"Well, you see, we've made very good friends here," I explained and then waited a decent interval before looking up from my plate to Lynette. When I finally did, she was grinning broadly with that characteristic squint-eyed sparkle in her eyes. Shortly after that she had to leave the table because of a coughing spell that would not end.

We stopped at Curtin Springs to use the facilities. On its welcoming sign it noted its size—1,028,960 acres. I found that impossible to conceptualize, like *googol* or *quark*. Another sign pointed to a bird aviary. Yet another to an Internet station, the www accessible even out here.

Back on the road, we passed the first of several "Ayers Rock Scenic Flight" signs. Then a dead kangaroo. Dave grabbed his microphone. "Did you see the wasaroo we just passed?"

Everyone groaned.

The next sign read, Yulara…80 km."

"What's Yulara?" I called out.

"Our destination," Dave said, "But first we're going to The Olgas. They're a bit past Uluru. We'll have lunch there."

I checked my sources and learned that these were 36 round rocks of varying sizes called Kata Tjuta, the Anangu people's words meaning *many heads*.

"This area is very popular with Germans," said Dave, and I pondered that particular bit of trivia without understanding.

"There it is, folks," Dave said about ½ hour later. But I had already glimpsed Uluru as we crested one of a series of seriously undulating hills. It looked a lot like Mount Connor/er except for its uniformly strange color that would be impossible for the maker of Crayolas to duplicate.

"Geologists believe that Uluru is like an iceberg with only the top exposed. They think that the base is about 6 kilometers under the surface," Dave said in his authoritative voice that I had come to know so well.

The road from this point on was as celebratory as Uluru itself, a series of rapid rises and falls with young desert oaks on both sides raising their feathery branches as if in tribute to some monarch. They appeared newly sprung from the earth that was an even more intense red than any I had seen until now.

As we neared The Olgas, fleecy clouds appeared above, the first interruption of pure domed blue in 11 days.

During lunch a cold wind sprang up and sent us for jackets. It was, after all, still winter in The Outback. Perhaps this is normal here, some natural force. The main walking path circling The Olgas *was* named Valley of the Winds. It reportedly took five hours to make the circuit. Since our focus that day was Uluru, 30 or so miles back down the road, we had to content ourselves with the easy Gorge Walk. It crossed over huge boulders, ever upward to a crevice with a water hole.

I loved The Olgas, which were quite different from The Devil's Marbles. The tallest outcrop, Olga herself, was more than 100 feet higher than Uluru. Surrounded by gigantic, haphazardly tilted boulders that looked like an abandoned Olympic field for Titans, she was already what Connor/er and Uluru will look like after another million years of erosion.

Michael shared my enthusiasm and asked Dave if we might linger a bit longer, but Dave insisted, "Sorry, mate, we have a date with a guide at Uluru."

Aboriginals were given title to Uluru in 1985 when Commonwealth law finally recognized that the Anangu were the traditional and rightful owners of the land. The Government agreed to grant title on the condition that the Anangu lease the Park back to the Australia National Parks and Wildlife Service for 99 years. That's why we had to pay a separate fee to enter Uluru-Kata Tjuta National Park, the only attraction not covered in our National Trust package.

The Rock once known as Ayers was of huge cultural influence to the Anangu. So was alcohol. *Grog* sales were forbidden to locals at the one liquor outlet in the settlement of Yulara so that the dependent locals relied on tourists for help, lurking like hoping-to-party teenagers outside a liquor store.

The next attraction on our agenda was the Uluru-Kata National Park Cultural Centre. I found it well planned but culturally abstruse. It showed quite explicitly the utter simplicity of life among historical Aboriginals whose lives seemed to be mostly about food gathering and role playing. There was an innocence about the displays, which included a lot of contemporary images that said, "Here we are, naturally. This is our reality."

Quoted in one display, Billy Wara said, "I grew up on rabbit, kangaroo, goanna, perentie. I didn't know what school was, I didn't even know it existed. I was a real bush boy. I was almost old enough to live off the land by myself when I saw a whitefella. It was Lasseter on his camel." Harold Lasseter was the man who in 1930 died while trying to find the "reef of gold" he had seen earlier but lost track of.

If the displays were any indication, it appeared as if most Aboriginals either wanted no part of it or continued to struggle with adjusting to life in the Instant Messaging Age. Even here where they were in control of the message and its total focus, I couldn't tell if they were victims of intentional neglect or merely highly independent fringe dwellers. But this Cultural Centre seemed to lean toward the latter.

I went through the displays three times trying to understand and relate to their lives, but, again and again, their world proved elusive to me. Heretofore, I had struggled with understanding the Dreamtime concepts that are key to understanding them. And *here*, I was experiencing an entire museum for me not to understand.

But the art displayed on the walls throughout the Centre was magnificent, and the Maruku Arts & Crafts shop sold reasonably priced works with certificates of authenticity. Here for certain patrons *were* buying directly from the artists, not like in Sydney's trendy shops with low lighting and high rents where even small, simple paintings had big price tags.

I wasn't the only one who had cultural whiteout. I found our group rather glumly sprawled on benches and along the walls outside the Centre long before our time to explore was up.

I joined the others while Dave arranged for our tour. The guide was a local man, affable Wally Jacob, Senior Aboriginal Guide. After introducing himself in Anangu, he took us back through the Centre to explain the displays that we had already seen, which was definitely a good idea. They were only a bit less inscrutable after his explanations, which were given strictly in the Anangu language.

Wally's words were translated by a young whitefella named Darrin. It was interesting to listen to Wally's cascade of sounds being interpreted by Darrin, who stood at his side and listened intently to Wally as if afraid he would miss something. The flow of Darrin's English words consistently made his explanations seem far more complex than the original. He frequently asked Wally questions in Anangu, clearly seeking further clarification of something Wally had said. Looking like the perfect calendar boy for the straight-arrow Outback Male, Darrin took his job very seriously. He was surprisingly fluent in the little used, strictly regional language, and I wondered how he had mastered it.

Many of the depictions of the Aboriginals in the Centre showed them without clothing, and Darren, through Wally, explained that many native words showed Western influence without affecting customs. *Naked*, for example, was *niggedy* in Anangu, and apparently still the way to go, for some.

The explication of the displays dealing with their belief system was, to me, a confusion of ancient myths having to do with generations of shape-shifting ancestors. One, for example, was about some poisonous snake men who could change from human to animal form. It reminded me of Greek Mythology, the Arthurian Legends, and, well, the Old and New Testaments. God did, after all, appear to Abraham as a burning bush, and Jesus performed many transformative miracles affecting lepers and, in one case, a dead man named Lazarus.

Wally talked about ceremonial dances. He showed us an Anangu man's weapons, primarily the usual boomerang and club. But, strangely, in many stories the women were bashing men.

All laws among his people, Wally explained, were passed on orally. And he made it seem as if they were a self-contained tribe with both suspicion of and limited contact with neighbors. The Mala people north of the Anangu, for example, spoke another language, and Wally spoke only of their differences, calling them wallabies instead of people.

I later checked on this to discover that the Mala *were* considered the hare-wallaby people. Since some wallabies, a kangaroo about the size of most rabbits, were small, I figured that this reference had something to do with the Mala's physical size. Or was it their rapid movements? Perhaps this reflected some god/human connection. More mysteries leading to more questions that seemed somehow inappropriate to ask in this setting.

I later found a well-told story on JoyZine, a website that offered an impressive number of Dreamtime legends. One particular interpreted local tale seemed to give me, finally, a bit of insight into the Aboriginal human-animal-nature connection. Someone named C.P. Mountford retold an Anangu legend, calling it *The Kuniya and Liru*. Briefly, he related the story of how the Kuniya, non-venomous carpet snakes, migrated from Mount Connor/er and found a waterhole. The men hunted and the women gathered seeds until the end of the creation era when they were turned into boulders, the very features of what was now known as Uluru. Before that, however, some wandering Liru, poisonous snake men, attacked. Pulari, who had just given birth, went ballistic. "Enraged and desperate to protect her child, she sprang at the Liru with her baby in her arms spitting out the essence of disease and death." Another woman, the mother of a just killed youth, "rose in a fury and struck Kulikudgeri a great blow on the nose with her digging stick." A great warrior, he died in agony. And so on.

The building we were standing in, Wally told us, was designed to represent a slithering serpent, and then he called it the *carpet* snake. At the time I had no idea what he meant, but now I have a glimmer of understanding since I have read several Dreamtime stories.

Wally explained the commonly used designs in native art. In Aboriginal paintings, for example, circles represented water holes, and gracious Wally said that he was now taking us to particularly significant water hole to tell us more about his people.

We parted at the Centre and rejoined Wally and Darrin for the Mutitjulu Walk, one of four possible at and around Uluru. This easy lope took us to permanent water on the southern side. Since the Centre was not especially near Uluru, this was our first opportunity for a really close up view. Standing right below it, Uluru looked nothing like the glossy travel literature photos of it. It was pocketed by deep recesses for one thing.

As we gathered near the entrance to a cave by the precious waterhole, Wally encouraged us to closely study the sheer cliff behind us as he told the tale of this place's particular cultural importance. As usual with Dreamtime stories, it sounded more like a *flu*time fantasy. At least that's the way I felt as I listened to a tale of a violent clash between Kuniya and Liru whom Wally identified as two Rainbow Serpents. One of them seemed to be a woman with an especially nasty disposition. Wally kept pointing to the erosion holes in the cliff's surface as evidence of deep weapon penetration on the part of the combatants during the battle.

Wally then spoke of a native tobacco growing inside Uluru's caves, and I wondered if *that* might partially explain Dreamtime. Perhaps the local blend contained hallucinogens.

"These caves were used as shelters in rainy times," Wally explained. "Then the tribe would head back out into open country to live." He gestured toward the flat bush where the food was. "They would, of course, return here for water regularly."

Wally pointed to a native fig tree. The fruit was the size of a marble. "When they've gone red, they're ready to eat," Wally said through Darrin.

My grasp of native foods was certainly becoming extensive. After listening, I now knew about unturngu—bush bananas. And thanks to Jane, who showed them to me at The Olgas, I could now recognize grevillea's bright yellow flower. Aboriginals sucked out its sticky nectar without picking the flower and mixed it with water to make a sweet drink. Maku—grubs. Tjala—honey ants. Wally's forebears were omnivores who also ate goannas, echidnas, and pythons, with bush raisins for garnish.

Many of Wally's words at the waterhole were about life in the shadow of Uluru—food gathering, tracking animals, using spears. He showed us a simple digging stick and, after demonstrating its use, he began beating the ground with it. Darrin didn't explain why, but I suspect it had something to do with bothersome snakes.

He said that snakes were generally avoided, but then he showed us how his people determined which ones were poisonous, something having to do with how they slither. I hoped I would never have to be tested on the differences. This detail of daily life made perfect sense, and I felt like I was making headway towards understanding.

We went into the cave and Wally pointed to a faint, fragile ocher and charcoal painting on a wall. Due to increasing darkness and the painting's age, I couldn't make out what it depicted. But Wally grinned and gesticulated in its direction as Darrin explained, "All painting was done using fingers. The women painted mainly on their bodies, not on the walls. Ceremonies followed. Men played with their boomerangs while the women danced."

I watched Darrin's face to see if he intended a double entendre, but he was completely serious.

"The women clapped hands and sang," he added.

"Surely because of the sight of all those boomerangs," I whispered to Ruth. She gave me a dark look and shushed me.

Looking for and failing to find something recognizable in the cave painting, I asked Wally through Darrin how old the drawings were and he said, "My people have been here for 22,000 years." Another source I found said 30,000 years, but more than likely no one knows for sure. Beat that longevity record for staying in one place, anyone. Anyone?

Wally said something that sounded very much like a farewell, and then he grinned.

"Wally thanks you for visiting his home," Darrin interpreted. "He says that it's OK to take a photo of him as long as you send him a picture of *your* home when you return to it." This surprised me because the Welcome to Uluru-Kata Tjuta National Park information sheet said boldly, "**Anangu do not like to be photographed, and ask you to respect this wish.**"

As we walked back to the parking area, I caught up with Darrin, took him aside, and pummeled him with questions, the first being how long it took him to learn the language.

"Four years. Nothing's written down, so the only way to really learn it was to listen," he told me. It had proved difficult for him to grasp the meanings of words since they were only spoken, especially those sounds implying deeper concepts. He said he got very tired from just paying attention. He seemed very young and said he was a newlywed.

When I asked about his plans, he said, "I've been doing tours for five years now," as if that explained his future.

I asked how many human beings spoke Anangu, and Darrin answered, "2,500 or so." I told him that I admired his tenacity.

No one knows how many Aboriginal languages there have been. Estimates range from about 300 to 750 or more. But most authorities agree that only about 20 are still in current use, and all are endangered.

It was getting late in the day, so we scurried to a viewpoint where a line of tourist busses, caravans, and cars made it difficult to find a place to park. Dave wedged into an impossibly small space and pulled out a picnic cooler as the rest of us staked out places to watch the sunset, the Super Bowl of attractions at Uluru.

Dave passed around champagne in plastic glasses, then a platter of cheese, crackers, and sausages. We had a perfect tailgate party as distant Uluru, a postcard view of its entirety stretched before us, morphed from ochre to henna.

"I'm at a loss for descriptive words," I told Michael as we sipped champagne together and watched Uluru darken. "How would you describe it now?"

"Brown velvet," he replied without hesitation.

But then it segued to milk chocolate, to big bruise, and then mauve before finally becoming dark mocha just before disappearing from view.

It was way after dark by the time we found our assigned room at the Outback Pioneer Motel, which was too bad since it was an elegant accommodation. "Best of Trip" we knew 7 days later. We had only a few hours to enjoy it because an early bedtime had been recommended. Tomorrow meant an early call and a long ride to one of the strangest communities in the world. No joke.

Chapter Fourteen

Coober Pedy

During next morning's glorious sunrise, we were circling Uluru. Not on foot but in the bus.

I really wanted to walk around the rock, but that would have taken about five hours. Had I the time, I would have done it. There were, reportedly, many sacred sites along the trail, some off limits to visitors, even to some ineligible Aboriginals. That might include women and tribal members who were not seniors.

I wouldn't have climbed to Uluru's top, however. That was discouraged by all local tribes because, according to *Frommer's*, "The climb follows the trail their ancestral Dreamtime Mala men took when they first came to Uluru." If visitors to Uluru chose to become *mingas*, the Anangu word for *tourists* or, interchangeably, *ants*, Aboriginals would look the other way and endure the insult. And many mingas, especially those who refuse to call it anything other than Ayers Rock, ignored the request. Two pages in the official visitor's guide were devoted to dissuasion in which Barbara Tjikatu pled, "If you worry about Aboriginal Law, then leave it, don't climb it. The chain is still there if you want to climb it. You should think about Tjukurpa and stay on the ground. Please don't climb."

Tjukurpa was the Aboriginal word for Dreamtime or Dreaming which, to them, had nothing to do with sleep so far as I could discern. It had to do with all human relationships and with plants, animals, and the environment, the very landscape they inhabited. To them Tjukurpa had nothing to do with imagination either. It was real, existence itself.

If I were Aboriginal, I would call those who actually attempted to climb Uluru the *birdbrain people*. As we cruised by the trail on the bus, I was shocked by the verticality of the single pathway's 1,142 foot rise. In the early morning light it looked to me like a primitive T-bar for the very, very naïve. Yet it's clear and present danger plus warnings of heart attacks, high winds, fatal falls, and outrageous heat or cold were still ignored by a number of visitors. But that number was dwindling, and no one was climbing toward the top this dawn.

"There are 720 kilometers between us and Coober Pedy," Dave said a bit groggily as we left Uluru-Kata National Park. They turned out to be the bleakest kilometers of the trip. Except for three fly infested roadhouse stops, there was nothing to break the monotony of scrub and red earth as we traveled south. And our destination, hard to believe, would be even less connected to civilization than Uluru, which at least had regular air service to and from Alice Springs, Perth, Cairns, and several other cities.

One of the roadhouses was Erldunda, where we reconnected with the Stuart Highway and turned south again. After morning tea.

For once I didn't want refreshment, so I wandered about taking pictures of the parked, unoccupied Road Trains. There was quite a concentration of them at Erldunda, a big meeting place for truckers. I spent my time studying the rigs closely while swatting at flies on my arms and forehead, the Australian salute to everyone, including me, who endlessly repeated this already tired joke.

Less than ten miles south of the Kulgera complex, we crossed into South Australia, but its bustling, culturally rich city, Adelaide, and the lush vineyards of the Barossa and Clare Valleys were still far away.

Marla's roadhouse was a dismal, low slung affair, and there I spied a young woman with a small child. She was Caucasian and seemed distressed as she attempted to make a call from a pay phone. I really couldn't hear her words, but her every facial expression and her slumping body showed that she clearly didn't like what she was hearing. She had no suitcases, and the little boy was dirty from play, so I had the impression that she lived here at Marla. As I watched her hang up desolately, I couldn't begin to imagine what her life must be like in this barren landscape at this nothing outpost.

Several miles north of Coober Pedy, conical mounds started to appear on both sides of the road.

"You can see, left and right, the beginnings of the opal fields," Dave said. He hadn't spoken for so many miles that I feared he might have dozed off at the wheel. But then I relaxed because, if he veered off the road, there was nothing to hit anyway. "These mounds would be some of the newer stakes," he continued.

I knew by his tone that an often given lecture was commencing, and I got my notebook out just in case his stories about his opal hunting trips contained some useful or interesting information. My tiny voice recorder had quit on me long ago. It had proved impractical anyway with road noise and distances from speakers.

"Opals resulted from wind and erosion at least 100 million years ago," he droned on like a dutiful, documentary host.

I studied the curious mounds while Dave rambled. At first sporadic, they became more numerous quickly and stretched to the horizon on flat red plain, numbering in the hundreds and in full view by the time we reached town, where they were even more numerous and closer together.

"These ones are abandoned opal digs since mining in town is now illegal," Dave mentioned.

The cones I could see were pretty uniformly three feet high and white, virtually all the same except for an occasional grey one or a mini-pyramid the color of brown sugar. In their evenness, they looked assembly line produced, ready for packaging.

"Those piles are called mullock," Dave continued. "They result from drilling as much as 30 meters down."

Michael saw me scrambling for my conversion table and said, "Just under 100 feet, Hank."

Bulldozers remove the dirt, tunneling machines with revolving cutting heads expose the opal seam, if one is there. Spotters follow behind watching for opals, which are worked by handpicks."

"What's the name of the biggest company here?" I asked.

"There's no company," Dave rejoined. "All the mounds you see represent the efforts of independent miners."

I was amazed at their industry. As I watched, occasional trucks with round scoops were working the mounds. But there were no humans to be seen. It appeared as if the entire operation was automated. It was a bizarre, unprecedented-in-my-experience sight.

But not as bizarre as the town of Coober Pedy, which announced itself with a road sign sporting cut out camels for a Stuart Highway caravan park and another for the charmingly named Mud Hut Motel.

"Coober is distressed and weird," I wrote in my diary later that day, an unfair judgment that would be amended before I left. I crossed out the negative adjectives and wrote above them *defies the ordinary*.

We pulled up to our accommodation, surely the most unusual Comfort Inn in the entire chain. It was in an abandoned opal mine and completely underground. The only door leading to sunlight was the one in the reception area.

Michael took an instant dislike to the "Comfort Inn Cooper Pedy Experience" and its tomblike ambiance and spent most of his time sitting in a lawn chair on the cramped patio outside the entrance. He didn't lack for company because many from our group, especially the men, experienced mild claustrophobia inside. Sometimes I found that Michael had moved into the reception area, which at least had shafts of natural light, unlike the guest rooms.

Ruth and I dumped our bags in our cave like accommodation and immediately took pictures to record and validate its strangeness. A cloth bag sagged from the light fixture over the bed to catch whatever grit fell from the ceiling. The bag appeared heavy, as if ready to fall during the night and splatter some very surprised guests. I recalled the pioneer women in sod huts on the Midwestern prairie who were driven literally insane by the rain of sod on their face, in their hair, and on everything they owned.

The bed was covered by an incongruous, frilly bedspread replicated from, likely, a 1947 *Better Homes and Gardens* pattern.

I kept looking up at the ceiling, perhaps hoping it would open to sky. It was quite high, probably to counterbalance the feeling that guests were being entombed alive.

The TV was in a hole sculpted into the wall just next to another alcove covered by a curtain. It concealed an area for hanging clothes.

Both the white ceiling and walls were shot through with veins of color that I dubbed Martian Orange.

The room was equal parts homey and alien.

We quickly craved openness and set out for a walk. Most of the storekeepers in this hilly town of 3,500 seemed to be opal merchants, and I wondered how so many survived. We did find two grocery stores. They looked like provisioning headquarters for risky expeditions. Both were under-stocked, or over-shopped, and noticeably dark inside despite the fact that neither was underground. Perhaps the long-term locals were evolving and required less light, developing echolocation skills similar to bats.

We wandered through elegant Desert Cave, which called itself, "The World's only International Underground Hotel." We browsed its interpretive center, underground, of course. It was actually a museum about, what else? opals, and we bumped into John and Jenny, who wanted to talk to us, really wanted to chat, for the first time. Actually, they wanted to complain, the first of many times as it turned out, about the tour. "We're not learning enough from our guide," they said, sounding like participants in a round song. Jenny was particularly hot and went on about Dave's deficiencies as

John, continuously smiling through gritted teeth, backed her up like a high-powered lobbyist.

"He does take care of the routine chores, like buying food for our lunches," Ruth said in his behalf.

"He's doing his best," I said, "but the commentary is pretty lame," I agreed.

"Well, we're going to talk to the others," Jenny said. And I sensed trouble ahead.

It occurred to me that their sudden dissatisfaction might be due to the influence of this creepy burg, but later at dinner—pumpkin soup, the usual tasteless chicken, and commercial ice cream at a local restaurant called, not surprisingly, the Opal Inn—Roger and Jan did the same thing. Used to scholarly guides, neither was happy with the tour. I began to wonder if our bus would turn into the Bounty before we reached more temperate surroundings.

It was true that we were learning little from Dave other than the predictable. What he told us was readily available in common tour guides. But he *was* affable and caring.

The citizens of Coober whom we passed seemed to be colorful characters, the kind of people you'd want to watch unobserved for fear they would not take kindly to interest in them. In a couple of cases we whispered about or crossed the street to avoid what appeared to be wild-eyed, dangerous oddballs. It was hard to tell just by observation, but as we went in and out of stores, more and more my instinct was not to engage to find out. Without question, I was finding Coober a great place for discreetly done, if potentially risky, people watching.

I learned from a free tourist booklet named "Coober Pedy: Opal Capital of the World" that about 60% of Coober's citizens were of European descent, the offspring of immigrants after World War II from southern and eastern European countries like Greece. Other straggled in daily from other end-of-the-road type places hoping to find opals, bringing the total in this international olio to about 50 nationalities, all independent and armed with attitude and explosives. The rest of the citizens were Aboriginal.

Unlike other towns with big, largely unseen native populations, here in Coober Pedy Aboriginals were very much in evidence. They mingled with other ethnic groups freely. They had always called this place *Umoona*, which meant "long life" and/or mulga tree, about the only plant that could survive in this desperately dry and hot environment.

The total mix came to about 3,500 citizens, most of whom spent their time in their little underground kingdoms hunting for the opals that make this town the globe's largest producer of this gem. About 85% of the world's opals come from Coober Pedy and nearby Mintabie and Andamooka.

I asked practical Ruth, who by choice had little valuable jewelry, if she was interested in buying an opal here, and she stared at me as if she couldn't understand how I could ask such a dumb question. I now understood why there were so many opal sellers in town. She disappeared into several opal shops while I stood outside pretending not to watch while watching the townspeople walk and drive by.

The town's buildings were either cleverly adapted constructions or dilapidated eyesores. It was often hard to say which description was more accurate. They were almost all one story affairs, not too close together, like a planned housing development in the middle of the Mojave Desert that went bankrupt after only a few houses had been built and sold.

The town clearly had only one thing on its collective mind—opals. There were already 250,000 holes and, as a result, mullock heaps everywhere. Locals claimed that they would not fill in the holes even though they were hazardous to walkers. I wondered about the reason. "They're something to look at," one local commented, at least partially cluing me in. Something is always better than nothing, I suppose. Visitors were constantly advised by signs, "Don't run. Don't walk backwards."

And don't tempt fate. "It's illegal to go on a pegged claim without the miner's permission," we were frequently warned.

Special areas were set aside for innocents like me to pretend to hunt for overlooked, valuable opals, an activity that was called *noodling*. This *could* become profitable, however. Even many locals sifted through mullock for gems missed by miners. Some claimed to make a living from it. Or so I was told.

But once a visitor decided to use tools, machinery, or explosives, in other words, *get serious,* he, sometimes even she, needed a permit. Ruth, therefore, only hunted for opals in stores. Waiting if front of each, I always expected her to emerge with a very small package and a big smile. But that didn't happen.

Opals are considered precious stones between 5 ½ and 6 ½ on the Mohs hardness scale that rates the scratch resistance of minerals. Composed of basic silica and water, 3 to 10 percent, 90% of those found around Coober Pedy were worthless, or potch. The other 10% revealed bits of fragmented rainbow when rotated, an enticing kaleidoscopic play of many colors. But which opals were valuable and which were not was a total mystery, at least to me, even after listening to Coober Pedy experts and suffering some unavoidable sales pitches. Ruth, on the other hand, was becoming quite erudite on the subject after visiting most of the dealers in town.

Opal fever began here in 1915 when 14-year-old William Hutchinson kicked up a few pieces of surface opal. It's been boom or bust ever since.

For five years the place was known only as the Stuart Range Opal Field. But apparently the opal hunters heard the locals calling them "kupa piti", loosely translated "white man in a hole", and the name became Anglicized and stuck. This fact, by the way, seemed to be in absolutely every tourist brochure and travel magazine in Australia as if required by law.

The same coverage applied to "The Big Winch", a Coober Pedy landmark that served no earthly purpose and was so over-promoted that any interest in seeing it died.

But don't tell the locals. Today's hole people can be prickly. They are probably the most territorial souls on the planet. Part of that results from both personal and geographic isolation. A paved road into their town didn't happen until 1987 when the Stuart Highway was sealed. Part of it is that 70% of them reside underground. The other part, of course, is the result of living *The Lottery* 24-7.

What did unify this community, oddly, was the Open Air Outback Cinema, a community run drive-in movie. Unfortunately, it only showed four films per month on every other weekend. I wondered if it showed only films like *Treasure of the Sierra Madre* and *Romancing the Stone*. We were there on a Friday, which was not a cinema night, so I couldn't find out. And there wasn't anything of interest on TV.

So after dinner Ruth and I had to content ourselves with reading in our room, which after a while seemed like a sepulcher with motel décor. Ruth read soberly about opals while I tried to figure out what else made this place, the town not the motel, seem more bizarre than almost everywhere else I had ever been.

Things really became weird when we turned out the lights and experienced total darkness. It was an eerie feeling for both of us. Ruth kept reaching over just to touch me as if she feared I'd been snatched away by the Mole People. She finally admitted that she couldn't sleep until I turned a light on.

The silence then became the issue, so I switched on the fan. Earlier I had noticed it and wondered why it was there in a temperature controlled environment that definitely leaned toward coolness but, surprisingly, not dankness. Now I understood the fan's function—white noise.

I wondered how Michael was doing in the next tomb, er, room as I opened and closed my eyes pointlessly.

"The expression 'sleeping like the dead' was probably first uttered here," I whispered to Ruth.

She was not amused.

Chapter Fifteen

The Road to Marree

The next morning brought a Nyngan-like change in attitude about Coober. After traditional fare in the motel/cave's breakfast room we went, en masse, to the Umoona Opal Mine and Museum to meet our guide.   After a tour of the town, we would be treated to underground demonstrations in the mine, according to our itinerary.   Umoona, Coober Pedy's largest privately owned attraction, had been a tourist magnet since 1974. Before that it was an actual opal mine, worked as early as the 1920s. Ruth leaned forward with anticipation when Dave said, "Umoona's showroom and retail shop is the largest underground opal retailing complex in Australia." Oh.

I couldn't help but notice a similar reaction in six other females, who made cooing sounds as their heads bobbed noticeably. Only Lynette, who was not herself, seemed indifferent to the lure of unlimited opals for viewing and sale at their very source. The truth was that she was not well enough to enjoy shopping.

On Rob's last trip to the United States, he had some very old travelers' checks he wanted to cash in so Ruth helped him pick out gold earrings for Lynette. The 3 of us enjoyed an excursion to the Rose Garden and downtown Portland, and, afterwards, I watched from the sidelines as Rob and Ruth selected a simple, elegant pair. I regretted that Lynette and Ruth could not now share a similar spree Down Under.

"Does Lynette wear the gold earrings Rob bought her?" asked the typical man.

"Of course! She wears them all the time when we go to formal occasions. I can't believe you haven't noticed," replied the horrified woman.

Before I could be supplied all the details of what outfit Lynette had on each time she wore her earrings, Dave said, "We'll return to Umoona in a bit, but first, here's Sandy."

A middle aged woman who looked like she could wrestle crocodiles and win every time climbed aboard. Wielding a microphone as if she had done this a million times before, she greeted us. "Mornin', everybody. My name's Sandy and I've been a miner here in Coober Pedy for 12 years."

Much to my disappointment, she moved quickly away from the topic of herself and began an informal, colorful description of her town.

As we cruised its streets, which didn't look quite as strange as they had the previous day, she scrolled back to Coober's beginnings and described a typical street scene in 1922 as "one hundred people and one hundred and fifty camels."

It didn't take Sandy long to get around to the practical side of life in this isolated, desiccated place. "Fresh water comes from 27 kilometers outside of town. The source is artesian, and a pipeline brings it to our water treatment tanks before we get it in our holding tanks. It's the most expensive water in Australia. Water's so precious here that you think twice before flushing the toilet. It costs 8 cents every time, and that adds up. The four inches of rain we get per year is welcomed but…."

I mentally measured 4 inches and gasped. At home, it was not unusual for us to get four inches of precipitation in a few days during an average winter month when it typically rained almost every day.

"Despite that, we have a public swimming pool on Paxton Road," Sandy said with obvious civic pride.

We pulled up to some modest houses surrounded by what appeared to be standing pipes. "Those white pipes take air underground. Each vent that you see represents a room in somebody's house underground, so we know how many rooms our neighbors have by counting their pipes."

She talked like a *Variety* reporter about the many movies that had been shot in her town, mostly apocalyptic epics like *Mad Max, Beyond the Thunderdome* and Vin Diesel's *Pitch Black*. She told us about the movie currently shooting. "You may have noticed the Christmas decorations on Hutchinson Street last evening. That's because of a film being made here by the producer of *The Full Monty*. It was shooting there yesterday. The men in town are all hoping they'll be hired on as extras."

As we pulled up to the cave like entrance to St. Peter and Paul's Catholic Church, Sandy was inducing mirth with her tale of just having signed a contract to allow a film crew of yet another upcoming movie to use her elaborately decorated bathroom for a graphic sex encounter. "I know you'll be paying attention to my taste in décor when you see this scene," she deadpanned.

Inside, St. Peters was just like any other small town church, except for the fact that, being underground, it had no stained glass windows. When it was built in 1967, it was non-denominational and the only church in town. But now Coober had, in keeping with its riotous individuality, three more— Serbian Orthodox, Assembly of God, and a Revival Centre. Then there was something called the Catacomb Church, which we passed on the tour but didn't stop to see. Given its frontier appearance and feel, I wasn't the least bit surprised to learn that Coober existed for 50 years without a single house of worship.

"Our priest covers an area the size of Germany and The Netherlands, half of South Australia. He visits all thirty Catholic families every two weeks," she said as if this situation was normal.

Ruth was enamored of St. Peter's crystal chandelier and poked my arm and pointed to it just in case I hadn't seen it.

Sandy bragged about her community's 20 bed hospital and Coober's single doctor, a Japanese/Canadian named Takohara. "But we call him Dr. Kamikaze," she added. In the Outback you don't have to be politically correct apparently. "For emergencies, the Flying Doctors come in from Port Augusta."

She took us by the public noodling area on Jewellers Shop Road "where tourists can hunt for their own opal."

She pointed out the giant mining winch, Coober Pedy's Eiffel Tower, and said dryly, "The bucket goes down and dirt comes up."

There was pride in her voice continually, but it escalated when she directed our attention to the drive-in. "It belongs to the community and was our only entertainment before TV arrived. We've bought fire engines with the proceeds, $15 entry for a car full."

"You can buy fresh produce and explosives at the same time," Sandy noted without the least hint of irony as we passed one of the not-so-supermarkets on the main street.

She was telling us about Dusty Radio, run by local students 18 hours a day, as we returned to the Umoona Opal Mine and Museum. "We have 310 school aged kids here," she said of the student body.

Umoona's entrance was through a hillside and down a sandstone tunnel that wound 100 meters into the non-working mine that was especially busy in the 1920s.

Sandy led us into a theater where we watched a slick film named *The Story of Opal.* Before the credits rolled, she turned us over to Gina, who afterwards gave us an opal cutting demonstration. The women on our tour, even Jenny, ringed her like groupies at a rock concert as she used a diamond cutter to show how experts get rid of dirt around a just-mined opal. She sanded it to form a dome and vacuumed it vigorously.

Among the second ring of viewers, the men had their hands protectively over their wallets.

I could clearly see an emerging gemstone as Gina talked about the range of value among different types of opals. "A solid opal is white and milky," she explained. "A black opal is very hard to find. Potch is an opal with no color." The iridescent colors began to reveal themselves as Gina worked.

Satisfied, she applied serum oxide, the tooth polish used by dentists and a necessity during multiple opal sandings, and began speaking about singlets and doublets.

I was lost and, admittedly, a little bored, so I looked over at Ruth to see if she was too. Oh, oh. She was on high alert and clearly absorbing every bit of information. Her head was nodding knowingly.

Sandy returned from somewhere and gave us a limited tour of an underground dwelling, not a model home for tourists but someone's actual living quarters. She challenged us to determine our depth and, after several wrong guesses, she told us that we were 33 feet below the surface and that it was 24 degrees at this depth at all times. "This consistent temperature is appreciated in a place where we've had 56.7 up above for eight days in a row." I did a hasty calculation and figured 134 degrees outside, 75 degrees inside. I flashed on Cloncurry where the supposed record high temperature for Australia was 128°, so I wondered if Sandy was exaggerating a bit. Perhaps it just felt like 134°. Or maybe my metric wasn't as good as I thought it was. Either way, both places sounded impossibly hot.

As if no Coober Pedian could go for fifteen minutes without thinking of mining, Sandy said, "90% of our opals are hand dug with a pick. You can't tell by looking now, but these rooms were once a mine shaft. Before moving in underground, we have to use a white glue to seal the walls to get rid of airborne particles. Result? We never have to dust furniture. The largest home in town has 44 bedrooms."

"44 rooms?" Angus asked, either not trusting his hearing or giving Sandy a chance to correct an error.

"*Bed*rooms," Sandy repeated as we viewed a fairly routine kitchen and living area. Its only slightly unusual features were no windows and dull, artificial lighting.

"We own the ground on top and 100 feet below," said Sandy, a proud mine dweller herself. Never too far from tongue-in-cheek humor at the strangeness of it all, she made life as a human mole seem both real and surreal with stories of drilling accidents where home extenders found themselves suddenly in someone else's kitchen or, embarrassingly, bedroom. She said something that I didn't catch about bulldog shale and summarized, "The only other place in the world with the same kind of underground structures is under the Pyramids in Egypt."

She scraped her hand along a wall and rubbed something on her face before extending her hand to the nearest woman. "This is alunite, the same stuff used in cosmetics to absorb oils and smooth the skin. It really is 'dirt cheap' until they put it in a jar."

Sandy ended her very entertaining tour with a tender, childhood reminiscence. "Sunday night was bomb night. The whole family would gather around the kitchen table to make our explosives for the rest of the week's mining. Now we use nitropril and a fuse."

I wanted to follow Sandy home and talk to her for hours but didn't even try because we had just a little time left to see Umoona's museum. I was the only one who had a cursory look and it was disappointing, largely about local Aboriginal life and not the fascinating subject of daily living in Coober Pedy. It was thoughtful but anti-climactic after Uluru.

Ruth began looking at the exhibits with me but quickly became bored and left to explore the opal showroom. As my interest in the not too varied life of local natives waned, I flashed on the shop's earlier description, "The largest underground opal retailing complex in Australia." Oh, oh, oh.

I went to see if I needed to call and beg for an increase in our credit card limit and found that the men, many experiencing mild claustrophobia, had drifted outside. The women had disappeared into the Wal-Mart of Opals.

I entered it expecting to see Ruth dripping in rainbow jewelry from ears to fingertips, but I was mistaken. Actually, more like relieved. She was completely opal free. "What happened?" I asked, amazed.

"Follow me," she whispered.

Outside, she confided, "The others all bought. But I didn't."

"Why not?" I asked, shocked at her restraint.

She looked left and right to see if any of the other women were around, leaned toward me, and said, "Their opals are very expensive and most of the settings are not current styles." Then and there I realized that Ruth had somehow deeply internalized the art of opal acquisition and would return home with just one souvenir that would perfectly fit her personality. But her opal would not, surprisingly, be bought at the source.

Since we had lingered quite long at Umoona, we headed out of town at a bracing clip while Dave talked about the extra time he had given the ladies to shop. He added the urgency of getting the ten passengers aboard who wanted a flyover of Lake Eyre to the runway. "We have to be in William Creek by early afternoon," he said with a bit of tension.

Within a minute we passed a sign that clearly indicated, at least to me, that we were on the road to Oodnadatta, almost due north. Lake Eyre was to the east. I looked at my map and sensed that there was something wrong. But I hadn't planned the itinerary and didn't know the roads so I kept quiet.

A few miles out of town we passed through the dingo fence, the longest continuous construction in the world. It ran haphazardly from just west of the town of Nundroo in the part of South Australia known as the Great Australian Bight to near Surfer's Paradise in Queensland, a 3,307 mile fence meant to protect sheep from wild, native dogs. Made possible by the Dog Fence Act of 1946, it wasn't completed until the 1980s. The idea of it, twice as long as the Great Wall of China, was far more interesting than the sight of it. It was, after all, just an ordinary fence.

The road, or track, was unpaved but well maintained, smoother actually than many of the paved roads we had been on for the past several days. There were many floodway signs, the only vertical objects in sight. The Outback here was absolutely treeless with a perfectly horizontal horizon line in the vast distance bumping against blue sky. Vegetation had completely disappeared because we were on the edge of the Simpson Desert. But, typical of the always subtly changing Outback, mesas suddenly loomed before us. And although the place appeared lifeless, I glimpsed a single dead roo by the road, evidence that they lived almost everywhere in out back Australia, even in the most forbidding places.

Suddenly Dave said, "I think I've got a bad tire, mates," While I began praying for a decent spare, he pulled over and got out to check, and I noticed what I hadn't seen before, wispy grass sparsely spreading away from the road, tenacious flora that had not been observable when the bus was in motion. I looked behind the bus to see Dave pacing back and forth furiously. Oh, oh, oh, oh.

He climbed back in and, without explanation, turned the bus around and headed back in the direction from which we had come.

"I thought we were on the wrong road," said Angus, who was seated in front of me.

"I did too," I agreed.

"Now we have a 400k diversion instead of a straight 166," Angus noted. He looked at his watch and sighed.

Dave was apparently too embarrassed to say anything. He tried to compensate for his error by driving rather too fast for the road, and the back window just behind my head shattered with a stunning report. Luckily the glass shards held together, a crazy fragmented mosaic for the rest of the trip.

The same can't be said of the passengers. Tempers were clearly rising, at least among the ones who had paid a lot of money for a daylight flyover of Lake Eyre this Friday afternoon.

We were not among them. Rob and Lynette had decided against this adventure; so Ruth and I opted to forego what sounded like an amazing experience to spend some time with them. We had had very little of that since the trip began, and we were hoping for an insider report about Lynette's condition. She did not seem to be getting worse, but the cough persisted and Ruth and I hoped for candor once we were away from the larger group.

We drove back through Coober Pedy and, south of town, turned east on the William Creek Track, which quickly became a spine jolting proposition. The landscape was pretty much the same as on the other road with, perhaps, a bit more vegetation.

Within a few miles, the bus screeched to a halt at the dog fence, a twenty second stop, and I could see this time that the fence was well-maintained.

Dave speeded up again, going as fast as he possibly could without careening out of control. Suddenly I was aware of a kangaroo, a big grey, hopping purposefully and powerfully parallel to the bus about ten feet away. I couldn't tell if this was an impromptu race or a mere coincidence, but this roo and two prancing emus were the only moving objects visible for the entire 103 miles to William Creek, except for one tough looking Ute-type vehicle pulling a trailer.

I had become used to seeing the true but unassuming beauty of The Outback because I had learned to look for what was not obvious to the unpracticed eye. I now spotted occasional water holes, hills blanketed by nearly invisible wildflowers, and huge, flat salt pans that I might have missed before. The Outback was nothing if not a multi-sensory experience. I closed my eyes and tasted dust, heard the roar of an overworked engine, and felt the heat of the Outback afternoon even through a closed window and despite the bus' laboring air-conditioning.

Dave did a decent job of making up for the lost time, and we pulled into William Creek, population 10 and the take-off place for the Lake Eyre experience, only about an hour later than expected.

We had a fast lunch on an open patio where I discovered that a porch swing, vigorously pumped, kept the flies away, at least temporarily.

The ten who had signed up for the fly-over took off at a not-so-unreasonable 2:30 p.m., so the prior dark atmosphere became less tense as anticipation rose.

The three couples who didn't go included also Gwen and Angus, who gravitated to the porch swing. The six of us had more time at William Creek than the flyers, so with an hour to kill I went inside and entertained myself with a video about Lake Eyre. In it, a grinning Australian man stood way, way far out in what appeared to be an impossibly huge body of water…up to his knees. It looked like trick photography but wasn't. He lifted one leg to show the depth, and I suddenly experienced glum regret. Seeing something, Lake Eyre for instance, in a video just wasn't the same as seeing it in person.

The time spent with Rob and Lynette was, however, worth the sacrifice even though nothing truly of consequence was discussed. We only had to drive a short, straight-shot 60 miles to pick up the fliers at Coward Springs, an old railroad stop and makeshift landing strip. I barely noted the scenery because I was engrossed in conversation with Rob. Friendship trumped all else, even occasional glimpses of Lake Eyre.

All of the deplaning walked toward us excitedly glassy-eyed. From their demeanor, you'd think they had witnessed a miracle. And, actually, they had. Rain preceded our visit, so there was some water in this huge salt expanse which has completely filled only three times, most recently in 1984, since Western eyes first saw it.

Karin and Brian reported being totally thrilled by the sight of Lake Eyre from the air, and even John and Jenny admitted that they instantly forgot their annoyance due to the delay when Lake Eyre appeared in all its vastness below them. Everyone assured us that the experience had been worth the risk and expense.

According to World Lakes Database, "Lake Eyre Basin is one of the largest areas of internal drainage in the world." Its lowest part is almost 50 below sea level, not all that impressive compared to the Dead Sea's 1,340 feet, but nonetheless notable. There are actually two lakes. Lake Eyre North is 90 miles long and 48 miles wide, and Lake Eyre South is about 1/3 its neighbor's size.

Because we lost time on the wrong road, we didn't arrive at our overnight destination, Marree, until after dark. This town of less than 100 people seemed closed for the night, but the Marree Hotel was brightly lit and looked inviting.

Dave, still a bit subdued due to the delay, opened the luggage carrier sheepishly and began to set our suitcases on the steps. Upon impact with the ground, a cloud of dust arose comically from each one. Someone on the hotel staff brought us a few brushes, and we all got to work ridding the outsides of our bags of as much dust as possible.

Stepping into the Marree Hotel's entry hall was like time-traveling back to the 19th century. Standing at the check-in desk waiting for my room number and key, I felt like I was in a painstakingly re-created western-movie-set bordello.

All of the guest accommodations were upstairs, so I hefted our suitcases up some steep, carpeted steps to our assigned room where I found the western town whore house theme from downstairs continued. But what was fairly charming in an elaborate entrance hall was depressing in a guest room. It was historically authentic, down to old furniture, miniscule size, and minimal lighting. It was the kind of serviceable room that only those focused on sex for as long as it took would find tolerable. The bathroom was down the hall and communal, but at least with separate male and female facilities.

Ruth went to investigate.

She returned, closed the door behind her, and said rather gloomily, "Only one of the toilets in the ladies' bathroom is working, and there's a sign that says water from the taps is not fit for human consumption."

I opened my suitcase and picked up the shirt on top. It sported a ring of dust exactly matching the suitcase's zipper. The red earth had defied the trailer's doors, the made-tough luggage zipper, and the suitcase's thick skin. I was soon shaking every article of clothing I took out and coughing. Red grit was in every crevice, each seam, inside every folded-in sock.

"I need to wash down the dust," I said, "so I'll check the men's loo and ask about drinks."

There were shower stalls and two toilets, both working, but absolutely no privacy. A couple of my mates were freshening up for dinner and I asked if they had found water.

"There's a refrigerator at the end of the hall with bottled," Michael informed me.

By the time I found it, however, it was stripped bare. It was Friday evening, after all, and the hotel was full to capacity.

I returned to our room to find Ruth testing the mattress. Her expression told me all I needed to but didn't want to know about the bumpy night ahead.

Our neighbors seemed to be having an in-room party. I thought of going down the hall, banging on their door, and demanding our share of any potable liquid they had acquired from the communal fridge. But it sounded like their drinks of choice were laced, and I couldn't tell if they had risen to an alcohol induced, butt kicking stage yet.

"No water," I reported to Ruth. "We'll have to drink a lot of beer instead." I pointed pointedly past the wall.

She was not tempted, not amused. "Let's go down to dinner early. Surely they'll have some water on the tables."

"Expect the worst," said I, a seasoned traveler who knew better. I had stayed in far worse accommodations and knew from experience that you can have a miserable night in a 5-star hotel and a great time in a hovel.

I was certainly wrong this time. Our party of sixteen was seated at a single, long table and served a sumptuous gourmet meal, the undisputed best-of-trip. The service was sensational too. I savored Tasmanian smoked salmon salad. The marinated rib fillet of beef in red wine reduction was exceptional, but I coveted my neighbors' pan fried fillet of perch with Maitre d'Hotel butter on homemade tartar and mild Malay lamb curry with rice pilaf. My dessert, fresh peaches and ice cream with raspberry coulis, was as good as anything I had had at the Ritz in London. And here I was in a ramshackle hotel in an isolated town without even a paved road into it and having a succulent meal in the best of company.

Back in our cramped, stuffy room, however, Ruth announced, "I'm going straight to bed. I might as well be dreaming instead of looking at these faded walls."

I tried to read but the single lamp yielded little light. A candle would have been better. The party in the next room was almost drowned out by the party downstairs in the pub. This was, I presumed, a typically lively Outback Friday night.

At 10:30 I gave up and crawled into my single bed with no female companionship or comfort.

Wide awake and staring at the high ceiling, I listened to some amplified songs of heartbreak and hell bent living. I kind of expected to eventually hear Keith Urban, local kid who made good elsewhere. Keith was born in New Zealand but grew up in Caboolture, northwest of Brisbane. But instead of Keith, unfamiliar voices filled the night with twang and percussion. The classic sounding country from below was so loud that I couldn't imagine how Ruth slept through it. But then the juke box flipped to something familiar, and I could plainly hear every word as Arlo Guthrie warbled achingly about Massachusetts. Many Aussie voices, young and old, sang along. Nothing better to do, I joined them.

All of a sudden, it hit me. What the $%&@* was I doing? Just below me was an ideal, wholesome country pub. I could even hear children's voices in the mix. Who besides Ruth could sleep? All I had to do was knock on Allan's door, I even knew which one, and ask him if he wanted to join me. If not, at least I could have beer and bonding with some partying locals who lived in a very interesting, end-of-the-dirt-track kind of place.

I was halfway into my jeans when the music abruptly stopped. Voices ceased. Goodbyes were spoken. Even the party in the next room ended. It was as if a switch had been thrown and Marree was turned off for the night.

I had once again been denied, through my own fault, an authentic Outback pub outing.

Chapter Sixteen

The Flinders

I awoke in the dark ready for action. Eight hours of sleep in the single, not-too-uncomfortable bed had done wonders. I roused Ruth and we dressed and had a walkabout around Marree long before breakfast.

The sunrise, and the experience, reminded me of Nyngan.

I did the math. It was 13 days ago that we greeted the dawn in central New South Wales on our first full day of this splendid trip. That fact seemed incomprehensible in light of all that we had done, all of The Outback we had seen, in less than two weeks.

The sky to the east was stunning with every shade of red morphing into a complete array of golds. But the air was chilly, and on the south horizon storm clouds were gathering.

Ruth and I admired Marree's well preserved railroad station and platform that had been maintained to represent its important past. Sleepy, sleeping Marree was the start of both the Birdsville and Oodnadatta tracks. The first took the very brave north through three deserts and just across the Queensland border where it ended in Birdsville, population about 100 and one of the most isolated communities in the world. It was certainly the remotest town in Queensland. The pub in the Birdsville Hotel, not a family friendly place like the one here in Marree, had a legendary reputation. Birdsville was so in the middle of nothing that it was yet another 425 miles to the next nearest town—Mount Isa.

A lot of the Oodnadatta Track followed the defunct Ghan train line. Marree had been a regular stop as the old Ghan made a semi-circle from Port Augusta in South Australia to Marla just south of the Northern Territory border. That was where I had seen that forlorn, young woman attempting to make a phone call outside the fly infested road house. The vision still haunted me. We had been headed down Oodnadatta Track yesterday when Dave realized his mistake and turned back.

I liked Marree, but I couldn't imagine living here or in Marla or Birdsville or Oodnadatta, which had been the site of The Outback's first hospital. Once a thriving town, Oodnadatta lost most of its citizens when the old Ghan stopped operating.

Train-deprived Marree was hanging in there as a community. None of its houses or businesses looked deserted. It had once been a big camel train oasis too, and the old Ghan made regular stops at this station where passengers either switched trains because the track changed from broad to narrow gauge or hailed, not cabs, but camels. Those who went on ended up in Alice Springs, the end of the line.

It took from 1877 to 1929 for the old Ghan to extend from Adelaide to Alice, and what was in between became a bad-engineered and logistical nightmare. The track had been laid atop creek beds and flood plains that were normally dry, but when it rained…. The old Ghan, named for the Afghans who met it with caravans, was slow, expensive, and unreliable. It made its last run in 1982.

The sleek new Ghan now whisked passengers once a week all the way from Adelaide to Darwin in 47 hours in absolute comfort, but the new and far more reliable train track was not near Marree.

According to the folks in the Hotel, some of the displays in their historic train station provided information about the old Ghan, but it was way too early for it to be opened, so Ruth and I just studied an old train engine and the dilapidated shell of a mail truck. I took some pictures, not of them especially but of the volcanic eruption of a sunrise.

Jan had mentioned as we pulled into town the previous night that she had heard that Marree's cemetery contained some historically interesting tombs. The hotel's brochure had listed it among the town's must-see sights. "The history of the townspeople is written on the headstones," it enthused. But, alas, we were not destined to learn if this was true.

By the time we came across Marree's numerous cattle pens, we had seen every building in town, but we had failed to find the old cemetery. As small as the town was and as incredible as it seemed, we couldn't find it. We did, however, visit the stockyards where the town's current history was being written.

The pens were populated with lowing livestock. Marree's main source of income, after all, was cattle. Identical enclosures stretched to the horizon, not exactly a thrilling sight, so we were quickly done with them. No one was around yet to answer questions about the whereabouts of the cemetery, so we gave up on the local, so-called *best* tourist attraction.

As we zigzagged back to the hotel, citizens began to appear and greet us. People got into cars and waved goodbye when they pulled away as if we were kin. Children emerged from doors, ran down steps, and headed for school. This could have been 7 a.m. anywhere. Marree's small town spirit trumped its appearance and rumored economic woes.

Back in the lobby, I learned a bit of trivia that amazed me. The Marree Hotel, built in the 19th century and never altered, attracted an impressive number of international visitors. I was especially surprised to learn that French couples liked to come here for honeymoons. I supposed that they appreciated the isolation and the gourmet meals. But how did they find it in the first place? And how did they get here? The nearest paved road, other than the town's streets, was almost 50 miles distant. And why did they choose a dinky town with absolutely nothing to do? Oh. Of Course.

"Did you see the roos?" Barbara asked when we returned to the lobby after a breakfast far humbler than the previous evening's sumptuous dinner.

We said we hadn't, so she led us to the hotel's penned backyard where three greys, one a joey, were foraging. I knew by this time not to get too close no matter how domesticated they seemed. It was, however, certainly the closest proximity I had experienced to date. But, alas, the thrill of seeing roos had somewhat faded. And these were, after all, confined semi-pets and not accidentally sighted wild and free ones.

We mustered at the bus and headed south across a landscape of abandoned homesteads toward the gathering clouds.

Marree had fared better than Farina, our first stop of the day. Named Government Gums in 1878 when it was established as an experiment in growing wheat, it now spilled across open prairie like a town long after Armageddon.

Farina began promisingly. The railroad arrived six years after the first settlers. Merchants followed farmers and started businesses. But like the old Ghan, it was a poorly conceived mistake. The climate quickly proved unsuitable for agriculture, but the railroad didn't stop running until the 1980s. After that closure the town was soon deserted. At one time 300 Farinians and a few Afghan camel drivers made their homes here. But now all that remained were an abandoned bathtub, an old tire or two, and the shells of a few buildings. It was a genuine ghost town on a windswept plain.

South of Farina were the Wilpoorina and Witchelina homesteads, according to my road map, but we only stopped to view a second ochre pit. I still don't know if Wilpoorina and Witchelina were deserted experiments like Farina or just interesting names for ventures that sounded like characters in a *Wicked* sequel. Both were off the unpaved track we were traveling down, on side roads, and not visible.

The ochre pit was much larger than the one we had seen in the MacDonnells, which we had seen from below. This one we viewed from the top, and it was deep and deeply impressive. Its vivid colors reminded me of Utah's wondrous palate in places like Bryce Canyon. There was absolutely no one around but us, yet I imagined ordinary looking men carrying spears climbing down the multi-hued cliffs and coming back up a bit later with make-overs, ready to party or go to war.

Where the dirt track ended and pavement began at Lyndhurst, we stopped for morning tea. Lyndhurst was no more than a few buildings at a place where two roads came together. A monument on one building that appeared abandoned attracted everyone's attention. It was a stirring tribute, not to a war hero, a stellar athlete, or a prominent politician, but to a publican, John Henry Edwards, who ran a drinking establishment and hotel here for 25 years. I had to suppose that living in a place like this for that length of time made you something of a hero.

I wandered over to where the roads met and became fascinated by three signs, all pointing down the intersecting road. One announced the Strzelecki Track, the second gave the distance to Moomba and Innamincka, and the third pointed to the Elsewhere Hotel. Like a new rookie in spring training, I sought my geographic expert, Michael. As usual he was staring up at a flag.

Having no clue as to how to pronounce the Track's name, I pointed to the sign.

"The Strzelecki," he said, "handles mostly heavy transport because it passes through Moomba where you find the natural gas fields that make Canberra and Sydney possible,"

"What's the Track like, Michael?" asked a man who never saw a road he didn't want to take. Me.

"Look at the sign again," he instructed.

"NEXT FUEL...INNAMINCKA 500 km."

"Oh. There's nothing of great interest."

"Correct."

"And you have a big problem if you have car trouble."

"Correct again."

"Buggered," Dave said, overhearing me and looking over his shoulder.

Michael looked slightly offended by this word but said nothing.

I studied the sign again and went back to Michael, who was now discussing the attention-getting flag with Angus. "Moomba is 376 kilometers and must have workers with families. Why are there no services there?" I asked.

"It's a restricted area. Very security conscious," he explained before turning me around and pointing to the flag, a far more dynamic subject for him, on a pole just across the road. "Did you notice that South Australian flag?"

I squinted upward and saw a large bird. "It has an eagle on it."

Michael chuckled, his suspicion confirmed. "Most people from America assume it's their national bird, but it's a piping shrike."

Until the bus left, I learned about shrikes and listened to the history of the South Australian flag. And the Northern Territory flag. And the Tasmanian flag. And shortly after I returned home, a wall sized poster depicting every flag in Australia's history arrived in my mail.

Serious rain, the first in 15 days, began to rearrange the dirt on our increasingly grimy and battered bus windows as we passed a Leigh Creek coal mine sign. We had left desert and were now in foothills that promised approaching mountains. A few miles further, Dave turned off the paved road onto a twisting, jouncing track that took us to Beltana. Once a telegraph station, it was now mostly a ghost town where we tromped around looking through windows at deserted, empty rooms. Curiously, one building turned out to be an art gallery featuring the works of local artists. A woman in her 60s greeted us as if we were her first customers in many years.

Barbara quickly dismissed the art, which was strictly amateur if well-meant, and engaged the woman in friendly conversation while the rest of us looked around, pretending interest, and listened. "How many people live in Beltana?" Barbara asked after listening to the woman's truncated life story.

"Three, since my granddaughter moved to Adelaide."

Only Jane, who felt sorry for the woman, made a purchase.

"No Hans Heysen's in there," Barbara observed as we walked back to the bus.

"I suppose that's another Australian artist I should know about?" I asked.

"He lived here in The Flinders."

Indeed. Wilhelm Ernst Hans Franz Heysen brought himself and all of his names from Germany to Australia in 1884 when he was only 7. At 16 he went to art school and was soon entering his works in Adelaide exhibitions and winning awards. He studied art in Paris for 3 years. He married Selma, and despite fathering 8 children whom he had to feed and educate, he became a full time, self-supporting artist before he was 40. He loved the Flinders, the mountain range we were entering, and painted them in every medium. After his death in 1968, some tunnels, a mountain range, and a scenic 1,500 km hiking trail in this area were named for him.

Our next stop, Blinman, had the appearance of a town that had just been abandoned five minutes before we arrived. Long ago a copper mining town, Blinman was now surviving as the service center at the northern approach to The Flinders. But there were no services available today. It was Saturday but also winter with storms threatening, so no one was on the streets. I walked past a hotel/pub with cars parked in front, but no sound emanated from within. Unlike Farina, the town did look occupied, and I sensed the presence of people as I stared through the window of the tiny, closed community library.

It became kind of eerie to know there were people about but to not see anyone. I sensed that if I walked into any house, I would find a hot dinner on the table, the back door open, and fresh footprints disappearing into the bush.

We didn't linger long in Blinman and were soon heading south into what would prove to be, for me at least, the most unexpected and spectacular destination of the trip, the drop dead gorgeous, even in heavy rain, Flinders Ranges.

Many years ago I was standing on a prominence about the Barossa Valley when a tour guide pointed north and said, "The Flinders are just over there." I looked in that direction but saw nothing except for miles of low yellow hills beyond the vineyards below us. As a result, I had always wondered what, and where, they were.

The only clue between then and now was a comment I had read somewhere about The Flinders. Surveyor General Colonel Edward Charles Frome reported in the 1840s, "A more barren sterile country could not be imagined." Now that I have been there, I must assume that this man was completely blind.

What they were, at least in this Australian winter, were really ancient looking mountains, like Noah's corrupt earth at the beginning of The Deluge, sporting native cypress pines, twisted eucalypts, and occasional prickly pears. Mostly dry streambeds crossed broad valleys. Although semi-arid, these valleys were currently alive with abundant grass being trampled by prancing emus and leaping kangaroos.

The uplifts were, according to Dave, limestone inter-layered with siltstone. "They're even older than they appear," he added, driving cautiously along a narrow, challenging, unpaved track.

I later investigated to learn that The Flinders birthday cake would have 500 million candles atop. Three hundred million years before that, give or take an eon or two, a sea rushed in and flooded this area for, oh, 300 million years or so. After another cataclysmic change, the rock layers we now witnessed were squeezed upward and folded into a long mountain chain. The peaks and ridges were resistant quartzite, but the siltstone and shale underneath eroded, so time had done its work and exposed the interesting formations that made The Flinders so very unique.

The first Western explorers of the area were a party that dropped anchor in the Spencer Gulf, an arrowhead shaped inlet south of these mountains. Matthew Flinders, exploring the coastline aboard his ship, the Investigator, led a group up here in 1802 and they climbed Mount Brown to get an overview.

He apparently wasn't as impressed as I was because it was another 37 years before Edward John Eyre's party further explored the region. Squatters began to appear in 1845, and leases were granted 6 years later.

The road we were taking through The Flinders would be difficult to drive on the best of days, but this one had turned nasty with a grey pallor and horizontal rain driven crazy by the wind. Dave did a masterful job of negotiating the Range's descents and curlicue turns giving me the freedom to gape in wonder at unparalleled beauty despite the weather.

No one else was on the road, probably due to hazardous conditions and wintery murk, but nothing could diminish my appreciation of all I surveyed. Without hesitation, The Flinders moved up to near the top of my list of favorite places.

We stopped at breathtaking Brachina Gorge where a sign read, "Here are Trezone Formations and 630 million year old escarpments."

We traversed the Aroona Valley that was once threaded by Aboriginal trade routes. Early people judged the Flinders to be sacred. They knew. They gathered a plant called pituri here that, when chewed, had narcotic and stimulating properties. They made shields, boomerangs, and work tools in this valley and used them for many purposes: digging, tending fires, time beating, and, of course, fighting and hunting. Along the trade routes were centers of exchange, like medieval fairs. This was one busy, prehistoric place.

As we neared our stop for two nights, the Wilpena Pound Resort, we saw an especially big wallaroo, yet another species of kangaroo that inhabited rocky areas such as this. But we never spied The Flinders reportedly cutest resident, the Yellow-footed Rock Wallaby, which almost became extinct but had somewhat recovered. And we didn't see a euro, yet another small marsupial. The best named of the local fauna, however, had to be the fat-tailed dunnart, which was described in the literature as a marsupial mouse. They're all lucky to still be around. Within 50 years of European settlement,

2/3 of the area's land-dwelling mammals moved to the endangered species list. For shame.

The Resort sat below Wilpena Pound, a natural bowl shaped by erosion caused by weather and uplift. There was only one easy way into this remnant valley surrounded by jutting peaks, a trail that followed a creek bed that, today, probably contained a raging torrent. Most of us hoped that the weather would clear by tomorrow so that we might hike up to the Pound.

Most of the peaks in Flinders Ranges National Park were between 2,000 and 3,000 feet, but this basin topped out at only 1,500. The highest elevation in the Flinders was 3,901 foot St. Mary's Peak.

The area had been home to the Adnyamathana People for eons. In their language, Wilpena had two meanings—the place of bent fingers or camping shelter. Whitefellas arrived in 1851 and started a sheep station in the grass filled bowl. The sheep, unlike the native animals, thrived. But from 1864 to 1866 no rain fell causing huge stock losses. So even here the rain gods were either parsimonious or spendthrift as in the rest of Australia. Today they were being far too generous.

Despite the weather, The Resort was wonderful, and we had two full days to explore it and the surrounding area. There were all sorts of different accommodations in several building clusters. Ours was a typical but comfortable motel type room decorated, not intentionally I suppose, in 1950s Holiday Inn style.

Ruth and I drifted down to the Visitors' Centre to see what there was to do. Most of the brochures were about bush walking, the best way to observe the roughly 1,500 plant species, 120 birds, and 20 mammals that made homes here. Camping was popular as were scenic flights. These were, however, grounded due to the rolling storms.

We sloshed next door to the resort's store in search of exotic souvenirs, but it proved to be a fairly ordinary convenience-type store for visiting campers. The only exotics were some Internet stations that we couldn't figure out how to use correctly. There was no mouse and the weird looking contraptions were expensive to use, so our messages home were both clumsy and short.

Poddy Dodger's Bistro and Bar, the anti-roadhouse, was busy, and not just because of our group. Dinner in Captain Starlight's à la carte restaurant was traditional buffet style. There was a mind-boggling selection, but it was the kind of place that made it virtually impossible to have a fresh, hot meal. By the time I decided what I should eat, lots of chunky, root-type vegetables, and found a spot at a table, my bland food was unavoidably cold. Then too, memories of our Marree feast from the previous night lingered, diminishing the Starlight experience. The adjacent swimming pool looked inviting, but it was still raining, after dark, and unpleasantly cold.

By the time we returned to our room it was close to 10 p.m. Not especially tired, Ruth and I talked about tomorrow's possibilities at Wilpena, assuming a break in the weather, the main topic at dinner. Everyone wanted to bushwalk. Especially popular and anticipated was the trek up to the Pound, but we would have to do it in reeking, still dusty clothes, or niggedy, unless someone did laundry. Not having had a chance to wash our few repeatedly-used articles since Alice Springs, we had zero clean clothing.

Ruth was tired. "I should head for the laundry room, but…," she said, yawning.

"I'll do it," I offered.

"Do you know what time it is?"

"Of course, but do you want to spend your time tomorrow listening to the spin cycle or spoonbills?"

"But you'll need help," she said, wary of my laundry skills.

"They told us that winter was the best time to spot animals, and we have exactly 24 hours to see as many as we can." So I gathered up the dirty pile and headed for the coin operated machines provided by the resort.

Luckily, no one else was using the washing machine at this hour, so I dumped in all of our duds, stuffing it full, and scanned the instructions. There was a strange message scrawled on a piece of paper either by a guest or by the management and taped over the usual do-this-but-don't-do-thats. "You may find some marks on laundered whites and lighter garments, so use this machine at your own risk," it warned.

What did that mean?

There was no one around to ask, and the warning did clearly say "may." So I decided that this was probably a rare phenomenon, and the staff was just avoiding liability or attempting to head off an occasional desperate housewife. I inserted the necessary coins and listened to the rain while the machine did its work.

Following the final rinse, I opened the door to find that every piece of clothing that was not originally black was shot through with angry slashes of what appeared to be tar. I was, needless to say, shocked. And it didn't take long for my mind to register problems 1, 2, and 3. For the rest of the trip we would look like we had run through an ink sprayer. There was no chance that rewashing the clothes would get rid of the problem because there was apparently something odd in the water here. Rewashing would surely only make things worse. And number three…how would I reply when Ruth held up her white blouse that now looked like an unfinished Jackson Pollock and asked, "Why didn't you pay attention to the warning?"

Indefensible. And there was no hiding the evidence, so I walked as slowly as I could back to our room and immediately confessed.

Practical Ruth, who had revived and was reading about Wilpena's unusual marsupials, only said, "Well, at least we got rid of the dust and dirt. And our clothes don't smell." She stoically grabbed the in-room iron and began to, at least, get rid of the wrinkles in her once white blouse.

Chapter Seventeen

Soggy Wilpena Pound

When I peeked behind the curtain, there was no rosy dawn so I burrowed back under the covers with Ruth who, luckily, didn't waken.

When 8 a.m. rolled around, I looked again. No change. The rain, I guessed, would continue all day. Just like at home.

I gently poked Ruth. "It's going to be a quiet, off-season Sunday at Wilpena Pound Resort. The rain will not let up," I said like a Weather Channel reporter.

"Too bad," she said.

"Not so bad. I declare a day of rest."

Some of our favorite travel days had been like this. I recalled a similar day in Tasmania. The weather, not unusual for a place that outfitted Antarctic expeditions, had turned nasty 24 hours before our departure. We had seen all the local sights and especially enjoyed Salamanca Place and the Saturday market. We were staying in an exceptionally lovely hotel, Lenna of Hobart, just up the hill from Salamanca. By noon on Sunday we were back in our room, wet down to the skin. So we changed back to sleepwear, read books, listened to the ABC on the radio, and enjoyed our cozy room to the max for the rest of the day.

"We can still enjoy the Resort," Ruth said, "and I can finish the ironing."

After breakfast, she did just that while I went back to the Resort's convenience store. Normally, I'd have been in and out of a place like this in a minute, but this time I browsed, finding, much to my surprise, a respectable selection of Australian wines. But no Cover Drive. I bought The Weekend Australian, the newspaper that was "Keeping the Nation Informed." Standing in a long line of customers, I felt a bit like a guy in the police line-up expecting to hear, "That's the one, Officer! The one with the weird blotches." But no one looked twice at me or commented on my shirt, which made me look a bit like a Dalmatian.

It took most of the morning to work my way through this very serious newspaper with fear of terrorist attacks and homeland security on its mind. Australia had, after all, been targeted in Bali and Indonesia. As usual, there was very little news from or about the United States and page upon page of Aussie football, which still seemed to me like a combination of soccer and rugby played by men who looked like serious hell raisers.

"How is it?" Ruth asked, folding her last dappled top.

"No decent comics," I groused.

At noon we joined a jolly group for a Resort sponsored ride up a nearby canyon. Dave had the day off. Only Jane and Michael from our gang were aboard this bus that routinely took visitors up to the Pound Gap trail from where they could access the bowl on foot. The landscape was impossibly green due to the rain, and the mountain stream paralleling the road was a tumbling, rushing torrent. The canyon floor had the look of a prehistoric forest and was populated with truly wild kangaroos.

A few hardy souls wearing plastic ponchos and carrying umbrellas got off at the trailhead and disappeared into the bush. Their destination, Wilpena Station, had survived several droughts and managed to be a going concern for 135 years, ceasing operations only in 1985 when the last lease expired. The entire Pound was then purchased by the Federal Government and added to the already existing National Park system. According to the Park's website, "Preserved at Old Wilpena Station is the most complete group of early station buildings in South Australia in an authentic pastoral landscape." But the wheat fields, which were not a good idea in the first place, were gone and the foragers had gone back from cattle to kangaroos.

Ruth and I didn't mind not seeing the Station because we had already vowed to come back to The Flinders the next time we visited Australia. On our own. In the summer.

The driver took the same paved road back to the Resort, following the gum lined creek. The trees too were benefiting from the abundant rain. It was almost September, and spring's arrival next month was already being announced by an array of golden wattle trees that were just starting to bloom. These low-growers are a branch of the acacia family. They produce vivid yellow flowers and sneezes for about six weeks beginning in late winter.

Despite the fact that they are a bane to anyone who suffers from allergies, the wattle's bloom is much loved and it has become the National Flower. It can be seen on tea towels, in jewelry designs, and everywhere all over Australia.

We had spotted a lot of foraging kangaroos up in the wild canyon, but more interesting were the emus in the groomed park down below. The driver responded to our pleas and eased in as close as he could to the flock without disturbing them. He was most knowledgeable about these flightless natives, the second largest birds on the planet.

The large group we were quietly observing consisted of a single adult emu herding a large number of undisciplined babies. They were apparently being taught how to forage among the trees for grains or grubs. But few were paying attention. They were far more interested in chasing each other into the road.

"You might be surprised to learn that the parent you're seeing is a male," the driver began. "Female emus are terrible mothers."

I watched and, sure enough, the guardian looked like a weekend dad on playground duty.

"After mama lays the eggs, she goes off with another male and does it again. A bit of a tramp, she is. Then sheila leaves him and finds another larrikin. She likes to root and has absolutely no interest in child rearing. Fair dinkum dad raises the young. He even goes through hormone changes as he builds a nest and sits on the eggs. Dad lives off his body fat for about eight weeks, sips only morning dew, and loses a lot of weight. There can be seven or more of his offspring running around as the result of his go, and he's been known to adopt others too. But predators, mostly eagles and cats, keep the population down once they're born. Good old dad defends his brood as best he can and teaches them like a good mum until they're ready to survive on their own."

He told us we could get off to take pictures, but he warned us not to try for a close-up. "Emus can get tetchy and attack if you get too close to the children," he said, "and they can run 40 miles per hour."

I took him up on it and stayed close to the bus. I counted eight rambunctious chicks from a comfortable distance as the father of the brood watched me warily.

When I climbed back on, the driver was telling his very focused audience that emus had lived in Australia for 80 million years. "That bloke's ancestors had to watch out for dinosaurs," he added.

The friendly driver, who had surely given this emu report to countless busfulls and still seemed interested, dropped Ruth and me at the store again and I browsed it for the third time.

"Since this is a National Park," I told Ruth, "I was surprised to discover an excellent selection of Australian wines this morning." I showed her my find and I looked again for The Cover Drive without success.

We strolled about the Resort and found many of our group hanging out near the unused pool. They had just had lunch together and were also enjoying a quiet Sunday afternoon, except for Jan and Roger, who had headed up to The Pound despite the rain. Jenny and John, who were never around for impromptus like this, were absent and no one knew where they were.

Allan, a successful lawyer, was telling everyone about his work on the Australian Law Reform Commission. Then, for no apparent reason, he spoke about the time 18 years previously that he had gone to Sydney for a routine check-up and ended up having coronary bypass surgery. "I'm a member of the zipper club in long standing," he said, a bit sheepishly, not quite sure why he had told us.

Barbara saw his discomfort and changed the subject. She told stories about events when she had played the organ and sang.

"She's much in demand as an accompanist," said her proud husband.

Barbara warned us about using the washing facilities at Wilpena. "I've heard that it dispenses a nasty black substance that is visible on light colors," she said.

"Did you discover this by using the machine?" I inquired hopefully.

"No, of course not. I read the warning and heeded it."

Ouch. Luckily I had put on a jumper, er, sweater because of the cold so my embarrassment was well hidden.

Seeing *my* discomfort, Ruth now changed the subject by asking, "Barbara, do you know "The Kookaburra Song?" Ruth had been looking for the sheet music because she wanted to use it when teaching children about Australia.

"No, but I know most of it." And Barbara treated us to an almost complete rendition of this delightful, child-friendly song. Some of the others joined in.

The subject turned, as it often did, to travel and Jane began comparing this trip to other experiences. "4 weeks in India and 2 international flights were a breeze compared to Central Australia."

I was shocked, not having found our travels especially arduous.

But then Jane added, "But in all this time in strange beds and bumping along, I haven't had a twinge of arthritis. To be pain free, I fear that I may have to spend the rest of my life driving about Central Oz in a small bus."

Gwen and Angus reminisced about the cricket match that we had attended together in Melbourne on our previous visit. One half hour before the end of the eight hour game, the Australian team was far, far behind.

New Zealand, a major rival, batted in the first half and had scored 245 runs. Yes, 245.

Rob, embarrassed by the rout, had suggested that Ruth and I return to our hotel and skip the rest of the match since the Australian team had no chance of closing the gap. In cricket, one team bats, or whatever they call it, and then, after a long break, it's the other team's turn. There are no competitive back and forth innings as in baseball. Despite the fact that the Australian team was way behind, Ruth said, "Don't you believe in miracles, Rob?"

They reminded Ruth of that comment and recalled how, suddenly, the team came alive. Thanks to a miracle worker named Bevan, The Australians not only caught up, they surpassed the other team's score by 3 runs, winning the match in the final seconds. Ruth and I were as jubilant as the 40,000 fans in attendance even though we had little understanding of this complicated sport despite patient, intensive, and expert instruction.

"Australia won by two wickets," Rob reminisced.

"Wickets. Does the term *sticky wicket* have something to do with game of cricket?" I asked.

"It has something to do with the way the ball bounces off a wet playing field," Angus explained.

"Rain makes it harder for the batsman," Lynette added.

"It's more difficult to play in a wet, or sticky, pitch, "Angus said.

There was silence as the group pondered this.

The subject turned to family and Gwen spoke of their son, who lived in Brisbane but traveled to Iowa on a regular basis for business.

"Speaking of business," Karin said, "We're just out of the wine industry, and I'm beginning to dread the mess we're about to return to."

"What mess?" Barbara asked.

"After Brian and I booked this Outback trip, a young couple came to our door and asked if we were interested in selling. We had absolutely no intention of leaving our beloved land, but…" She sighed regretfully.

"But you did," Barbara surmised.

"Yes, and this meant moving back to Canberra right before leaving for The Outback," Karin said. "So we decided to be flexible. We might just as well unpack our suitcases along with the entire contents of a house after we return."

The conversation segued into names. By this time Karin had begun to call me "Hank the Yank" on a regular and affectionate basis. At least it seemed affectionate, so I asked her where this term came from.

"That's what we've always called American men," she replied. She may have been right about the *always* part, but the term came into far wider use during World War II when lots of American servicemen passed through Australia, a least a million by some estimates.

The conversation turned to names, given and married.

Gwen said, "My maiden name was Hansord, and I can't find any Hansords anywhere!"

"Keep looking," I advised her, "You'll eventually have success." I told her about looking for Harbaughs, a name so rare that 99.9% of phone books contain none. "I know because I search all over the world and have had only two surprises. I found 70 Harbaughs in a telephone directory in a small town in Maryland and a distant cousin…in Alaska." I told her about our good friend Tom who thought he was pure Irish until he took a trip to France and found branches of his family tree that he didn't know existed.

"What's his last name?" Gwen asked.

"It's a very unusual surname, Rochford."

"I know someone named France Simone Rochford!" Gwen said excitedly.

6.7 billion people, small world.

Ruth and I looked at each other and shared a wordless thought. In three days we would leave these wonderful Aussies, these great friends, and probably would never see them again. We were suddenly rueful but grateful for times like this, times of casual sharing and friendship.

Dave came by and asked, "Is anyone interested in a trip up to the Sacred Canyon?"

The rain had stopped temporarily, so several of us stood up to follow him. But not Lynette and Rob.

Lynette said, "You go on Rob," but he refused.

"Would you like to play bridge later?" Ruth asked.

"I might be up for a game if I have a bit of rest first," Lynette replied, so Ruth and I joined the others for a Sunday afternoon adventure.

About 12 miles from the Resort, Sacred Canyon turned out to be an Aboriginal engraving site, one of three in the area. Our group of 9 followed yet another gum lined creek bed up to what would always have been an ideal camping site. Caves provided shelter and there was fairly permanent water from a spring. Natives long ago had carved crude circles and lines into the walls of what had become known as Sacred Canyon.

"The Adnyamathanha were known as the hill or rock people," Dave instructed while pointing to the faded designs. "Up there on the canyon's sandstone walls they portrayed water holes, animal tracks, and each other. Some local Abos believe that those drawings were done, not by people, but by spirits who passed them on as part of Dreamtime."

Try as I might I couldn't put the primitive curlicues and slashes into any meaningful picture, but it was clearly the work of human hands.

"They used granite pieces for carving and that's why they remain."

"Impervious to rain, wind, flood, erosion, and tourists," I said, and the others laughed.

"Is it known how old they are?" I inquired.

"Oh, maybe 40,000 years. See the arrows there?"

"Where?"

"There."

"Next you'll tell me that there are roos up there too, Dave."

"Good on ya. Roight there!" he said, but I think he was yanking the Yank's chain.

The South Australia Park's website that I later visited called Arkaroo Rock, another of the carving places in the Flinders, "An important Aboriginal art site featuring ocher and charcoal images depicting the creation of Wilpena Pound."

Now, I didn't get to see Arkaroo, but if it was anything like what I *did* see, this sounded like overstatement, but perhaps I didn't get to observe the best of the local carvings. And, I suppose that what would turn an archeologist on might not have the same affect on unpracticed eyes. Mine, for example.

The third site was the Yourambulla Caves that reportedly had some of the best rock paintings.

Meanwhile in the Sacred Canyon, I was having...what? A major failure of imagination? Maybe it was simply time to have my eyes checked.

I looked around to see if I was the only one struggling. The others were respectfully silent. Perhaps they were experiencing awe.

Dave could see that I was having difficulty interpreting, so he added, "It's best to see them in early morning or late afternoon. They're clearer then."

It *was* still grey and gloomy even though the rain had ceased.

"I believe there are more up there," Dave said pointing up the canyon. "Shall we have a go?"

The cleft became narrower and more boulder strewn as we climbed.

Three other people, a young guy and two girls, had been just ahead of us when we stopped to study the Aboriginal art. While we were discussing the primitive scrawls, they had disappeared. But we caught up with them at the edge of the water hole, which was the color of suede. They appeared to be traveling together, perhaps backpacking their way around the interior of Australia during a study break.

They were only as friendly as they had to be, and one of the girls was clearly frightened by the prospect of continuing.

I was with her. We were all stymied by a rain swollen water hole that completely blocked access to the trail on the other side.

The group split up and we all climbed atop boulders looking for ways around the water filled depression. Other than swimming across, there was no safe way to continue without climbing equipment.

A shout from above drew everyone's attention. Far above and skittering along bare rock like a mountain goat, the athletic male was about to jump down onto dry land beyond the water hole. "Here's the way!" he shouted.

One of the girls made a half-hearted attempt to follow, but the rest of us decided it wasn't worth the effort to see a few more sandstone squiggles.

We headed back down the canyon, and, lo-and-behold, before we left the parking area, Ken and his two Barbies emerged from the canyon entrance. Apparently, seeing the engravings was not as important as proving that he could get to them.

We went back to the Resort, pulled an impromptu card table to the center of the room and hailed Rob and Lynette. We played riotous bridge from 4 until almost 7 p.m. while listening to the rain, which had returned just as we left Sacred Canyon. Lynette was in great spirits and seemed to be a bit better after all the rest time.

Dinner was longer than usual, and the Captain's food was again in large quantities but cold. Ruth sat across the communal table from me but not within hearing range. However, I heard her laughing often to Allan's entertaining stories. I sat next to Michael and across from Lynette and Rob. Since we were nearing both of their hometowns, they were beginning to reminisce about their childhoods and how they met. Lynette told about living in New Guinea as a newlywed and having to always remove weevils from her flour before using it.

Whenever a group of adult humans with no common family history assemble for a period of time, at some point everyone in the group will provide an outline of his or her life, including those details that had a lasting impact. If you get to know someone well, you're likely to hear these stories more than once.

This day had not been one of exciting experiences or great discoveries, but it had been important for building relationships.

Our second dinner at Wilpena Pound ended with Michael telling about royal visits by the British monarchy and other historic events at his family's castle in Ireland. He told us how his ancestors had resisted Oliver Cromwell in 1649 after Cromwell seized the nearby town of Drogheda and headed in their direction. He was his usual animated self, but later that night, like his ancestors, he would experience a misfortune that would alter the next day's itinerary for everyone.

Chapter Eighteen

Small Towns After the Fall

At 3 in the morning Michael awakened in an unfamiliar motel room and groped his way to the bathroom without light. He reached the door without incident but then stumbled and fell into the shower. He didn't realize it at the time, but he had broken his left wrist in two places.

When we assembled for breakfast, Michael, being a trooper and a team player, claimed he had only sprained it. And maybe he believed it, maybe he didn't. In any event he made light of the injury and insisted that we go on.

For the very first time, Dave didn't show up at the scheduled time of departure.

We all sat on the bus, me near Rob and Lynette, waiting to leave. Michael's misfortune was on our collective minds. Inevitably, we spent the idle time talking about travel mishaps.

Rob reminisced about an aborted Alaskan cruise. He had told Ruth and me about it in a letter, but we had never heard a verbal account, and no one else on the bus within hearing distance besides Gwen and Angus had heard the story. "We were out on the ship's deck after breakfast on a cloudy, drizzly day when we experienced two sharp bumps. Shortly after that the Captain asked all passengers to muster in the lounge with life jackets."

"We had a roll call, Dear," Lynette recollected.

"Yes. Then we were told that the ship was taking water," Rob continued, "but the pumps were keeping up with it. So far. And the ship was being moved to a place where it could be beached, but the Captain assured everyone that there were other ships in the vicinity which could help."

"Then the lights and all power failed," Lynette interjected.

"Yes. We knew by then that we would be abandoning ship and transferring to another. Our damaged ship, The Spirit, was then beached, bow first, and we were moved in a very orderly manner in groups of 6 or 7 down gang planks to the rubber zodiacs, alternately on each side of the ship. Lynette and I were transferred to the Sea Lion, a somewhat smaller vessel than The Spirit, and we were taken back to Juneau."

Lynette continued, "We accepted travel to Ketchikan on another of the Company's ships, the Sheltered Seas, which left Juneau the next morning."

"What happened to your possessions?" I asked.

"The crew on The Spirit packed all of our belongings, and our luggage was transferred to us."

"Was everything in a mess?"

"No! It was quite orderly and we lost nothing."

At this point Dave, who had been trying to find a doctor to check Michael's wrist, boarded and announced that the bus was leaving.

Everyone had to wait to hear the end of the story. But I was reminded of my own incidents—a bad fall in Vienna, a mugging in Madrid—not quite as dramatic as a sinking ship but nonetheless bad at the time, that led to my first rule of travel: today's disaster is tomorrow's great story.

It was yet another lousy morning in Wilpena Pound, even colder with steady rain. Nevertheless, I regretted leaving. This had become one of my favorite places in Australia, as memorable as the Great Barrier Reef.

The morning's ride took us south through a series of small South Australia towns, some thriving and some not.

Barbara tapped me on the shoulder, passed me Alan Marshall's *Australia,* and said, "I thoroughly enjoyed reading this!"

"So did I. Do you know of anyone else who wants a look?" I asked about this fine book of essays about Australians and their collective character.

"No, I think that we've all read it, at least those who are interested."

I thumbed through it again and came upon this quote, "The Australian's capacity to tell a vivid story is born of open spaces, lack of opportunities to read, the need to express their reactions to tough experiences, and the bond of mateship."

I meditated upon this, recalling the hundreds of wonderful stories that I had heard from Australians over the past 16 days and on 4 previous trips. Why, just a few minutes ago I had been listening to "Abandon Ship!"

I read on.

"What's so funny, Hank?" asked Angus from across the aisle.

I hadn't been aware that I was laughing out loud. "I'm rereading this essay called "The Bush Bore". This drover is describing a man he knew, 'He can talk to you for two hours and you still know nothing.'"

"There's a fair share of *those* blokes around."

"True. But in my experience, he's not your typical Aussie." I recalled other books I had read and the tapes Dave played, and I asked Angus, "Why do Aussies like poetry, especially simple rhyming couplets, so much?'

"Give me an example."

"Here." I read from the book. "Jack looked upon the woman's face, the piercing like a knife, the awful truth came home to him, the woman was his wife!"

Angus laughed, but before he could answer my question, Dave raised his microphone and said, "Before we stop in Hawker to use the facilities, I have a joke. Did you hear the one about the two Irishmen in night school? Well, Patrick O'Shawnessy...."

I tuned him out and read instead what little information I had about the crossroads hamlet that we were entering. "Hawker, population 400, is a modern day transportation hub that was once a thriving railway town."

Words to this effect had been used often in The Outback and especially along its fringes to describe once thriving settlements. And the description of Hawker could just as easily have been describing the first non-native settlements in often dry Nebraska, or rust-belt Pennsylvania, or played-out Colorado. Perhaps that's why Americans get along so well with Australians. We have similar histories.

We pulled into Hawker Motors, a combination gas station, convenience store, and fast-food restaurant. We stepped off the bus, all except for Michael and Jane who remained seated and stoical, and the others headed inside. But I didn't. I took a brisk walk around Hawker, little more than a country crossroads. My jaunt was aborted due to Antarctic wind and slashing rain. On the brink of hypothermia, I went inside and joined the others.

There was a buzz. Something was afoot.

I found Ruth and asked, "What's going on?"

"Tea towels," she whispered.

"What?"

"I don't have time to explain," she said as she went to tell the other women.

I watched as Barbara took a cloth stack of something to the check-out, paid for her purchases, and left in a hurry.

I found out later that she rushed aboard the bus to tell Jane, who immediately came inside and bought some. In the store, somehow, word about Barbara's purchase spread rapidly, and for some reason known only to females, each of the women decided that she just had to have some of these towels stitched with native flowers, Ruth included. She bought several, which meant that as we rolled out of Hawker the women were busily exchanging towels, comparing their purchases, and complimenting each other on their good taste. Every woman aboard, every one, now had new tea towels to take home.

Did this ever happen with men? I envisioned the 9 of us passing our new athletic socks around for closer inspection. No, I don't think so. Well, maybe with golf clubs.

As we reached the edge of town on this Monday morning, I spied a sign: "Wilpena Pound, 56 km; Adelaide 400 km." I already missed the former and wished we had time for the latter. South Australia is the driest state, and Adelaide is a colorful stone, brick and mortar city with few trees. When we first visited, it had a bit of an inferiority complex that was not, in our opinion, in any way deserved. When I had told the lady at the hotel desk in Perth that I was headed there, she sniffed and said, "The city of churches."

That was its nickname at the time, but we found it, then and now, easy going and cosmopolitan with a number of fine attractions including a wonderful Migration Museum that delved deeply into Australia's roots. Its Art Gallery contained the largest collection of Australian art in the country. I had especially fond memories of Festival Centre, an entertainment complex, and Adelaide's huge Central Market, a gourmet's delight and, at the time, the largest in the Southern Hemisphere.

Going south towards but not to Adelaide, the sun came out, but fog was still draped over the mountains, which were all around.

We passed a "Historic Arkaba" sign without slowing. I searched my sources but could find no reference to Arkaba so decided I would probably not find out any time soon what earned it that sign.

Later, I learned that in 1851 two English doctors, the Brown Brothers, homesteaded here in the southern Flinders foothills. A sheep station survived with 7,000 grazing merino sheep, and its more than 150 years-old woolshed was still in use. Guests can rent the Assistant Manager's cottage for an unusual, scenically splendid holiday.

Occasional caravans whizzed past, heading toward The Flinders. I experienced jealousy.

The sky was suddenly alive with rainbows. We were clearly sliding back into the temperate Australia of sheep, wine, and open roads with few users. I always experienced a sense of real freedom from congestion here that was not an illusion. Australia's entire population was about equal to New York State's.

Dave slowed to a crawl as we passed the Cradock Hotel. Nestled in a valley surrounded by three mountain ranges—the James, the Black, and the Black Jack—its setting was picturesque. "The Old Cradock has been here since 1881," Dave said. "When it was built there were high hopes that this would become a wheat-growing area, but a hotel's about the only business that's survived."

I found a page about this might-have-been town in one of my Flinders Ranges visitor centre's pick ups which said, quite frankly, that the Cradock Hotel had survived drought, depression, two world wars, and a population decline. It described the town as an unrelenting Outback post and said that the human cost of staying became apparent quickly as family after family walked off their land leaving behind their hopes and dreams of a prosperous life. Not exactly your typical PR puff job, but honest.

We were apparently *still* on the fringes of The Outback. The hotel, as we passed by, looked like something one would expect to see on, say, Pitcairn Island. Or in the middle of Patagonia. I had to admire the grit of the current owners who were obviously still trying to make a go of a difficult business venture that looked like a frontier army outpost from the outside.

But I could have been wrong. Maybe, like the Marree Hotel, this was yet another hideaway for amorous French newlyweds and anorexic celebutants.

If not, and the owners were standing behind the check-in counter hour after hour waiting for guests who never arrived, their efforts at least preserved history and defied an inhospitable environment that was, despite it all, hauntingly beautiful.

Heavy rain returned as we drove slowly about the town of Orroroo, a fairly typical farming community with, as was usually the case, no one around. Dave was looking for a small park with a pavilion that he remembered from previous visits where we could have morning tea. "This town of 800 is an agricultural center," he said, rather distractedly. "There's lots of wheat grown around here."

Thriving wheat fields? There truly were potential waves of grain surrounding the town today, and it was nice to see early-spring green again. But it wasn't unusual for farmers Down Under to end up harvesting only seed from stunted stalks when timely rains didn't come. In appearance, this part of South Australia kind of reminded me of central Kansas' Flint Hills region.

I decided that somewhere between Cradock and Orroroo we had crossed an invisible border. Just as there had been no sign that announced ENTERING THE OUTBACK, there was no GOODBYE, Y'ALL COME BACK! billboard. But I did see a sign that said, "The Rendezvous of the

Magpies." I decided not to ask anyone what it meant since magpies are not loved.

"Ah, there it is!" Dave announced, spotting the park.

I thought this over, this sudden uncharacteristic failure to ask. Arkaba. Tea towels. And now.... "Tell me about magpies, Jane."

"Ha! In the spring they dive at you if they have little ones nesting. They're all over Australia, and their raucous call is most unpleasant," she huffed.

I dashed from the bus to the pavilion because it was pouring, and just in case the rendezvous was in this park. I looked in the overhead trees for nests.

We all huddled in the pavilion trying, and failing, to warm ourselves with tea. "That's Pekina Creek," Dave said, pointing to a swiftly flowing, up-to-the-brim rush of water just down the slope.

Rob, who rarely spoke of the past, suddenly said, "My father was born here in 1892."

"Was he now?" Dave responded, as surprised as the rest of us.

"He was one of 12 sons."

I was triply shocked—the revelation, the candor, and the number.

"How many daughters?" I asked.

"None. He was the village blacksmith, and his name was Septimus."

"Septimus! Why?"

"Because he was the seventh son."

I was curious about the other brothers' names, but our cups were empty and the environment harsh, so I aborted further questioning and headed back to the bus, dodging swooping magpies the way Hillary Clinton dodged bullets.

Everyone aboard knew that I was fascinated by, despite our common language, the vast number of word differences from my Hemisphere to theirs. So on the way to Peterborough, the small group around me became involved in a game of Australian Word Trivia. Angus nearby began it by asking, "Hank. Know what a floater is?"

"Yes, but in our culture it's rather crude, so the word probably doesn't have the same meaning here as in the United States."

"Want to guess?"

"Ivory soap? A daydreamer? Someone who drowned in the Murray?"

"Well, those too. But it really means split pea soup covered with a meat pie."

"Sounds unappetizing, especially when I connect it to the American usage." I mulled some recently noted language differences and said, "The bar back in Wilpena was called the Potty Dodger. Translation?"

"A potty is a hand fed calf, and *dodger*, well, The Artful Dodger?" supposed Brian.

"I heard someone refer to a *blow-in*," I continued. "Is that a sudden storm?"

"No, a stranger. Bunyip?"

"Hah, I just read about them! They're evil bush spirits, like gremlins."

"Good on ya. Chook?"

"A criminal?"

"No. Chicken. Cark it?"

"Don't know."

"Die. Pass on."

"Plonk."

"Haven't heard it used."

"Cheap wine."

"Mozzies?"

"Clueless."

"Mosquitoes!"

"Dave ends some of his stories and comments with the word *bugger*." "I've read some books about prisoners and sailors, so I'm pretty sure I know what *bugger* means historically, at least it's most common meaning, and, well, it's still not something you'd want to talk about in front of small children or easily offended adults. So, given how Dave uses it, uh, so liberally in general conversation, I assume that it doesn't mean, well, male bonding. But does it then, to put this nicely, basically just mean, 'I'm very disappointed that things turned out this way'...or...'"

"Yes, that and a bit of the other meaning too."

"The F word?"

"Exactly."

Jenny, joining in the fun, a rare occurrence, said, "Speaking of inappropriate words, I'm always embarrassed when Americans call their waist wallets 'fanny packs.'"

"Why? Fanny's only a mildly disreputable, kind of antique word for the posterior in the United States," I said. "And most people fill these reversible pockets with money, passports, swing them around, and wear them there."

"Not in Australia. Here it's female genitalia."

Before I had time to be amazed at Jenny, Dave interrupted, "We had planned to stop in Peterborough, but I think that we'd better focus on getting to Renmark early so that Michael can get his arm x-rayed."

I looked around at Michael, who was rather wan but smiling gamely. He was consistently embarrassed by his situation, not liking to be singled out and/or judged a problem for the rest of us.

I had noticed that he didn't join us when we stopped in Hawker, and he wasn't in the pavilion for tea. But this was the first real indication that the injury was more than a simple sprain.

Of course, no one objected. In fact, it was quite the opposite. Expressions of relief, sympathy, and support were heard up and down the aisle.

I looked through my travel materials, which needed serious winnowing again, to see what landmarks and attractions we would be missing. It didn't seem like a lot. The town of Peterborough was yet another agricultural community. It was also a railroad town and the junction of three different track gauges. Why there was such a lack of coordination Down Under in the steam era was and is still unknown to me. But at one time Peterborough had the largest roundhouse for turning engines in the Southern Hemisphere. All of this history was apparently preserved in something called Steamtown, which I wouldn't lose any sleep over missing. The mighty trains no longer ran, and *Lonely Planet* said, "The town is worth a visit as much for its lingering air of a bygone age, as for its wonderful, though sadly deteriorating, historic streetscape." And that's what I liked about *Lonely Planet* publications, consistent and well-put honesty.

We went on to Burra, where we stopped at noon. This town was clearly thriving.

But not Michael or our little bus. Its blinker lights were not working, and for safety and legal reasons Dave had to get them fixed. He also had to make arrangements for Michael. So he set us free on Commercial Street with instructions to find our own lunch.

It had stopped raining. As the others looked for restaurants, Ruth and I spotted an IGA. We bought apples, seeded bread, and almonds and had a private, spontaneous picnic.

Once a copper mining community, Burra had a host of well preserved 19th century buildings in a beautiful, hilly setting. A lot of the early settlers were from Cornwall, England, and the buildings, from cottages to stone business establishments, reflected their origin and their tastes.

Once a city of 5,000, Burra was at that time in the 19th century larger than Perth and Brisbane combined. Miners and their families created makeshift housing in the form of dugouts along Burra Creek, but the creek was prone to flooding so they moved into Australia's first company built housing.

On our exploratory walk we ran into a solo Jane, who said she was very worried about Michael. The wrist, arm, and hand were swelling alarmingly and she feared a severe injury had occurred even though Michael kept telling her not to worry.

We asked her to join us, but she said, "I'm not such good company today."

A bit later, Ruth and I were pouring over some brochures in the Visitor's Centre when Jane entered and said, a bit distracted and forlorn, "I at least want a postal card from quaint little Burra."

Heading east from this prosperous, very Anglo community, we passed through a landscape of low, treeless hills carpeted with green vegetation that reminded me of the Scottish Highlands. *Burra* even sounded like a Scottish name, or at least a variation on one, but according to the locals it came from an Aboriginal word for a creek.

We passed a sign that shouted, "Eat Fruit Now!" I checked to see if we were near a border checkpoint that might confiscate the produce of other states, but no. There wasn't a state line any time soon, so I had to assume rather too demanding orchard owners.

Next stop…Morgan, on the great elbow of the River Murray. Except for once flying over the place where it emptied into Lake Alexandrina and the Southern Ocean and glimpsing it far below, I had never seen the Murray, a river system that was often compared to the Mississippi. And as I stood on a bluff overlooking it, the comparison was, I now knew, apt.

The Murray begins in the Snowy Mountains and flows, erratically, for 1,609 miles to the ocean. If you add the Darling River, which joins it just west of Mildura, New South Wales, it becomes a 2,310 mile long river system that is just 30 miles shorter than the Mighty Mississippi.

At Morgan, the Murray made an abrupt turn south, and Ruth and I stood together with Lynette and Rob looking down at this impressive, swiftly flowing, wide river.

I grew up on the Mississippi and over time had explored its length on both sides by car and visited most of its towns, and Morgan looked like a typical American Midwest river hamlet. I could have been in Keokuk, Iowa, or Clarksville, Missouri. Behind us were warehouses and businesses that looked like they had seen better days. Below us were a paddle wheeler and a car ferry.

"I was born here, and my grandmother lived in Morgan," Rob said at my shoulder.

"And I lived in Renmark," Lynette said softly, "where I learned to swim by diving off boats into the Murray. We were living in my hometown when John was born."

"I thought you were in New Guinea," I said.

"I came home."

We crossed on the ferry we had been watching from above and entered a land of orchards, mainly orange and apricot trees in full spring bloom. It was like driving continuously through a van Gogh painting. Sprinkled among the orchards were vineyards, all showing vivid promise very early in a new growing season. We drove past a huge Berri Estates Winery that looked capable of supplying the world with wine.

Dave lifted his microphone and said, "I've made arrangements to drop Michael at a hospital just up the road since there are no x-raying facilities in Renmark. We have to be there before 5 o'clock because that's when they close."

He pressed the accelerator a bit more than usual, and the fruitful land whizzed past.

We were subdued as Dave drove up and down the streets of Berri trying to locate the unfamiliar hospital, which turned out to be in a hilly, residential area. Just before exiting the bus, Michael turned to all of us and said, "I'm so sorry for this inconvenience, and I thank you for your patience and forbearance." He bowed in a courtly manner, turned, and stepped off the bus.

Just a few miles further we entered Renmark, and Lynette turned and said to Ruth and me, "I was a bank clerk here before marrying Rob. I worked for my father. We used to live above the bank on the second floor. If I don't get to do anything else, I want to see the building." Lynette, in a weakening state, could not walk great distances.

Ruth and I had to explore Lynette's home town on our own, and it proved to be our favorite town of the trip, and not just because Lynette once lived there.

After we checked into the Citrus Valley Motel, which turned out to be a Best Western, Dave told us that he would tend to the bus's burned out lights and then check on Michael. He drove off.

Earlier in the day Allan noted that we were two days away from the end of our time together. On the bus he had begun to privately solicit ideas, the thrust of which was that it was time to decide on an appropriate gift for our guide, if any, and *if* the group desired to reward him. This dual mission that took Dave away could very well be the last time we would be without his hovering presence.

Allan knocked on a few Citrus Valley doors, but no one seemed interested in volunteering to organize this tip. Some said frankly that he deserved nothing. So Allan and Ruth, the more compassionate souls among us, formed a committee of two to take care of this.

Ruth, frequent co-pilot, had noticed that Dave ate candy all day while driving. "I think he does it to stay alert," she told Allan. She had even noted the brand names of his favorites. So any gift, she suggested, might include a selection of these.

Motion immediately seconded, Allan offered to take up a collection that evening during pre-dinner drinks, if Dave was still away.

"Someone has to buy the candy," Ruth reminded him, "and Renmark might be our last opportunity."

Sensing the mood of the group, Allan cautioned restraint as Ruth and I set out in search of a grocery store or lolly shop.

Dave had been so conscientious that he had dropped Michael at the small hospital at four, so we were here in Renmark earlier than expected and still had lots of daylight and, hopefully, opened stores.

A town of slightly more than 8,000, Renmark was the largest community that we had been in since Alice Springs. The name *Renmark* sounded very British, or maybe like the name of a lost New England colonial settlement savaged by natives. However, it came from an Aboriginal word that meant *red mud.*

As we headed toward the center of town, we walked some residential streets that looked exactly like the set where *Leave It to Beaver* was filmed. I wouldn't have been surprised to pass June Cleaver on the sidewalk. Or George Bailey.

We needed to check our e-mail too, but there was no place in Bedford Falls, er, Renmark to get on the Internet. This became harder and harder to believe as we checked out likely places—coffee shops, business stores—without finding access. When we asked about a library or store with Internet connections, we were met with blank stares that seemed to infer that the citizens of this time-warp town had yet to enter the Instant Information Age. It was a late-night-movie kind of small town, perfect and quietly affluent. Everyone was friendly in a Stepford kind of a way, and everyone looked to be of about the same social strata—successful middle class. A woman with shopping bags pointed us to a shopping center.

We found the mall quickly and bought an assortment of sweets. We also found a 50's era Catholic Church named St. Therese that was right next door to the local Masonic Lodge. We began looking for the synagogue and the mosque, but instead we found a delightful small park on the River Murray right in the middle of downtown and, next to it, the bank where Lynette worked so many years ago. It had been lovingly restored.

When Allan attempted to collect money one hour later, many from our normally generous, culturally enlightened group grumbled. Both Ruth and Allan pointed out how, just that day, Michael had shown both compassion and good judgment in helping Michael get the best treatment available in an area of only small towns. He also kept us on schedule and well fed. But many still thought he had been inadequately prepared to lead a Trust group and gave accordingly.

As we sat down to dinner, Michael appeared with Dave just behind him. Michael had a full cast on his arm, but he was grinning in relief. He now knew the extent of his injury and was no longer in pain. Lightheartedly, he joined us for dinner as if already on the mend.

Ruth and I liked Renmark so much that we took another stroll after dinner looking for the soda fountain and the sock hop. First we followed just about the same route we had taken earlier and revisited the charming park, now illuminated by street lamps. Lights stretched up and down the placid, glistening Murray.

Then we sought unexplored streets. Night was kind to Renmark. The people entering restaurants, the locked stores with brightly lit display windows, the Thomas Kincaid-like cottages, they all gave it an aura of small town perfection. We returned reluctantly to the Citrus Valley Motel and reality.

Chapter Nineteen

Alas, the Last Day

Dave surprised us by driving, not out of town, but into central Renmark and dropping us at the attractive River Murray Park that Ruth and I had visited twice the day before.

"OK, mates. I'll pick you up at the far end of that walkway in about half an hour," he said, seeming somewhat preoccupied. He pointed to the right and drove away.

Did he sense the conflict in the group or overhear something? Was he trying to get away from us, if only temporarily? Was he so tired of us that he was leaving, never to return? He had called us *mates*, though.

"What's this all about?" I asked Jane.

"He's just being very good because he's rid of us tomorrow, and we all have evaluations to write."

"Good?"

"Yes, he knew that it would be difficult for Lynette to walk this far and he learned that she longed for the chance to see where she lived as a young, single woman."

"Sounds more like kindness than manipulation," I said. But I wasn't sure.

Jane and Ruth set off down the walkway along the river chatting amiably about Michael's apparent progress.

I walked over to Lynette, who was staring at the bank with a big grin on her face. "It really looks quite well," she said pointing to the white, white art deco building adjacent to the small green space. "We lived up there," she said gesturing toward the windows on the park side. "I was a clerk. But then I married Rob and we went off to New Guinea, where I got pregnant with John. I didn't come back to Renmark until I came home to have him."

"You seem to love it here. Do you wish you had stayed?"

"Not really. Rob had lots of offers. We had opportunities to travel, see the world, live in Washington. Canberra is our home now."

She lingered a bit though, looking at her past while the others drifted on down the path toward our pick up point.

I hung back too, taking a few pictures of the park's interestingly sculptured fountain that bespoke civic pride.

I saw Lynette shrug, turn resolutely and head toward the others without looking back. That's the Lynette I know and love. Visit the past but don't stay there.

The morning was fine, cool and sunny. I was the last to reach the bus. Dave had been busy so the windows had not been cleaned for a couple of days during which time we had driven through torrents and mud. Those windows were exceptionally grimy, almost opaque. Dave had, after all, lots of priorities superseding grimy windows.

Ruth and I were sitting near the back this morning, and I had noticed from the inside that we could barely see out, so I had dug through my carry on bag like a gypsy peddler and found a couple of slightly used paper towels. They were stuffed in my back pocket, just in case I had an opportunity.

Now back at the bus, Dave motioned for me to board quickly. The engine was running. But instead, I counted down to our window and wiped it as clean as I could without water and proper equipment. When I stepped back, Barbara was staring down at me through her dirty window. So, feeling a bit selfish, I wiped hers too as best I could. But then I realized that I had started something I had no choice but to finish.

As quickly as I could, I went around the bus and swiped every passenger's window. The results were far from perfection but better than nothing.

As I climbed aboard, the entire bus burst into applause, and, taken aback, I bowed from the waist and went sheepishly, grinning all the way, to my seat.

"Do you do dishes?" Karin asked.

"Of course!" I responded.

"Well then, come to dinner Friday night."

"But you just moved. We'd be a bloody nuisance."

"No. We'll just move some boxes. But do expect clutter."

"I'd like you to try some of the wine we made ourselves," Brian added, making it an offer no one in their right mind would refuse.

"We'll ask Lynette and Rob to join us too," Karin added. Of course, she turned out to be a sparkling, unflappable host, and Brian a generous pourer with a genuine talent for making wine.

We headed east on the Sturt Highway and soon crossed the border into Victoria, a state which we would visit for only about 70 miles before returning to New South Wales. After flat farm country with regimental rows of recently pruned grape vines receding into the horizon, we came to Mildura, which would have been a desert city were it not for the River Murray and a 19th century irrigation system. Two Canadians, George and William Benjamin Chaffey, came from California to devise it. Renmark received their expertise too.

City was the right word for Mildura. Along with Wentworth, which was just across the Murray in New South Wales, Australia's most populous state, Mildura had an area population of about 60,000 making it the largest metropolitan area we had been in since leaving Canberra. We drove down a grand boulevard heavy with traffic and lined with royal palm trees, passed groomed parks, and glimpsed busy downtown stores.

Mildura had a Mediterranean climate, but it was more about work than sun bathing. There were few tourist attractions. About 20% of both Australia's citrus and wine grape production was here, and 100% of its dried fruit was processed and packaged in Mildura.

We crossed the Murray again and stopped for morning tea in a riverside park lined as far as the eye could see in both directions with house boats. This area's blindingly blue skies and consistent sun made it ideal for renting a vacation boat and drifting with the current.

After tea I was photographing the scene when Angus sidled up behind me in his shy way and said, "*White Butterflies.*"

"Where?" I asked.

"It's a book I think you'd like. It's about a man from Burma who suffers incredible hardships in an attempt to escape to India with his family during World War II. Allan has read it. Roger too."

I had discussed a lot of Australian literature with the group and had endlessly encouraged recommendations, but this was the first from outside the culture. "Is there an Australian connection, Angus?" I asked.

"Yes. He emigrated here after the war."

"Thanks. I'll find it before I leave." And this is what visitors must do. Just because a book is popular Down Under doesn't mean that it will find its way to the American market, so finding it in US bookstores can get difficult. And I did find *Butterflies* by Colin McPhedran in Melbourne. And it was a fascinating read.

On the road again, Dave stopped at a roadside stand and bought a bulky bag of local oranges just before we entered another town.   Balranald was a nondescript burg on the nondescript Murrumbidgee River.   Balranald's biggest claim to fame was that the oldest human footprint in Australia, made 30,000 years ago, was nearby. This would only have been interesting to me if the human was still alive.

We had lunch in a riverside park. The oranges were sensational.

In the next town, Hay, we had our last tourist attraction experience of the trip at Shear Outback, or The Australian Shearers' Hall of Fame. Its puffed up brochure described Hay as "a delightful and friendly town" with "five museum experiences and a whole host of other attractions." But a shortage of exclamation marks, apparently.

We only sampled the one attraction, and it was ho-hum, but, then again, I'm not the product of a culture that treats sheep shearers like rock stars. Or as Ruth said, "This is what we did with cowboys."

This Hall of Fame had an "award winning" Interpretive Centre made of corrugated iron. Shear Outback was a community project involving both the Commonwealth and Federal Governments. Our host, a woman who didn't share her name, told us that 4.6 million dollars were spent on Shear as if spending money made this project automatically soar into the winner's circle. Anyway, Shear Outback opened in 2002.

Mildly interested, I studied the five recent inductees into the Hall of Fame and other shear heroes, like John Hutchinson. In 1969 he won his first of six Australian championships. He demonstrated his shearing skills at the Osaka World Expo. Who knew such an event existed? Did Japanese youth, as a result, aspire to become world champion shearers?   I flashed on thousands of Japanese families in rapt silence watching Hutchinson denude a sheep while a clock ticked and then taking millions of digital photos of themselves with him and the fleecy pelt.

Then there was Keith Sarre. "He did 200 sheep, left-handed, in one day…just to prove he could do it."   I wondered if *did* had the same sexual connotation that it did in our explicit American culture but decided not to ask Jenny, who was nearby and studying shearing equipment like Queen Elizabeth at an agricultural fair.

Then, of course, there was a lot in this museum about Aussie icon Jackie Howe, still the blade-shears record holder, still dead since 1920.

There was a magnificent 1860s wool wagon with six foot wheels that could hold up to 150 bales, a floor to ceiling circle including practically every type of commercial shear ever manufactured, and an art exhibition of water color paintings of historic wool sheds. Really. Someone traveled all over Australia drawing and coloring in virtually identical wool sheds. I wondered if there might be a market for, say, paintings of free-standing garages in the US. Andy Warhol, after all, made a fortune with Campbell soup cans. I made it through about 1/3 of the painted sheds before my interest plummeted to zero.

I also made it about 1/3 of the way through a time line named Important Events in the History of Australian Shearing before my eyes started to glaze and I almost fell asleep standing up.

Not for the first, but for the last time on this journey, I realized that I was in a museum alone.

By the time I found the others out back in the wool shed, I was thinking that Shear Outback's claim to be "an entertaining, informative and fun-filled interpretive centre with interactive exhibits for all ages" was a bit of an exaggeration. But don't tell Hay.

The others had already found something somewhat more interesting. Behind Shear Outback was the Murray Downs Woolshed, a historic relocation from the Swan Hill region. It was built in 1926 for $7,000. Inside a sheep shearing demonstration was about to begin, and I was the last to take a seat for it.

The Woolshed was huge, reflecting the importance of sheep rearing in Australia. The National Flock reached its peak in 1969, 180 million sheep. Put end to end, you would have...a bloody mess to clean up. These sheep represented 900 million kilograms of wool. That's enough to knit, well, how many sweaters? I'm not sure numbers go that high.

One Shear Outback ad had invited, "Meet a real shearer, he'll show you how it's done!" So I was expecting to be wowed when a middle aged man came from behind some stalls, reached into one of them, and grabbed a sheep that was so placid it seemed triple-dosed on Lunesta. The man hefted the animal against his mid-section, an act that looked as awkward as grappling a burlap bag containing an adult anaconda. However, he held it against his burly chest as if a full-sized sleepy sheep was nothing. He wore a sling that went around his waist. "This eases the strain on my knees and helps with weight distribution," he said of the harness. He set to work shearing and had no trouble removing the sheep's heavy coat while commenting continuously on what he was doing and what happened to the wool. It went like this: "The guesser grades it. A baler bales it. The presser presses it. That's the hardest work, so pressing is now done with hydraulic presses." His work was as methodical as his words.

The Hay area grew medium wool, and a bale at the time of this demonstration was worth about $600. As a commodity, wool somewhat unraveled in the 1990s causing a lot of job losses. But demand for high grade wool was on the rise in Asian countries.

A single, 200 pound bale of high grade Australian wool with a fiber width of 11.6 microns was recently bought by an Indian fabric maker for $247,480. That's enough to make 50 men's suits. They'll sell quickly.

After the wool lay in a heap on the floor, the shearer extracted a tuft and passed it around, encouraging us to appreciate the natural lanolin in the fibers. He then called for questions, and the answer to Ruth's was, "Not too bright. Many sheep die because they huddle together when it gets cold and they suffocate."

We headed east on the Sturt Highway following the Murrumbidgee River all the way to Narrandera. The land was flat, a rice growing region. "The rice is exported to Japan," Dave told us. "So is high quality Australian made sake."

Then he announced a contest. "My mates at Shear Outback gave me two posters, and I'm going to pass them along to you through a contest. The money collected will go to my favorite charity!" he added without specifying which one. However, he had told us almost daily that he was taking a fishing trip to the Northern Territory with his son-in-law as soon as he returned home.

Dave explained the rules. We were all to bid on the suitable-for-framing posters showing Shear Outback's gigantic, out-front shears and its, to some, architecturally brilliant building. The highest and lowest bids would receive the posters, whether the bidders wanted them or not. *Who wouldn't desire these prizes?* Dave implied. He handed a paper bag to the pair behind him, and it passed from couple to couple up and down the silent bus so that we could toss in our bids, paper preferred.

This extortionate game highly embarrassed Michael and Jane, who resented making a more-or-less forced "charitable" contribution. They put in $1.60, and won a poster along with the announcement of their paltry gift. Dave collected $76 and thanked us for being so…charitable.

The Gateway Motel in Narrandera was right in the center of downtown and a two story affair with a tiny parking lot not suitable for large caravans or busses, especially those towing carryalls.

Michael was at my side during the last supper. Ruth sat at the mostly-ladies' table. At my right were Allan and Rob. Michael was chipper, well past his ordeal and already learning how to use his cast encased left arm. He spoke of his fine treatment at the hospital the day before.

I asked all assembled to explain the Australian health care system, which is considered by some to be the best in the world.

"We've had Medicare for about 30 years," Allan began.

"Medicare!" I exclaimed that's the name of our program for over 65s in the United States."

"At first it was called Medibank, but they changed it," said Michael.

"Does it work?" I asked.

There was absolute silence all around the table.

"What's the problem? Is it too expensive?"

"Well, no," Allan admitted finally. "There's a simple income tax surcharge of 1.5% that everyone pays."

"Surely that doesn't cover operational costs," I said. "And might that go up?"

They all shrugged.

"Higher income Australians pay an additional amount in the form of a Medicare Levy Surcharge."

"How much?"

"One percent."

"Is the system fair?" I asked.

"Well, it gets complicated. There are several tiers of service," Rob said.

"Yes," Allan agreed. "Most well off Australians have private health insurance."

"A lot of treatments aren't covered by the universal plan, and it can take a long time to schedule certain procedures," Rob explained.

"Give me an example of something that's not covered," I said.

"Emergency ambulance transport."

"A lot of people who can afford it purchase their own health insurance and become private patients," said Michael.

"Why?"

"It reduces waiting time, and you can choose your own doctor."

"So not everyone is treated equally," I surmised.

"Oh, it's a fairly good system," Allan argued, and he took me through a series of for-instances that made my head ache. In operation, Medicare sounded like the government program equivalent to advanced calculus. But everyone at the table agreed that it worked relatively well and they were generally satisfied with the results.

My only experience with Oz health care was second hand. A good friend and ex-neighbor had a mild heart attack while attending a performance at the famed Sydney Opera House. When I asked about his medical treatment, Richard began by saying, "The hospital's food was marvelous. I asked for recipes, and the kitchen provided them." Marvelous *hospital* food? Perhaps the Aussies are on to something.

Ruth seemed a bit down after the final dinner with her well-bonded Australian female friends, all with new tea towels. She wanted nothing more than to watch a bit of TV and turn in.

But I wasn't the least bit sleepy, so I decided to take a solo walk up Narrandera's sloping main street to where a town-bypassing highway slid past the commercial center. As I climbed, closed stores segued into auto repair garages and insurance offices before becoming main street apartments and finally humble houses. Narrandera's hospital was at the top of the rise.

As I turned back, it occurred to me that the only places opened for business at this late hour were three or four lively bars.

Then it hit me. This was our last night on the road and Allan and I hadn't had our authentic pub experience. It was too late to go and wrest him, probably, from bed.

It was a wintry night with a chilly canopy of stars above.

I pressed my nose against the window of the pub across from the motel. Several patrons, mostly men, were engaged in animated conversation. The atmosphere appeared smoky, the music loud. I could tell that from the vibration without actually being able to identify the juke box song. If someone had waved and motioned me in, I would have joined him. But no one did. This was, after all, not my home and not my neighborhood pub.

Oh well, wherever I go in the world I always leave some important landmark unvisited or some activity undone. That way I have reason to return. So a drink with mates in an Outback pub was, and still is, my "Outback Rosebud."

Chapter Twenty

The Circle Closed

After our last breakfast on the road, Ruth and I had time for a walk around Narrandera. It was still very early, so most stores were not yet open, but we found a news agent already busy with customers heading for work.

After we browsed magazines, I bought two *Australians*. Newspapers, that is. I wanted to give them to Brian and Allan, who often shared theirs with me when they could find them, however infrequently, in The Outback. It was Tuesday, but they were bulky like weekend editions, so Ruth offered to take them back to the Gateway and find both men.

I wasn't ready yet to return to either the Motel or Canberra. This trip had gone much too fast, and part of me whispered that, if I was still in Narrandera and kept busy, it wasn't over yet.

I repeated my stroll of the night before and watched Narranderans approach from residential streets and walk to businesses. I watched as several used keys to unlock doors and turned signs to announce OPEN. They looked relaxed and purposeful, just going about their daily routines unaware of the stranger, me, who found their lives exotic and foreign to his experience for no reason other than geographic placement. If I had been in Sioux Falls, I wouldn't have given their lives a second thought.

I returned reluctantly to the Gateway for a final room check and the stowing of our road gear for the last time.

Instead of the Sturt Highway, Dave took a back way to our last morning tea stop at Junee. The trafficless country road curved through cultivated hills in this temperate, pastoral part of Australia known as the Riverina because of the Murray, the Murrumbidgee, and their many tributaries. This was some of New South Wales best farming country. In the Harefield area of the Murrumbidgee River Valley, for example, pistachio trees thrived, adding further credence to Rob's assertion that everything grows in his country.

The town of Junee, where we stopped for tea in a community park's bandstand surrounded by dormant rose bushes, began as a pastoral lease named Jewnee Run. Its name changed over time for rather obvious reasons and despite the fact that the word was Aboriginal for "speak to me."

Junee blossomed into a town in the 1860s during gold fever, but it owed it continued prosperity to the railroad. Workshops moved here, lines cut through, and Victorian buildings went up. Today its 6,000 people depended on agriculture and transportation for their jobs.

We purposely lingered over tea and coffee, and I decided that I wasn't the only one who was in no hurry to "get back."

But we had to. Ominously, Lynette's chest-rattling cough was worse then ever. She seriously needed medical attention. Nevertheless, with a big smile on her face she gamely posed with the rest of us for a group picture. Then Dave gave us a slow tour of the town before taking us up to Bennett's Lookout for a fine view of the entire community.

Perched on a rock above the group for a better view, I suddenly realized that I had not taken a single picture of my friends on the entire trip. Lynette and Rob were in deep conversation with Ruth, probably discussing details of our imminent return to Canberra. I snapped away. But most of my other friends were too far away, just as they are today, for me to get good pictures of them.

"One final recommendation, Hank," Angus said, easing up behind me, "You might enjoy *My Love Must Wait*."

It sounds like Victorian Chick Lit," I said.

"What do you mean by that?" he asked, and I for once was not on the receiving end of language instruction.

After hearing my explanation, he said, "No, No. It's by Ernestine Hill, and it's about Matthew Flinders. He left his new wife in England and didn't return to her for 9 years."

"So, who speaks the title?"

"He does. I think. Oh," he added, "Henry Lawson's short stories will give you insights into us too."

Except for a few poems, that name meant nothing to me, but I recalled that Matthew Flinders was the first person to circumnavigate Australia and chart its coastline, so the book might have been interesting. But then I remembered finding Ernestine's *Water Into Gold* a tough though ultimately rewarding read. I thanked Angus for the two tips, but made no effort to find the books. Maybe next time.

We headed for Gundagai, a place Ruth and I had visited with Rob and Lynette on our previous trip to Australia. At the time I dubbed Gundagai the most purely Australian town I had discovered in four trips, and nothing changed that perception on this second visit.

Gundagai was home to between 2 and 3 thousand people depending upon which source you accepted as more accurate. The town didn't look like a mountain or oceanside resort community with a seasonal migration, so I couldn't account for this 1,000 people difference. Either no one had bothered to count accurately or people came and went as the economy waxed and waned. It looked like the kind of town where that might be the case. In any event it was the location of several singularly Aussie cultural curiosities.

The dog on the tucker box for instance. Two years previously when I asked about this curious memorial to a mutt, Rob literally broke into song. He knew every word to "The Dog on the Tucker Box".

Australian Jack O'Hagan penned this popular tune in 1937 about an enigmatic dog, and the song's continued popularity put it up there near *Waltzing Matilda.*

The story went back, way back to the 1880s, some said even as early as 1850, and there were several versions of what happened in the original incident that inspired the song. Some said a loyal dog refused to budge when its owner's team of bulls got stuck in a creek, and the dog died heroically as a result. In some versions the dog, to show its displeasure, *shat* on the tucker, or food box, to demonstrate its disdain for its situation, but then some 19th century pc policeperson dropped the *h.* In other versions, the man's faithful companion, out of loyalty to his master, refused to leave the tucker even after the man mysteriously disappeared. One theory suggested that he gave up on extracting his team from the muck and left without the box that the mongrel dutifully guarded until it starved to death.

Whatever happened, there was a popular monument to this dog five miles from Gundagai that was generally described as a tribute to an icon of Australia's past, or words to that affect. Unveiled in 1932 by Prime Minster Joe Lyons, no less, this memorial showed a life-sized stone, mixed breed, anything but cute dog atop a pedestal. He, or she, was surrounded by a pool with spouting fountains. I watched as visitors stopped to pay their respects, taking the experience very, very seriously.

Jack O'Hagan, who had never been to Gundagai, also wrote two other wildly popular songs, one called "When a Boy from Alabama Meets a Girl from Gundagai" and the other "Along the Road to Gundagai". The latter became the theme song of a very popular and long running radio show about a family—Dave, Dad, Mum, and Mabel—who lived in a place called Snake Gully.

My only exposure to these characters was a film named *Dad and Dave: On Our Selection* that Ruth and I saw in Sydney on its opening day in 1995. We hadn't purposely gone to the premier. It just happened to be the last day of our trip, and I found twenty dollars lying on a sidewalk, so we decided to blow it on a movie. It was pure coincidence that we saw this stunningly Australian film starring Geoffrey Rush, who won the Academy Award for Best Actor the following year for *Shine*. Leo McKern, a wonderful character actor best known for playing Rumpole, stole the movie from the other actors, including Joan Sutherland. Yes, *that* Joan Sutherland. *Dad and Dave: On Our Selection* apparently never found a US distributor, and I don't wonder why.

In any event, the radio series and its cast were immortalized in copper in a family group near the stone dog. The original characters were created by a novelist with an action-figure name, Steele Rudd. Although I hadn't read the original or heard the radio show, my general impression was that it was kind of like the Beverly Hillbillies, but without the wealth and taken more seriously.

Captain Moonlight also sounded like a fictional character, but he was real. A flamboyant local lay preacher, Andrew George Scott, who originally hailed from Ireland, turned from saving souls to bank robbery and gave himself this interesting new name. In 1868, when he was in his mid-twenties, he grabbed a revolver, took a bank manager hostage, and made off with two bags of gold. The manager recognized his voice and went to the police, but Captain Moonlight was so clever that he convinced the authorities that the banker was lying. The innocent manager was arrested and tried. Moonlight was caught, however, when he tried to work the gold into the system. He was tried, convicted, and sent to jail in 1872. After 7 years he was released and resumed bushranging. *Bushranger* was the Aussie term for a robber who struck suddenly and then disappeared into the bush, like an Aussie Robin Hood. Moonlight formed a gang, eventually killed someone, and was tried and sentenced in Gundagai and hung in Sydney at the age of 37.

Walter McGill, a phrenologist who made his death mask, claimed that the Captain's head was peculiarly formed and added, "It was impossible he could speak the truth or be honest…devoid of all moral courage…a lover of life and its pleasures." Lonely Planet called him *notorious* and dubbed him, "leader of a gang of gay outlaws." I have searched in vain to learn if this meant that they were happy and carefree bandits or unable to quit each other, but I haven't come up with the answer. Apparently the Captain left behind some personal letters, so maybe he was out and proud way ahead of his time. Colorful indeed.

Captain Moonlight's body was returned to Gundagai, and he was buried in its cemetery.

So was Frank Rusconi, creator of the Marble Masterpiece.

We *all* went in to see this singular attraction at the Gundagai Visitors' Centre. I was surprised to find that entry to Rusconi's obsession would cost me a couple of dollars more than the first time I saw it. I wasn't particularly interested in seeing it again, but I *was* interested in studying the others' reactions, so I paid and entered.

Nothing had changed except the admission price. The song "Along the Road to Gundagai" still filled the air, driving the employees crazy I must assume. I immediately knew that the Masterpiece hadn't been dusted or cleaned in the two years since I had seen it because the little marble piece that looked like it had escaped from a chess game was still on its side, the one component among 20,948 pieces that was not in its place. Perhaps Frank did this on purpose to play with the minds of orderly individuals, like me, who would notice this one tiny flaw and be disturbed. The entirety still looked like the work of a slightly crazy individual with too much time on his hands and a drive to build a miniature Burmese, English, Disneyland, Japanese, Xanadu temple from scrap marble.

The literature called it a cathedral "created by the dexterous hands of the late Frank Rusconi and represents 28 years of work by this craftsman in marble." He finished it, I would assume gratefully, in 1938. Frank was a mason who purposely used only marble mined in New South Wales in his Masterpiece in an attempt to show that the Italians weren't the only ones who had beautiful stuff. Mr. Rusconi also created the dog on the tucker box at the memorial just outside of town.

I watched the others and listened for comments, but none were made. Not a single word was uttered among the sixteen people staring at this temple/cathedral. A group that, by the way, always had plenty to say about everything we had seen before. I concluded that it was either a kitschy curiosity, like a house made from beer cans or a miniature ship containing a million toothpicks, or a genuine treasure. That judgment was in the eyes of the beholder, and no one in my group would commit by commenting.

We had a brief tour of Gundagai, which was the scene of Australia's worst flood disaster in 1852 when the Murrumbidgee suddenly rose in the middle of the night and swept 89 pioneers to their deaths. Local Aboriginals in bark canoes saved 49 other settlers from a similar fate.

As we headed for Yass, our very last town, Dave announced, "We have driven 8,200 kilometers since we left Canberra nineteen days ago." I did the math and discovered that we had covered roughly the equivalent of a trip from Boston to Seattle….and back again.

Yass was a nondescript city of 5,000. It was so anonymous that there were no guidebooks or tourist brochures listing its charms and insisting that everyone *must* go there. Most travel directories didn't even mention it. There were no websites touting its attractions. Even assiduous *Lonely Planet* could find only one thing to do in Yass, visit the Hamilton Hume Museum. It was so perfectly plain and normal that I knew there just had to be something weird going on here. And it took me a while to find out what.

Yassians were perfectly ordinary folks. Maybe that's why they were being observed by aliens. Perhaps inhabitants of another planet did clandestined research and found ideal human specimens in Yass.

According to the Australian UFO Research Network, Dean M of Hobart, Tasmania, was spending the night in a motel here when he went out for a smoke at 10:20 p.m. Perhaps it was a funny cigarette, but he claims he saw an orangish light flickering in the sky that took off at warp speed. "It also turned very fast without slowing down and made very sudden turns, and went red when turning," reported Dean. It was soundless, he insisted, and had the ability to split into two and recombine. He alerted his wife, and she came out and saw it too. They watched this strange phenomenon for an hour so amazed, I suppose, that they didn't think to bring it to anyone else's attention.

Risking alienation, we stopped at a pretty park for our last lunch during which Allan presented Dave with the monetary gift and the candy that Ruth bought in Renwick. Allan diplomatically wouldn't divulge how much had been collected, but I suspect it wasn't enough to underwrite a fishing trip to the Northern Territory.

We boarded our battered, broken, and dirty bus for the final time for the short ride to Canberra and headed down the Barton Highway. The increasing traffic cut a swath through vineyards and gentle mountains, and we were soon pulling into the parking lot of the IGA.

John was there to greet us, and since it was already 2:30 and a bit past our scheduled time of arrival, we had little time to say farewell to the Australians with whom we had spent almost every waking moment for the past 19 days and weren't sure we would ever see again.

I made the rounds of my mates and missed saying goodbye only to Michael, who was using a public phone apparently to call his ride to report that he and Jane were back. I waved to him through the back window of John's car as we swept past, but Michael didn't see me.

Ruth wrote in her diary later that day, "Hank was in tears saying goodbyes." But I don't remember it that way at all. If it seemed so, it was probably because I was back in a city and had to get used to air pollutants all over again. I had, after all, been way, way out in the Australian Outback, where the only things sharing the air with me were flies and, occasionally, red dust made furious by Road Trains.

It had been an experience as big as the landscape, and as we inched forward in the first traffic I had seen for almost 3 weeks, I flashed on the day at Kings Canyon when I hiked the gravel road that took only travelers with permits in tough vehicles to Alice Springs. I had walked to the point where civilization completely disappeared behind me. I wished now I had kept going.

Postnotes

The next day Lynette went to doctors and learned that she was well on her way to developing a more serious heart problem. She had never completely recovered her health after her Scandinavian crisis, so she was still vulnerable and had perhaps picked up a virus on the road. No one knew for sure. Her heart's rhythm was not in any way normal. Experts drew blood, scheduled tests, and began considering methods to correct the irregularities. The next day she was back for x-rays. A team of specialists informed her that she had, among other concerns, an enlarged heart.

To prove that good and bad news frequently occur at the same time, as we were hearing a report on Lynette's health, the phone rang. It was our son Matt calling from Argentina to inform us that our daughter-in-law Jennifer was eight weeks pregnant. Since they had been married for ten years without children, this was equal parts shocking and ecstasy inducing.

Her heart issues didn't prevent indomitable Lynette from dressing up like a Central Park East matron to attend dinner with us at Karin and Brian's new home the next evening. Boxes were piled everywhere and the dining area was cramped, but the company was peerless and the meal—a smoked fish appetizer, Australian veal, and walnut cake with strawberries—was exceptional. Everything had been made from scratch with proper utensils still unpacked and just one day after returning from an extensive, tiring trip.

Pouring the cabernet sauvignon he had made, a relaxed Brian said, "I loved the process—growing the grapes and seeing it become wine—but I never liked the marketing." Nevertheless, it was unfortunate that he and Karin abandoned their dream because they were both fulfilled by and extremely good at producing excellent wines.

That day Ruth did some laundry, and the black spots that had been on our light clothes since Wilpena Pound miraculously disappeared down the drain. So we now had two mysteries—what had they been and why had they gone?

The next day we were scheduled to fly to Melbourne, a city which Ruth and I love and had visited every time we had gone to Australia. While there, I never had to set an alarm or be awakened early.

On our final morning in Canberra, we were having breakfast with Lynette and Rob when the phone rang. Qantas had some good and some bad news. Our afternoon flight had been cancelled, but, if we could get to the airport within the hour, there was room on the 10 a.m. flight. It was now 9 a.m. and we had yet to pack. As hard as it is to believe, we made that flight. And in retrospect it was a very good turn of events. We didn't have time for prolonged, sad farewells with dear friends who, unfortunately, live more than 8,000 miles away from us.

I went to Dymock's in Melbourne and bought both *White Butterflies* and Thea Astley's *Drylands*. Vexed and amazed, I read the Astley book before we landed in Los Angeles.

That evening we called from Melbourne to learn that Lynette was not responding to what had been tried so far. Her heart irregularities were proving difficult to treat, perhaps because she had experienced almost three weeks of increasing dysfunction without intervention.

The next day Ruth and I went to the fantastic Queen Victoria Market, where we bought three items—a miniature, crib-sized plush puppy for our newly expected grandchild, a ridiculously expensive jumper (sweater) made of Australian merino wool for me, and an opal for Ruth. Because she had learned how, Ruth found and bargained for a largely iridescent blue/black wonder that will always cause smiles when she wears it because it radiates mysteriously from within and reminds both of us of Coober Pedy. Mainly from Lightning Ridge in New South Wales, black opals are the most valuable with a red/black combo most desired. The value of an opal is directly related to its brilliance with red/orange colors highly prized.

The next day, we checked on Lynette again and learned that she had been put on beta blockers and was already responding positively.

Two days later after a 13 ½ hour flight to Los Angeles followed immediately by a shorter one heading north, we touched down at Portland International Airport. Not as catatonic as we expected, we went to the carousel to claim our luggage.

Ruth's suitcase came with the others but mine were missing. As we were deciding what to do, my name was called over the loudspeaker. I was instructed to report to lost and found. The good news was that my two pieces were there. The bad news was that they were covered with honey. Someone had packed a huge, unprotected jar of it, and it had exploded, proving that honey, like red Outback dust, knows no barrier and is without a doubt the stickiest substance on earth.

An apologetic airline employee was attempting to remove it with dry paper towels while only managing to make matters worse. I laughed and told him, "This is the worst thing that happened to me during 33 days of travel to the other side of the world and back."

"Send the cleaning bill to the airline," he said.

But I never did. I managed to solve the problem myself. Apparently, being in the Australian Outback enhanced both my self-reliance and my problem solving skills. It probably did that for anyone who passed through.

The Outback was hauntingly beautiful but also harshly unforgiving, like projectile honey.

So. What, and where, is The Outback? I still don't know for sure because, unlike the land on either side of the dingo fence, it isn't demarcated. Some say that it's any place in Australia beyond a large urban area. Others suggest that it's that inhospitable, infertile desert region out there, somewhere, down that unpaved track. Some are sure it's beyond the Stump, just past the bush, in the red center, the land of the Never-Never, and so on.

It clearly didn't have a perimeter. No map that I saw outlined it. No signs announced it. It was largely, I decided, a state of mind. And that means it's part of the Australian identity, that part of Down Under where a man or a woman doesn't have to live by the rules imposed by urban living. Humans out there are free to live as they want, as long as they can get used to self-imposed isolation and the risks—fire, flood, the sting, the submerged rock, the stalled vehicle, and so on.

The Outback is where the independent spirit thrives. And, like other landscapes, it will change. Because of the insatiable world demand for minerals, mining is exploding. Modern highways to connect towns are being proposed. Settlements are becoming towns, towns are turning into cities with shopping centers and Wi-Fi. All too soon, "The Outback" will be that place beyond human colonies on a distant planet with another sun.

But, at least for now, it is still that vast, incredibly majestic region with its own kind of beauty, a dream-time place that makes one feel like life can still be led on Earth without limitation or restriction.

I want to return to The Outback. And I will.

In the meantime, Lynette's heath has stabilized and she and Rob have crossed the Nullarbor Plain on the Indian Pacific. With us.

Karin and Brian have moved again. But they have not resumed wine-making. Instead, they travel, most recently to Turkey.

Allan and Barbara have taken the new Ghan to Darwin where they boarded a boat and explored the Coral Coast.

Jan and Roger have studied wild flowers and the Silk Road in China, twice.

Jenny and John met us for dinner in Canberra and we had more friendly conversation in two hours than we had in 19 days in The Outback. They are lovely people.

Michael and Jane have revisited her childhood home in Cyprus. Ruth and I recently tracked down Michael's family castle in Ireland and sent pictures. He wrote back to say it looked better maintained than the last time he visited. Jane wants us to go to Western Australia with her.

Gwen and Angus lost almost everything they owned as the result of a water leak that became a flood in their condo while they were away. But they are indomitable and back to normal.

And Ruth and I are, of course, planning our next trip to Australia.

Dave? He's probably gone fishing.

Printed in the United States
131016LV00002B/289/P

9 780595 533862